Cost Recovery and the Crisis of Service Delivery in South Africa

T0347718

Cost Recovery and the Crisis of Service Delivery in South Africa

DAVID A. MCDONALD & JOHN PAPE

HSRC Publishers

Zed Books
London and New York

Published by the Human Sciences Research Council Publishers
Private Bag X9182, Cape Town, 8000, South Africa

Editors: David A. McDonald and John Pape

© 2002 Human Sciences Research Council

First published 2002
Produced by comPress www.compress.co.za

Published in the rest of the world by Zed Books, 7 Cynthia Street, London N1 9JF
and Room 400, 175 Fifth Avenue, New York, NY 10010, USA

ISBN 9781842773314 paperback

A catalogue record for this book is available from the British Library
US CIP data is available from the Library of Congress

Contents

ACKNOWLEDGEMENTS vii

PREFACE viii

LIST OF CONTRIBUTORS ix

INTRODUCTION 1
by John Pape and David A. McDonald

CHAPTER 1

The Theory and Practice of Cost Recovery in South Africa 17
by David A. McDonald

CHAPTER 2

Debt, Disconnection and Privatisation
The Case of Fort Beaufort, Queenstown and Stutterheim 41
by Greg Ruiters

CHAPTER 3

"Massive Cutoffs"
Cost Recovery and Electricity Service in Diepkloof, Soweto 61
by Grace Khunou

CHAPTER 4

Cost Recovery and Prepaid Water Meters and the
Cholera Outbreak in KwaZulu-Natal
A case study in Madlebe 81
by Hameda Deedat and Eddie Cottle

CHAPTER 5

"They are Killing us Alive"
A Case Study of the Impact of Cost Recovery on
Service Provision in Makhaza Section, Khayelitsha 101
by Mthetho Xali

CHAPTER 6

The Struggle Against Encroachment
Constantia and the Defence of White Privilege in the "New" South Africa 123
by John Pape

CHAPTER 7

Viva Prepaids, Viva!
Assessing New Technology for Cost Recovery
in the Rural Northern Cape 143
by Hameda Deedat

CHAPTER 8

The Bell Tolls for Thee:
Cost Recovery, Cutoffs, and the Affordability
of Municipal Services in South Africa 161
by David A. McDonald

CHAPTER 9

Looking for Alternatives to Cost Recovery 183
by John Pape

INDEX 195

Acknowledgements

We would like to thank the contributors to this volume for their commitment to a research methodology that not only sheds light on the growing crisis of service delivery in South Africa but also contributes to change through the development of participatory processes and action-oriented dialogue. We extend these thanks to those citizens, workers, NGOs and bureaucrats who assisted with and/or participated in the data collection and analysis. We owe particular gratitude to Maria April, Dudu Khumalo, Steve Seloane and Lance Veotte of SAMWU, Simphiwe Dada of the Alternative Information Development Centre (AIDC), and to Youth for Work. We dedicate this book to all those involved in the struggle for a more just and sustainable system of service delivery in South Africa.

Meshack Khosa, formerly of the Human Sciences Research Council (HSRC), was instrumental in establishing the initial links between the HSRC and the Municipal Services Project and in establishing the basis for this joint initiative. To him we extend a warm thanks. John Daniel and Garry Rosenberg of HSRC publishing have been professional, courteous and supportive in the production of this volume, as has Robert Molteno of Zed Press.

Finally, we would like to thank all of our colleagues at the Municipal Services Project.

Funding for the research in the volume was provided by the project partners and by the International Development Research Centre of Canada (IDRC).

Preface

At present millions of South Africans face severe problems in accessing even the most basic services: water, sanitation, electricity, and refuse removal. All of us understand that the democratic government faced great difficulties and enormous backlogs due to the apartheid legacy. But unfortunately, the problems confronting many citizens today are not simply the result of historical factors. Much of what the authors of this book refer to as the "crisis of service delivery" is actually a result of the pro-market policies adopted by the South African government since 1994. This text goes a long way toward explaining this process. The authors have successfully combined rigorous theoretical analysis, copious statistical information, and a broad range of case study material. At the same time, the inclusion of numerous "live" interviews lends the book a quality missing in so many academic works.

But the book does more than just chronicle the complexities of our society. The writers included herein have also taken the initiative to further the discussion about where we might find opportunities to reverse this crisis. This book deserves to be widely read. I warmly commend it. The contents are not only relevant for those interested in the transition to democracy in South Africa, but for people across the world who are confronting the processes of a corporate driven globalisation which continues to swell the ranks of the poor in all countries of both the South and the North.

Dennis Brutus
Professor Emeritus, Professor of African Studies, University of Pittsburgh
Former Robben Island Political Prisoner

List of Contributors

Eddie Cottle is the Director of the Rural Development Services Network (RDSN). The major focus of his research has been water service delivery in rural areas.

Hameda Deedat is a researcher at the International Labour Resource and Information Group (ILRIG) which is affiliated to the Sociology Department at the University of Cape Town. She has written on service delivery and gender issues.

Grace Khunou has completed a Master's in Sociology. She is currently a Doctoral research fellow at WISER, a social research institute at the University of the Witwatersrand.

David A. McDonald is Director of Development Studies at Queen's University, Canada, and Co-director of the Municipal Services Project

John Pape is Co-director of the International Labour Resource and Information Group (ILRIG) at the University of Cape Town.

Greg Ruiters completed his Ph.D from Johns Hopkins University on the privatisation of services in the Eastern Cape. He is a lecturer in the Political Studies Department at the University of the Witwatersrand.

Mthetho Xali is a researcher at the International Labour Resource and Information Group (ILRIG) which is affiliated to the Sociology Department at the University of Cape Town. He has written extensively on public-private partnerships.

Introduction

by John Pape and David A. McDonald

Urban and rural development have been presided over by state bureaucrats and have been designed to entrench apartheid. It has been developer-driven and often carefully organised to disempower communities. The result is that development has failed, not only in our terms but in their terms as well.

That era is ending. People-driven development is now our watchword. But how do we transform a set of institutions consciously designed to prevent people-driven development and harness them to support communities?

Moses Mayekiso, National Chairperson of South African National Civics Association, April, 1994 (SANCO 1994)

The task for progressives is to formulate a development approach that builds on the best traditions of the democratic movement, and at the same time takes into account probable future realities. There are two primary points of departure: that organised communities must be the driving force of social progress; and that redistribution must guide economic growth policies. Although the growth-centred and spend-and-service development approaches are dominant, an alternative-community-controlled development has started to emerge within the civic movement ... current community-controlled approaches to development suggest that the past traditions of the mass movement can be appropriate for today's new challenges.

Planact, an NGO that worked closely with civics (1992)

In February 1995, the South African government launched Operation Masakhane (let's build together). According to Jay Naidoo, who was Cabinet Minister responsible for the African National Congress's (ANC) Reconstruction and Development Programme, the main aim of Masakhane was to facilitate "the restructuring of governance institutions so as to put the country on a path of sustainable development" (Naidoo 1997).

A key component of Operation Masakhane was urging residents to pay for services such as water, electricity, sewerage, and refuse collection. The logic of Masakhane was understandable. During the dark days of apartheid many residents had joined in the ANC's call to make the country "ungovernable". A central tactic for advancing ungovernability was withholding payment to unelected and unrepresentative "black local authorities" and "bantustans". Across South Africa, civic organisations and other democratic structures moblised on this issue. As a result, millions of residents simply stopped paying bills for rates and services in what was called a "rates boycott".

But when the first democratic elections took place in 1994 the "crisis of legitimacy" apparently ended. With a popularly-elected government in place, municipalities expected people to pay. At the time, Masakhane seemed like an inevitable step in the transition to democracy. There were few dissenters.

Yet while Masakhane may have had a broad developmental focus, by 1997 even leading ANC and South African Communist Party (SACP) stalwart Jeremy Cronin admitted that its message had simply become one of "black communities must pay up". Whether this was a misinterpretation or not, Masakhane became the first step in trying to impose a regime of cost recovery on impoverished residents. But even then Masakhane was the gentle kid glove of cost recovery with appeals to people's sense of responsibility and pride in nation-building. Leading figures like Archbishop Desmond Tutu and civic leader Moses Mayekiso were drafted for publicity campaigns. Yet, despite the millions of rands spent to hire advertising gurus Saatchi and Saatchi to promote Masakhane, the financial yields were minimal. In some cases, payment rates for municipal services actually declined.

This is not to completely disparage Operation Masakhane. Perhaps Masakhane was an appropriate programme and slogan to address the massive backlogs and inequities from the apartheid era. And some Masakhane projects likely helped communities to "build together". But in ideological terms, Masakhane became the lodestar in the building of a hegemonic framework of cost recovery. Since that time cost recovery has had a long, highly politicised journey in South Africa. To explain why we have chosen cost recovery as the focus of our research, we need to outline that journey in some detail.

The International Context

We must begin with an examination of the international context of South Africa's post-apartheid transition. Before 1994 the South African government was relatively isolated from global and continental trends. While Structural Adjustment Programmes were opening most African economies, the apartheid regime remained cloistered behind economic sanctions. While globalisation pressured governments to move away from direct economic interventions, the need to buttress white rule kept the South African regime away from extensive deregulation and privatisation (although there was certainly an increasing amount of contracting out to local firms in the 1980s and early 1990s).

However, as Patrick Bond (2000) has chronicled in detail, international financial institutions like the World Bank did not wait until the first democratic elections to woo South Africa's political and economic leaders into the market-forces camp. Throughout the early 1990s, World Bank delegations met frequently with key personnel in the African National Congress to ensure that the post-apartheid government would follow the so-called Washington Consensus in both macro- and micro-economic terms. By 1996, when the South African government abandoned the redistributive Reconstruction and Development Programme (RDP) for the neoliberal Growth, Employment and Redistribution (GEAR) framework, the World Bank's dark victory was nearing its final stage.

Under the market-oriented GEAR, South Africa embarked on a range of legislative and policy ventures that entrenched the power of corporate capital at the expense of workers and poor citizens in the country. While policies and laws often maintained some populist rhetoric, the underlying economic and political principles were informed by neoliberal principles of globalisation: fiscal restraint; export orientation; privatisation and corporatisation; financial and trade liberalisation, and cost recovery. This shift was nowhere more evident than in the area of local government and service delivery.

Local Government and Service Delivery: The shift to neoliberalism

Local government and service delivery were key points of engagement for the Mass Democratic Movement of the 1980s and early 1990s. As the transition to democracy approached, a wide range of organisations began to articulate post-apartheid visions of local government. These visions were a far cry from the neoliberal models which were eventually adopted. For example, the resolutions of the Congress of South African Trade Unions (COSATU) 1992 Economic Policy Conference included the following:

> There must be a redistribution of resources and power. This will have to be done by a process of state intervention combining nationalisation, anti-trust legislation, and other forms of legislative intervention including price control. A process of redistribution must be carried out by ... increasing the production and provision of basic necessities of electricity, water, transportation, housing, education, health and welfare, food, clothing and recreational facilities. The state must ensure that these basic services are retained in public hands and any such services that have been privatised should be renationalised.

This redistribution must be led by the state and financed by:
- redirecting existing investment;
- restructuring corporate tax in order to increase the tax collected;
- introducing progressive taxes such as land and wealth taxes; and
- increasing the level of savings both institutional and personal.

PLANACT (1992), a leading non-governmental organisation that worked closely with civics in the 1980s and early 1990s, drew a clear-cut dividing line on issues of municipal finance:

> It is internationally recognised that genuine development cannot work without a financial system that reinforces community control ... The role of the state, development agencies, service organisations and even business must be to operate in a way that builds a supportive environment for community-controlled development – even if this means going against what they perceive to be their immediate interests.

> The point of departure for any community-controlled development process is that finance and the financial system must serve the interests of poor communities and not the interests of those who control economic and political power (212).

This view echoed the sentiments of the South African National Civics Organisation (SANCO):

> Past attempts at "development" have failed and have actively undermined communities and prevented real development because they have been apartheid-driven and market-led. Funding allegedly meant to help poorer black people went to private developers and to prop up illegitimate apartheid institutions such as black local authorities and bantustan governments. Inevitably, private companies and better-off individuals have been the main beneficiaries of increasing ideological free-market funding systems...

> Most development finance in the past has given priority to private profit – of developers, contractors, individual homeowners and so on. This has proved corrupt and inefficient. Private companies ignore the poorest because they are less profitable. (1994, 6)

So hegemonic were the notions of redistribution, community control and grassroots democracy at this early stage of the debate that the ANC was prepared to defer to the powers of the civic associations. In the words of then-ANC activist Jackie Selebi:

> We think that the civic associations and some such structures dealing with local matters – water, electricity and such matters – must remain. Some members of the ANC will also be members of the civic associations because they also live in a particular township ... In the ANC they will deal with broader political issues, but when it comes to local issues like drainage and water, that will be left to the civic association (Seekings 1992, 232).

With regard to municipal economics, the ideas of the civics and Cosatu, as well as progressive academics, came to be embodied in the slogan: "One city, one tax base". At the local level, this slogan expressed perhaps the most fundamental economic premise of the liberation struggle: that the wealth of white individuals and white-owned businesses should be used to subsidise an improvement in the living standards of blacks.

These progressive ideas of mass organisation continued to carry considerable weight in the run-up to the first national democratic elections in 1994. Yet, at the same time, there were counter-pressures that became most evident in the transitional arrangements as spelled out by the Local Government Transition Act of 1993. The Act garnered a compromise that brought the civics and other mass democratic formations into multi-party structures with the new status of "stakeholder." For SANCO, long accustomed to being the sole legitimate representative of black communities, becoming one voice among many was a clear step toward disempowerment.

Over the next few years the stakeholder forum model was reproduced in many sectors. While the National Economic Development and Labour Council (NEDLAC) was the prototype, from 1993 to 1996 civic and youth activists flocked to RDP, Rural Development, and Community Development Forums in the expectation that these would be vehicles to bring services and genuine empowerment to their communities. But for the most part these structures were stillborn. They remained under-resourced and not given real political power. Decision-making gravitated upward.

While the 1996 Constitution guaranteed second-generation socio-economic rights, there was a highly contentious rider: affordability. The Bill of Rights granted all South Africans "the right to have access to sufficient food and water" (s27(1) b) and "to an environment that is not harmful to their health or well-being" (s24), but these "equality rights" are protected from "unfair discrimination solely on the grounds of race, colour, ethnic or social origin, sex, religion or language" (Table of Non-Derogable Rights). In other words, one's ability to pay does not factor in the Constitution. Nonetheless, the Constitution does tie the government's responsibility to deliver certain socio-economic rights to "available resources." This has subsequently been used as a constitutional justification for failure to provide access to certain rights.[1] As a result, citizens' rights are linked to the law of the market and cost recovery has sunk its claws deep into the Bill of Rights. From 1996 onwards, local government development paradigms shifted steadily from the redistributive state to the neoliberal "enabling" or "facilitating" state. At the level of finance, this meant moving from notions of redress and (cross-) subsidisation to full cost recovery (on which more will be said in Chapter 1).

However, the move to the neoliberal paradigm in general, and to cost-recovery in particular, was not a totally linear progression. Holdover pressure from the liberation struggle led to rapid expansion of infrastructure in the immediate aftermath of democracy. In particular, there were extensive rollouts of water and electricity infrastructure. The delivery of water was proclaimed a "miracle" by the Deparment of Water Affairs and Forestry and by 1999, it claimed to have reached the second million in terms of connections since 1994. Electricity also saw positive figures for connections. From 1991 to 1997 more than 1.5 million households were added to the electricity grid (NEDLAC 1999).

At policy level, even as late as the 1998 Local Government White Paper, some of the ideas of the RDP era remained. Hence the vision of local government as one that is "Committed to working with citizens and groups within the community to find sustainable ways to meet their social, economic and material needs and improve the quality of their lives".

Yet overall, the market continued to gain sway. The neoliberal model and its cost-recovery component gradually came to dominate both national legislation and local government practice. On one level this undermined many of the gains in infrastructure. For example, while two million households may have been given access to water between 1994 and 1999, cost-recovery measures and bureaucratic inefficiencies made many such projects inoperable. Peter Wellman estimated in 1999 that at least 50 per cent of the water projects were not functioning. In some instances failure was due to lack of maintenance. In other cases, government officials cited "vandalism". However, the "vandalism" often involved the destruction of meters – a likely form of resistance to cost recovery. Other researchers and even government officials acknowledged the severity of the problem of project failure (Wellman 1999).

---

[1] This has been the subject of heated legal battles in cases such as that of Christina Manqele in Durban, the Grootboom case in the Western Cape and the Soobramoney case in KwaZulu-Natal. In each of these cases citizens used their constitutional rights to access as a basis for gaining water, housing and medical services respectively. The Soobramoney case was the only one which definitively favoured the state's right to deny services. The appellant required dialysis for a kidney condition. His request was denied and he died within a few days after the denial. The cases over housing and water are subjects of ongoing litigation.

Apart from eroding some of the gains of service delivery, the ideology and practice of cost recovery became more dominant in a number of ways.

First, there is the question of how cost recovery influenced the then-Department of Constitutional Development's (DCD)[2] acceptance of the notion of basic service levels. In the Municipal Investment Infrastructure Framework (MIIF) of 1997, the DCD set basic services at the level of pit latrines and a five- to eight-amp electricity supply for urban residents with incomes of less than R800 per month. Applying such extraordinarily low standards to roughly 20 per cent of the population ultimately linked service delivery to cost recovery. The guiding principle had become one of "you get what you can pay for". And, since service infrastructure is typically a community rather than an individual provision, you also get the lowest common denominator (i.e. what your poorest neighbours can afford). In the context of South Africa, granting service quality along income lines was a guarantee that apartheid-era living standards would remain intact.

Apart from the question of basic service levels, access was further complicated by reliance on indigent policy. Indigent policy works on the notion that all households can afford to pay for services unless they can prove otherwise. Yet the process of "proving" poverty was often extremely complex. To begin with, there has been no standard national process or criteria for establishing indigence. Each municipality had to develop its own guidelines and admini-strative procedures.

Two examples from neighbouring municipalities in the North West province illustrate these difficulties. In 1999, residents of the former Eastern District Council area of Klipgat had to travel to Rustenberg to get information about qualifying as indigents. However, when they arrived there, they were informed that although the council had been allocated money to cover indigent subsidies, they had not yet developed a policy. Hence, there was no way to be declared an indigent. In nearby Ga-Rankuwa, a person's individual case had to be approved at a city council meeting before he/she become eligible for indigent subsidy. In the best of circumstances, indigent policies amount to harassment of the poor. But in many South African municipalities this harassment has been inserted into a process which makes it virtually impossible even to acquire indigent status. Yet without it citizens had to rely increasingly on the market to set their service tariffs.

With the steady cutbacks in central government allocation to local authorities as a result of GEAR, the market logic became more prevalent. For municipalities, reduced transfers from national government, coupled with expanded responsibilities, made cost-recovery and cost-cutting measures an almost inevitable choice. In many instances, the most direct and easiest methods were the harshest: cutoffs – either through direct administrative intervention or via installation of prepaid technology.

The hands of local authorities were further tied by the machinations of the National Treasury. Apart from cutbacks on central government grants to local authorities, stringent measures of fiscal conservatism were imposed. Through the GEAR-linked Medium Term Expenditure Framework, the Treasury imposed budget caps, limiting the percentage increase a municipality could make to any specific budget line item in a year. It also brought forward a draft Municipal Finance Bill which would bar national government guarantees for loans taken out by municipalities. In other words it was to be "sink or swim" for local governments, be they located in the industrial heartland of Gauteng or trying to survive on the meagre tax base in the rural Transkei.

These measures were complemented by the active promotion of public-private partner-ships (PPPs) through the Department of Provincial and Local Government's Municipal Investment Infrastructure Unit (MIIU). The MIIU actively undermined any notions of main-taining subsidised public-sector delivery. PPPs ensured that private-sector business principles, like cost recovery, were able to gain more and more influence on the ethos of local authorities.

This led to the outsourcing of functions in a bid to cut costs. The ultimate victims were retrenched workers or residents who ended up with higher tariffs. In some cases, outsourcing was the subject of very public contestation. For example, in Nelspruit in 1998, the South African Municipal Workers' Union (SAMWU) fought a long and bitter battle to block a

---

[2] Now the Department of Provincial and Local Government (DPLG).

30-year concession of the water service to the British transnational Biwater. But in the end the municipality handed over the contract to Biwater. Within two years, in many households, water charges had increased by more than 100 per cent.

But for every instance where privatisation and outsourcing were contested, there were dozens of incidents where functions were quietly outsourced – subtly moving the municipality farther along the road to business mode. Literally hundreds of services previously provided by municipalities were handed over to private providers – from bus services in Durban, to stormwater drains in Middelburg, to motor-vehicle registration in the Northern Cape, to street-sweeping in Cape Town. In some cases big companies with large amounts of capital were brought in. In other instances, a contract went to a local black-empowerment initiative. In still others, the service was handed to the "community" who were then expected to manage a library or park on volunteer labour and vastly reduced budget allocations.

Outsourcing was often complemented by a restructuring of departments which advanced the notion of the municipality as a set of financially ring-fenced units, each responsible for carrying its own share of the income load. Hence, whether it was electricity or a cemetery, a service was expected to cover costs or face the wrath of municipal powers. This was fully in line with the World Bank's vision of local government as a "conglomerate of firms, institutions, organisations and individuals with contractual agreements among them" (van Niekerk 2001, 67).

But perhaps the ultimate expression of the ascendancy of the local-level neoliberal model was the implementation of iGoli 2002 in the country's largest city, Johannesburg. Here, a management team led by contracted consultant Ketso Gordhan carried out a targeted programme of cutbacks, corporatisation, and selling off of municipal assets which changed the face of the city. In their drive to cut deficits (and also to earn performance bonuses), Gordhan and his team sent a signal to municipalities across the country: the developmental models forged during the days of the struggle were not in line with what was required in an era of globalisation. If South African municipalities were to take their place in the sun of bond trading and foreign direct investment, notions of redress and cross-subsidy would have to be sacrificed for market logic. Underpinning this shift was the alleged need for municipalities to adhere to a model of financial sustainability which required recovery of all costs, including those incurred through providing basic services to the poorest of citizens.

Not surprisingly, the efforts to implement iGoli 2002 met with considerable resistance. Organised labour, focusing on both job retention and affordable services, carried out a series of industrial actions in opposition to iGoli. At community level, a number of organisations began to emerge to defend communities against the knife edge of cost recovery. The most well-known became the Soweto Electricity Crisis Committee (SECC) which fought ESKOM's cutoff of more than 20 000 households per month in Soweto in early 2001 (Fiil-Flynn 2001) by launching Operation Khanyisa (light up). Under Operation Khanyisa, activists from the SECC defied the cutoffs by simply reconnecting citizens to the electricity grid, free of charge. In October 2001, the SECC was able to win a temporary moratorium on cutoffs, but the battle is far from over, with SECC protesters having been shot at and jailed for conducting a non-violent protest at the home of the Johannesburg City Mayor in April 2002.

While iGoli gained the most media attention, the implementation of cost-recovery measures and consequent resistance was not confined to Johannesburg. In September 2001, dozens of residents in Tafelsig, Cape Town, set up barricades to stop municipal officials attempting to carry out evictions. This was part of an ongoing battle with local government over service arrears. Like their counterparts in the SECC, Anti-Eviction Campaign members/activists did succeed in winning a temporary halt to evictions, but not a rejection of the policy.

Similar mass mobilisations against cost-recovery measures occurred in Chatsworth, Durban, and in Nelspruit, where an unlikely coalition, which brought together COSATU, the Pan Africanist Congress and traditional leaders, initiated Operation Vulaamanzi to re-open residents' taps after extensive cutoffs by Biwater.

A considerable thrust of organised labour's campaign against privatisation (as well as actions of social movements such as the Anti-Privatisation Forum[3]), is a manifestation of opposition to cost recovery. While the media tends to highlight unions' equation of privatisation with job losses, COSATU-affiliated unions in particular have repeatedly emphasised the fact that privatisation of service delivery leads to higher tariffs for the working class and the poor.

Explaining Non-payment

There are essentially two explanations for the shift toward cost recovery as a way of dealing with non-payment of services in South Africa. The first and most widely accepted within government is the so-called "culture of non-payment". According to this view, people became accustomed to not paying for their services during the years of the anti-apartheid rates boycotts, and stubbornly refused to change even under a democratic dispensation. Citizens, it is argued, have come to believe that it is their right to continue to receive free services.

Those who believe in the "culture of non-payment" see this as a serious threat to the viability of the South African political economy. They argue that service payment shortfalls will ultimately make the country's municipalities financially unsustainable. They extend their argument to say that financially unsustainable local authorities would not only be a problem for citizens but would also undermine the country's economic strategy. Without a solid financial base, municipalities are unlikely to have the potential to attract tourists and foreign investors who are deemed essential to economic turnaround in the GEAR framework. For those who see a "culture of non-payment" at the roots of municipal financial crises, stringent measures of cost recovery and cost cutting are the solution.

The alternative explanation holds that non-payment is actually related to issues of affordability and quality of service. Put simply, the affordability thesis holds that at the time of elections in 1994, roughly two-thirds of households were surviving on an income of less than R1 500 per month. Given the extensive financial burdens carried by most income-earners, rates and service payments are at times simply not affordable. Cyclical bills such as school fees, as well as unpredictable expenditure like healthcare or funerals, kept most poor households perennially in debt.

But the reticence to pay for services is further enhanced by equity considerations. Despite a democratic dispensation, people in historically black areas continued to have vastly inferior services to those in the historically white areas. This is what SAMWU President Petrus Mashishi has called "a culture of non-servicing" (Mashishi 1998). Critics of the "culture of non-payment" argue that willingness to pay is linked to the government's political will to upgrade service quality in historically black areas. As long as the "culture of non-servicing" and gross inequities persist, they would argue that payment levels are likely to remain low.

The research carried out in this book is based on the second hypothesis. In our view, cost recovery has already contributed to the perpetuation of poverty and inequality. Cost recovery has become far more serious than the early days of gentle arm-twisting under Masakhane. With cutoffs by remote control, and household invasions by ESKOM's "red ants", cost recovery threatens to unravel the very fabric of social and economic life in a democratic South Africa. This is an urgent issue, requiring both further research and social action.

---

[3] The Anti-Privatisation Forum (APF) began in Johannesburg as a response to the iGoli plan. Originally it included Cosatu, several of its affiliates, a number of community-based structures and a range of left-wing political organisations. In Johannesburg, COSATU eventually pulled out of the APF because of conflict with other organisations. In 2000 and 2001, APFs were formed in other municipalities. In late 2001 a national meeting of the APFs was held to develop a national programme of action. While COSATU is not active in most of the APFs, SAMWU, a leading COSATU affiliate, has taken a resolution to form APFs and has participated extensively in their development in most areas.

The Research

The research for this book forms part of a larger set of research activities under the auspices of the Municipal Services Project.[4] In tackling the specific issue of cost recovery we were informed by the following considerations:

a) **An appropriate mix of research methodologies**

This book consists predominantly of case studies. Examining a specific municipality or district should form the core of any such study. Without looking at the details of what happens at community, or even household level, there is little possibility of accurately assessing the impact of a sweeping policy such as cost recovery. But case studies have their limitations. Extrapolation and generalisation on the basis of what happens in Soweto or Bushbuckridge is problematic. Each community has its own particular set of dynamics which may make it the exception rather than the rule. Hence, we felt the need to combine our case studies with the results of an extensive national survey. At the same time, both case studies and national surveys typically provide little opportunity to elaborate a theoretical context. Cost recovery is not simply a policy of government. Furthermore, in South Africa, an examination of cost recovery must be situated in the broader context of the political transition after 1994, and the linkages between South Africa and the process of globalisation. Therefore apart from the case studies and the survey material, we have included chapters which consider the theoretical background of, as well as the vexing issue of alternatives to, cost recovery.

In addition, there is the question of quantitative versus qualitative methods. When we originally conceptualised the case studies, we envisioned random surveys of 200 households in the communities where we worked. However, we quickly realised the limitations of this approach. First, the sample size was insufficient to provide us with a statistically representative survey and would not therefore provide us with the ability to comment on national trends. More importantly, the strength of our research project resided in our political legitimacy. Most of our researchers have an extensive history of working with a wide range of community-based organisations, trade unions, and even political parties. The South African Municipal Workers' Union (SAMWU) is also one of the partners in the project. Our extensive networks and contacts in communities across the country provided us with access to residents and community leaders which is difficult for most researchers to replicate.

Hence, our starting point was our contacts with the community, not the demographic data of the municipality. This means that in many of the case studies we used "snowball sampling" methods – i.e. using our initial contacts to provide us with access to other people in the community who might be relevant for our research. For some researchers, such a method may be seen as inherently biased. However, we would argue that our work is a counter to the bulk of work done on these topics by consultants and researchers who never actually enter the communities they are researching, who rarely talk to ordinary citizens about their experiences of service delivery and policies like cost recovery, and who have a limited grasp of cultural and linguistic norms and nuances. We view our research as an opportunity to access the "voice of the voiceless" – those whose interests have not been adequately represented or even articulated in the shift from RDP to GEAR, from developmental local government to budget-balancing local authorities.

There is therefore an overall bias in our case studies toward qualitative research. Nonetheless, we have been rigorous. We have sought not only the views of those with negative

---

[4] The Municipal Services Project (MSP) is a multi-partner research, policy and educational initiative examining the restructuring of municipal services in South(ern) Africa. The project's central research interests are the impacts of decentralisation, privatisation, cost recovery and community participation on the delivery of basic services to the rural and urban poor. The research has a participatory and capacity-building focus in that it involves graduate students, labour groups, NGOs and community organisations in data-gathering and analysis. The research also introduces critical methodologies such as "public goods" assessments into more conventional cost-benefit analyses. Research results are disseminated in the form of an occasional papers series, a project newsletter, academic articles/books, popular media, television documentaries and the internet (the project website is at www.queensu.ca/msp). Research partners are the University of the Witwatersrand (Johannesburg), Queen's University (Canada), the International Labour Resource and Information Group (Cape Town), the South African Municipal Workers' Union, and the Canadian Union of Public Employees. The project is funded by the International Development Research Centre (IDRC) of Canada.

experiences. We have spoken with municipal officials, councillors, workers, politicians, and other researchers. Also, we have not relied simply on interview material, but like all professional researchers, have pored over legislation, policy documents and other relevant material.

Having made the case for the qualitative approach, we also acknowledge its limitations. Hence, we have included (in Chapter 8) the results of a national survey of more than 2 500 citizens, designed and conducted in collaboration with the Human Sciences Research Council (HSRC) of South Africa. This statistically representative survey is the largest and most comprehensive study ever undertaken in South Africa on people's experiences with, and attitudes towards, cost recovery on municipal services. The data provide an invaluable snapshot of the service delivery record of the ANC since the end of apartheid and serve as an important benchmark for future surveys on this matter. Most importantly, the survey acts as a reference point for the case study material, allowing us to extrapolate more confidently some of the conclusions from the smaller, qualitative studies, while at the same time enriching the otherwise narrow quantitative results of the large national survey. In the end, the two methods complement one another and offer a unique and powerful overview of the cost recovery situation on the ground.

The last issue we want to mention about our research methodology is participation. At the outset of the project, we agreed that our research should not be merely academic and detached but engaged and oriented toward action. Ideally, this participatory-action approach should involve citizens and social actors as researchers with the ultimate aim of breaking down the division between "expert" researchers and ordinary citizen-researchers. While we have held to this ideal, it has not been possible to implement it fully in every instance. Participatory action research is in all cases a time-consuming, process-intensive method. In some instances, such as the Makhaza case study done by Mthetho Xali, the conditions were suitable for high levels of participation by residents. But in other instances, either lack of time or the way in which a community was organised did not facilitate as extensive a participation and local capacity-building process as we would have liked.

b) **Geographical balance**

South African municipalities come in all shapes and sizes, but there are three legal categories: the large metropolitan areas like Johannesburg, Cape Town, Durban; smaller cities and towns such as Nelspruit and Queenstown; and rural districts.[5] In selecting our case studies, we attempted to strike a balance between the three categories. Key in this regard was ensuring a balance between urban and rural areas. Since research on local government and service delivery tends to be urban-biased, we wanted to avoid producing yet another study which uses findings in Johannesburg or Cape Town to paint a portrait of all of South Africa. With hindsight, we could perhaps have done better on geographical balance. Still, we have covered five provinces out of nine, represented significant rural areas in three of the case studies, and have collected information from all provinces and municipal category types in the national survey.

c) **Social justice**

We also wanted our case studies to focus on communities where central issues in the debates around cost recovery were evident. For example, Khayelitsha in Cape Town is a large township with many sections, but we chose to do research in Makhaza for two reasons: firstly, a large number of people in Makhaza had experienced cutoffs; secondly, and perhaps more importantly, the community had organised a vociferous response to these cutoffs. This criterion highlights our commitment to engagement in social action as researchers. While we make every effort to apply rigorous methodology to our work and to retain an appropriate distance from the communities where we do research, we also aim

---

[5] It should be noted that the categories of municipalities changed in the middle of our research. Categories A, B and C described here are those which were implemented with new lines of demarcation which took place simultaneous to the 5 December 2000 local government elections. This demarcation also reduced the number of municipalities from 843 to 284. The major changes of the demarcation were to amalgamate large cities into one metropolitan area and to amalgamate small rural municipalities into a single district.

for our research to enhance action and to promote justice. In an area like Makhaza, we hoped that our research would assist the community to assess the impact of cutoffs more systematically and also to develop the internal research capacity to monitor certain aspects of service delivery. On the other hand, in exploring the cholera epidemic in KwaZulu-Natal (KZN), we did not link up to specific local efforts at contesting policy. Rather, we wanted our research to impact on officials and policy-makers who were attempting to resolve the epidemic, and to aid in the prevention of similar outbreaks in the future as well. Finally our research helped inform a number of activities which emerged from the research. For example, much of the background research for this project was used to inform a series of workshops on service delivery conducted by the Internaional Labour and Resource Information Group (ILRIG) for SAMWU in 2000–2001. These workshops were aimed at assisting the union in developing its own policies on service delivery and the implementation of these possibilities through Local Labour Forums and the Integrated Development Plans.

d) **Gender and service delivery**

In tackling this research we were mindful that municipal services are a highly gendered area. The entire neoliberal model of the local state is premised on the availability of women's labour (formal and otherwise). When the state reduces service provision, it is women who typically take up extra burdens. This is largely because the range of municipal services is largely linked to household tasks which are often seen as "women's work" in the gender division of labour. Whether it be fetching water, collecting firewood, or looking after children, when access becomes more difficult, such as under cost recovery, women's workload increases. Hence, we have attempted to ensure that the gendered nature of the impact to cost recovery has been part of our analysis.

This, then, outlines the general issues we confronted in undertaking our research. Overall we have attempted to ensure that our design resulted in a participatory process that covered a wide range of communities in South Africa while striking a balance between the strengths and weaknesses of qualitative and quantitative methods. Having provided this overview, let us now turn to a brief summary of each of the chapters included in this study.

Review of Chapters

The book begins with David A. McDonald's overview of the theory and practice of cost recovery. It draws on international literature and practice in this regard – particularly as it has been articulated by the World Bank and its affiliates – and illustrates how and why these policies have been introduced in post-apartheid South Africa. The purpose of the chapter is to provide a conceptual overview of what cost recovery means in practical and theoretical terms, and prepares readers for the empirical case studies in the rest of the book. It begins with an overview of what cost recovery means in practice and then reviews the fiscal, moral, environmental and commercial arguments used to justify its implementation. The chapter concludes with a general outline of the problems associated with cost recovery in the South African context, particularly as they relate to low-income households. An examination of cost recovery takes us to the very heart of the neoliberal paradigm, and is essential to the promotion of balanced budgets, fiscal restraint, market discipline, and privatisation.

The first of the case studies comes from Wits Political Science lecturer Greg Ruiters. The author spent the better part of two years collecting information in three small towns in the Eastern Cape: Fort Beaufort, Queenstown, and Stutterheim. Even before the advent of democracy in South Africa, these municipalities had privatised water service delivery via a 25-year concession to Water and Sanitation Services of South Africa (WSSA), a wholly-owned subsidiary of French multinational giant, Suez-Lyonnaise des Eaux.[6] Because these concessions have been in effect for so long, it provides one of the best possible opportunities for assessing the medium-term effects of privatisation of services and the extent to which privatisation is accompanied by stringent cost recovery.

---

[6] The concession was signed in Queenstown in 1992, in Stutterheim in 1993, and in Fort Beaufort in 1994.

The chapter argues that the policy of cost recovery and the commodification of basic municipal services "pitted local bureaucrats and politicians against communities and destroyed reciprocity between citizens and the local state". In Ruiters's view, cutoffs of water, electricity and street lights have become part of the arsenal of state weapons wielded against the poor in a "low-intensity class war between desperate consumers and embattled local authorities".

Like Ruiters, Grace Khunou deals with the implications of cost recovery for citizenship in a democratic South Africa. A lifelong resident of Diepkloof in Soweto, Khunou became interested in the notions of service delivery and citizenship while completing a Masters' degree at Wits University. In this study she investigates her community's attitude towards, and experience of, the provision of electricity. She interviewed 33 people from various parts of Diepkloof: the working-class "matchbox houses", the more middle-class suburban-type houses and the informal settlement of Mandela Village. In Diepkloof, parastatal electricity provider ESKOM had carried out a programme referred to by one ESKOM manager as "massive cutoffs". Khunou's interviews reveal that service delivery problems, particularly those related to cost recovery and cutoffs, led some citizens to feel as if they had no rights. Most citizens who had such problems had little or no household income. For many, securing rights was not only about voting or even accessing services. Khunou then goes on to point out how under cost-recovery regimes, people's rights as citizens are conflated with the notion of "consumer" rights. Hence, they are only able to exercise their rights when they have an income which enables them to become a consumer. Khunou's conclusions and the comments by her interviewees tell us much about how far South Africa still has to go to become a fully democratic state where everyone enjoys full constitutional rights.

Chapter 2 is an analysis of the link between cost recovery and the cholera outbreak in rural KwaZulu-Natal. The disease affected over 100 000 people, more than 200 of whom died. Researchers Hameda Deedat and Eddie Cottle conducted interviews with citizens in Madlebe, a focal point of the cholera outbreak. Using a snowball sampling technique initiated through conversing with people at the nine communal taps in the community, Deedat and Cottle found an almost direct correlation between the implementation of a prepaid system and the cholera outbreak. The municipality initiated this system just a few months before cholera began to appear. Interviewees highlight the point that two problems in particular contributed to the usage of unpurified river and stagnant water: a registration/connection fee which was unaffordable to many residents; and the frequent breakdown of the entire system which left the community without water for up to three weeks at a time. The statements of residents are contrasted with the chilling disregard on the part of one uMhlatuze Water Board manager: "These people have been without clean water for years. They are used to it. What is a couple of weeks to them?"

From rural KwaZulu-Natal, we move to two very contrasting case studies in Cape Town. In the first, ILRIG researcher Mthetho Xali looks at water cutoffs in the Makhaza Section of Khayelitsha. Xali used the most participatory process of all the case studies. He worked closely with Youth for Work, a community-based organisation which had been working with residents of Makhaza on service delivery issues. Xali teamed up with the Youth for Work coordinator, Simphiwe Dada, and selected ten members of the organisation as research assistants. Xali and Dada provided training for these research assistants and worked closely with them in their fieldwork. The teams interviewed a total of 63 households who had experienced water cutoffs. Using a structured survey, the interviewers found that some people had been without water for almost a year. More than three-quarters (76 per cent) of the interviewees had also experienced periods where they could not access their electricity because they could not afford to "load" money into the prepaid system. Nearly all (95 per cent) gave affordability as the cause of their failure to pay their water accounts. Of this 95 per cent, nearly three-quarters were unemployed. Xali also found that community members had come together spontaneously to reconnect their water supply.

Like Khunou's interviewees in Diepkloof, respondents in Makhaza felt alienated from the local authority. In the words of one resident: "the action (the cutoff) shows that the council does not care about us". Not surprisingly, Xali concludes that cost recovery is "unlikely to succeed given the high levels of unemployment faced by most working-class communities". He predicts "an increase in struggles against it [cost recovery] and other neoliberal policies".

While Xali has predicted struggles against cost recovery, John Pape writes of another type of contestation in his chapter on Constantia: "The struggle to protect a certain form of race and class privilege". In contrast to the areas chosen for our other case studies, Constantia is extremely wealthy. In one survey it was adjudged the fourth-wealthiest suburb in South Africa, with individual house sales averaging R1.6 million. Primarily basing his conclusions on interviews with community leaders, Pape argues that, for these residents, cost recovery is not a problem. In fact, they have developed a strategy which attempts to protect their race and class privilege. Pape cites a number of ways in which organisations like the Constantia Property Owners' Association are actively involved in campaigning for Constantia to remain unchanged from the days of apartheid. Their argument is that "Constantia untouched" is a vital tourist attraction for the province (it is home to several famous wineries). The author, however, sees this strategy as one in opposition to the "encroachment" of the problems of the majority of South Africans. In his view, the privileged residents of Constantia have been able to avoid being the source of any real cross-subsidy because their interests coincide with those of policy-makers and bureaucrats advancing the neoliberal model. He argues that it is unsustainable to foist harsh cost recovery regimes onto the poor, whilst those who accumulated their wealth under apartheid reap further benefits of a liberation for which they did not fight.

The last of our case studies comes from Hameda Deedat. Working closely with SAMWU organiser Maria April, Deedat visited five small towns in the Northern Cape which had experience with prepaid meters. Although most residents had only used these meters for a short while, a large number reported widespread technical problems as well as periods where they could not afford to pay for services. In two of the towns she visited, the meters had been removed because of technical malfunction. But in Lennertsville, the prepaid technology had survived, much to the chagrin of nearly all those interviewed. Initially enthusiastic about the meters, even recalling the chanting of "Viva prepaids!" at a meeting where the council introduced the new system, the residents had subsequently become highly critical. Under the previous system, the residents paid R72 a month for all services. While they acknowledged that this was difficult to manage, particularly in households where no-one was employed, they could at least negotiate a schedule of payment with the council. With the prepaids, they simply went without. Particularly disturbing in Lennertsville was the way in which cost recovery had created tensions within the community. People were reticent to give water to those who had been cut off, since they had to pay for all the water they consumed.

After the case studies we move to a chapter by David A. McDonald which presents the results of the national survey conducted jointly with the HSRC. The survey findings reiterate the main points made in the case studies: i) that cost recovery measures are having a serious negative effect on the majority of households in South Africa; ii) that the major reason people are cut off is that they cannot afford to pay. Perhaps the most startling finding is that 13 per cent of the households interviewed had experienced water cutoffs, with an equal percentage having had their electricity cut off. Thirty-nine percent of these households had experienced cutoffs of both services. About three per cent of those sampled had been the victims of evictions for failure to pay arrears.

Apart from looking at incidents of cutoffs, McDonald also examines the attitudes of respondents toward cost recovery and service delivery. In particular, he addresses the need to "debunk" the "myth of a culture of non-payment". In supporting his argument he notes that 51 per cent of those who had arrears said they could not pay them "no matter how hard they tried."

The final chapter by John Pape takes us beyond a critical assessment of cost recovery and into the realm of "alternatives". In this respect, Pape offers two distinct possibilities. The first is a short- to medium-term set of alternatives and is somewhat "reformist" in scope, arguing for more equity-oriented models of cost recovery (i.e. more progressive block tariff structures, a better distribution of existing municipal resources, and job-creation strategies). But he also highlights the insidious effects of commodification, the role of the market in shaping the moral and economic fabric of service delivery, and the way we "value" essential goods such as water. In this regard he explores the longer-term potential for a more transformative vision of decommodified services in South Africa and what this implies politically, socially and economically.

A true decommodification of services is a long way off in South Africa (and in virtually every other country in the world), but it is useful to keep it in mind as an ideological antonym as we work our way through the theory and practice of cost recovery in this book. It is only when we fully understand the models within which we operate that we can hope to develop viable alternatives.

Conclusion

When we began this research project, we knew cost recovery was an issue that affected many people in South Africa but we had no idea of just how extensive its effects had been in terms of the sheer number of people affected, as well as of the impact it had had on their quality of life. We have spoken to people who have been evicted for arrears, people who have been forced to beg for water from a neighbour simply to wash a baby's nappy, people who for want of a mere R50 have been forced to consume water they know is infested with cholera. In the end, our research has strengthened our conviction that cost recovery is a threat to the poor and, ultimately, to the whole notion of a democratic transformation in South Africa.

Bibliography

Bond, P. (2000). *Elite Transition: From apartheid to neoliberalism in South Africa.* Johannesburg: Wits University Press.

COSATU [Congress of South African Trade Unions] (1992). Economic Policy Conference Resolutions.

COSATU [Congress of South African Trade Unions] (2001). Speakers Notes and memorandum on Privatisation, accessed at www.cosatu.org.za/speeches/2001/sn010816.htm.

Cronin, J. (1996). "Masakhane and socialism", accessed at www.sacp.org.za/umsebenzi/umseb9611.html.

Department of Constitutional Development (1998). White Paper on Local Government. Pretoria: Government Printer.

Fiil-Flynn, M. (2001). "The Electricity Crisis in Soweto". Occasional Paper 4, Municipal Services Project. Johannesburg:Wits University,

Mashishi, P. (1998). "Housing the masses". *Sowetan*, 23 October.

Naidoo, J. (1997). Speech given on Masakhane, 2 September, accessed at www.pwv.gov.za/ docs/sp/1997/sp970902.html.

NEDLAC [National Economic Development and Labour Council] (1999). Development Chamber Annual Report, accessed at www.nedlac.org.za/docs/socialreps/1999/development_chamber_se99.htm.

PLANACT (1992). "Transition and Development". South African Review 6,

Republic of South Africa, (1996). Constitution of the Republic of South Africa. Pretoria: Government Printer.

SANCO [South African National Civics Organisation] (1994). "Making People–driven development work". Report of the Commission on Development Finance. Johannesburg: SANCO.

Seekings, J. (1992). "Civic Organisations in South African Townships". *South African Review* 6, 216–238.

van Niekerk, S.(2001). "A commitment to developmental local government". New Agenda 2, 64–72.

Wellman, P. (1999). "Sustainability of South Africa's water miracle questioned". *African New Service,* May, accessed at www.thewaterpage.com/SAWS Problems. html.

People and Service Delivery

Mr Makhatini lives in Ngwelezane in KwaZulu-Natal. He currently resides in the sports field. The change rooms are part of the Ngwelezane soccer field that is situated on the border of Ngwelezane and Odondolo. According to Mr Makhatini he was granted permission by the former Empangeni Municipality to occupy the change rooms since they were no longer in use. For 17 years he had lived here with no incident, until two years ago.

One morning Mr Makhatini woke up and found that the Empangeni Municipality had ordered the removal of the infrastructure or water pipes surrounding his home. As a result the 17 years of access to purified water through an in-house connection, and water-borne sewerage, was removed from him and his family. According to Mr Makhatini he received no notification or warning of these developments, and no alternative water source or provision was offered to them by the muncipality. This situation left them with no alternative but to use the nearby river for their day-to-day water needs.

"We bath and do our washing there. We try not to drink the water; sometimes we come and boil the water, other times we walk long distances for clean water. The people of Ngwelezane cannot help me any more. The municipality has also started to cut off water in Ngwelezane, and people are scared they also won't have water since they cannot pay."

(Mr Makhatini, interview, April 2000)

Mr Makhatini also mentioned that he became ill from drinking water from the river. It was not clear from the interview whether he or any of his family had been treated for cholera.

He also added that despite his hardship, he did not have the right to free clean water from the trucks as a result of living on the border. According to the truck drivers he lived in Ngwelezane, and therefore had no right to the water. Mr Makhatini managed a successful appeal for compassion with one of the truck drivers, and has secured the delivery of clean water twice a week. He is however the first to admit that this situation is one of temporary relief and that his struggle to access clean water is far from over.

1

The Theory and Practice of Cost Recovery in South Africa

by David A. McDonald

Cost recovery refers to the practice of charging consumers the full (or nearly full) cost of providing services such as water and electricity. In direct contrast to the long-standing practice of the state subsidising these services, consumers around the world are increasingly expected to pay in full for service delivery.

This chapter lays out the theory and practice of cost recovery in South Africa as it applies to basic municipal services such as water, electricity, sanitation and waste management. It draws on international literature and practice in this regard, particularly as it has been articulated by the World Bank and its partners. It also illustrates how and why these policies have been introduced in post-apartheid South Africa.

The purpose of the chapter is to provide a conceptual overview of what cost recovery means in practical and theoretical terms, as well as to prepare readers for the empirical case studies presented in this book. I begin with a summary of what cost recovery means in practice and then review the fiscal, moral, environmental and commercial arguments used to justify its implementation. The chapter concludes with an overview of the problems associated with cost recovery in the South African context, particularly as it relates to low-income households. An examination of cost recovery will take us to the very heart of the neoliberal paradigm, with its focus on balanced budgets, fiscal restraint, market discipline and privatisation.

The chapter also prepares readers for the concluding section of the book, which deals with alternative approaches to cost recovery.

What is Cost Recovery?

The concept of cost recovery is a simple one: the recovery of all, or most, of the cost associated with providing a particular service by a service provider. For publicly owned service providers, this may or may not include a surplus above and beyond the cost of production, whereas for private-sector providers it necessarily includes a surplus (i.e. profit). In either case, the objective is to recoup the full cost of production.

Determining what to charge consumers is the difficult part. It is first to the pricing of services that we must turn, to better understand the basis of cost recovery.

For those services that can be accurately measured in volumetric terms (e.g. water, electricity, water-borne sewerage) cost recovery is achieved by charging end-users the (full) short-run marginal cost of production plus a portion of long-term operating and maintenance costs. To illustrate, if a person wanted to have electricity provided to their home, they would be expected to pay the cost of connecting the household to the electricity grid, a portion of the amortised operating and maintenance cost of the bulk infrastructure required to generate and distribute electricity, and a volumetric rate for the marginal cost of every kilowatt hour of electricity consumed.

There are several different ways of calculating these costs (Dinar 2000), but most models incorporate a downward-sloping marginal cost curve where, because of economies of scale, those who consume more of a service are charged less per unit of consumption than those who consume less. In practice, this has meant that poor households are in effect penalised on a per-unit basis because they consume less than wealthy households and industry.

In response to these equity concerns, progressive block tariffs have been introduced in many countries (including South Africa), in an effort to make the initial levels of consumption (or "blocks") more affordable, or even free, while charging increasingly higher prices as consumption levels rise. This rising tariff has the added potential benefit of curbing consumption at the top end, thereby introducing conservation incentives.

Block tariffs are not inconsistent with cost recovery, however. The difference with more orthodox pricing models is that block tariffs charge higher than marginal cost prices at upper levels of consumption in order to make up for lower-than-marginal cost prices at lower levels, effectively cross-subsidising the poor. Most importantly, they also provide individual consumers with a certain level of subsidised consumption.

It is important to highlight that not all services can be measured and priced on a volumetric basis. With services such as refuse collection and dry sewerage (as well as non-metered water or electricity), there is no way of accurately and easily measuring what an individual household has consumed. In such cases, cost-recovery models follow a flat rate that covers the average fixed and variable cost of the service. This can be done through a separate flat-rate charge or it can be included in a general rates account. Equity concerns can be dealt with through the application of differential rates, either along household-income lines (i.e. means testing), or through some form of property valuation (i.e. the higher the value of your home, the more you pay, regardless of your level of consumption).

Whether volumetric or flat, all cost-recovery models depend on "ringfencing" – i.e. the isolation of cost and revenue associated with a given service and the removal of subsidies in or out of that sector. Ringfencing means that resources – be they human or capital – cannot be shared between different service sectors unless they are paid for on a cost-recovery basis to the unit that provided them (e.g. a water department would pay the accounting department of a municipality for the cost of keeping its books). The intention is to ensure that a service provider knows all its fixed and variable costs and is therefore able to apply (marginal) cost pricing to its consumers.

Managerially, ringfenced units are controlled by officials who operate independently of all other service sectors, and at arm's length from elected authorities. Politicians generally retain the right to set standards and service delivery goals for a service unit, as well as monitor and evaluate their activities, but the daily management and long-term planning of the unit – including decisions about cost recovery – are carried out by the ringfenced management team, whose only concern is the management of its own sector.

In theory, therefore, the cost of water, electricity, refuse and sanitation can be isolated and applied to end-users (with varying degrees of equity considerations). In reality, the actual cost of service production is seldom known: costs are complex and difficult to measure; they are constantly changing because of the "lumpy" nature of infrastructure investments; there are inevitably joint costs that are difficult to apportion; accounting for externalities is constantly evolving, and so on (Renzetti 2000, 130). At best, cost-recovery models are an approximation of real costs.

In the end, it is *fuller* cost recovery that agencies such as the World Bank are after, i.e. charging prices that are as close as possible to the marginal cost in the short term, and to the average cost curve in the long term, with the aim of eventually achieving full cost recovery. We therefore use the term "cost recovery" in this book to refer not only to *full* cost recovery but also to the intermediary stages of *fuller* cost recovery.

How is Cost Recovery Enforced?

For any cost-recovery policy to be effective, a service provider must be able to measure the consumption of a particular service by an individual household regularly and accurately, and it must be able to collect payments. For volumetric services such as water and electricity, measurement is relatively easy with the use of increasingly sophisticated meters that measure the number of litres used and kilowatt hours consumed. Without meters it is virtually impossible to apply marginal cost pricing. For those services that are not measurable on a volumetric basis, it is necessary to approximate average consumption and to charge the average cost (with or without differential rates).

But the most accurate measurement and pricing systems in the world mean little if the service provider cannot collect the monies owed for services rendered. Effective administration is important here, including a good postal/payment system. Of equal importance are the punitive measures/threats used to persuade and force consumers to pay their bills. The most common form of punishment is to cut off a service to a household (or merely to threaten to do so). In the case of water and electricity this means disconnecting the household from the water and electricity mains. In most situations this is temporary. But in an increasing number of "delinquent" cases in South Africa, it involves shutting off services for weeks or months and sometimes the permanent removal of infrastructure to prevent illegal reconnections. Other enforcement tools include legal action, the attachment of assets, and, most controversially in the case of South Africa, the eviction from one's home for non-payment of services. Cutoffs are more difficult with services such as refuse collection and non-water-borne sewerage, but there have been cases in South Africa of households being denied these services as a penalty for non-payment of water or electricity (see Ruiters, this volume).

Cutoffs and evictions are expensive and politically sensitive enforcement weapons, however, which is why service providers interested in cost recovery are moving towards the use of prepaid meters wherever possible. A prepaid meter is a device that not only measures the exact amount of a service that is consumed – allowing for marginal cost pricing – but also forces users to purchase the consumption in advance. "Units" (be they litres of water or kilowatt hours of electricity) are purchased at a retail outlet and then entered into the prepaid meter with the use of an electronic "smart card" (the meters are usually located in or at the household, but can sometimes be centrally located and therefore controlled).

Prepaid meters are the ultimate cost-recovery mechanism. They collect money in advance, thereby earning interest for the service provider in the process. They also do not allow the consumer to go into default and, theoretically, they require no overt punitive measures to ensure payment for services. But there have been cases where prepaid meters were tampered with, and the system itself can be cheated. Service providers and meter manufacturers are actively working to develop more sophisticated meters, and to sell the prepaid meter as "pro-poor". The argument is that it allows low-income households to budget more effectively for services so as to avoid falling into debt. As one manufacturer of prepaid electricity meters stated to me in an e-mail on the subject, "Without controlling the meter it is not possible to control the [electricity] business".

The enforcement of cost recovery, therefore, requires a measuring system that allows a service provider to allocate costs to individual end-users, a billing system that informs consumers of their payment obligations, and collection mechanisms which ensure the payment of bills.

Cost Recovery in South Africa

Cost recovery for basic municipal services has not always been a policy of national and local government in South Africa. Only since the end of apartheid in the mid-1990s has full (or fuller) cost recovery been isolated as an explicit, widespread policy objective.

There were user fees, tariffs and general property rates for services under successive apartheid regimes, but for the most part these charges had little relevance to the actual marginal cost of providing them. This was partly due to the fact that it was virtually impossible to estimate the cost of a given municipal service because apartheid local governments were so fragmented. The City of Cape Town, for example, which is now a single "unicity", was composed of 25 municipalities and 69 local authorities prior to 1996.

More important was the lack of interest on the part of the apartheid state (national and local) to pursue full cost recovery. Indeed, the opposite was true, with heavy subsidies – both hidden and transparent – being provided for services such as water, electricity, sewerage and refuse collection. This was particularly true for white suburbs and industry. During the 1970s and 1980s, these areas received per capita infrastructure investments on a par with, or even higher than, most European and North American countries (Ahmad 1995). They continued, however, to pay extremely low rates for these services.

Even the black townships and "bantustans" received considerable subsidies for services (although much smaller in relative and absolute terms than those of white areas). Part of this subsidisation was direct – in the form of infrastructure developments and public housing in the 1960s and 1970s – but the bulk of it was indirect, extracted unwittingly from the apartheid state in the form of payment boycotts by township residents in the 1980s and early 1990s. In spite of the boycotts, the apartheid state continued to provide services to these areas for fear of the political fallout from not doing so, resulting in a *de facto* subsidisation of township services.

These service subsidisations were no doubt motivated in part by clientelist politics designed to win votes in white suburbs and maintain puppet regimes in the "homelands", but they were also driven by a "statist" vision of service delivery. In direct contrast to the neoliberal view of cost recovery and privatisation that dominates official service delivery discourse in South Africa today, the apartheid state saw its role as one of providing and subsidising the delivery of essential municipal services (albeit in a racially skewed manner).

The statist model came under attack in the mid-1970s with the formation of the Anglo American-financed Urban Foundation, began to splinter in the 1980s with the retreat of the National Party from state housing, and largely disintegrated in the 1990s. In fact, it has been under the post-1994 African National Congress – both nationally and at municipal level – that the push for cost recovery on basic municipal services has been most clearly and vociferously articulated. This shift has been supported and encouraged by an increasingly neoliberal civil service as well as by an ideologically reconstituted

New National Party (NNP), and an overtly neoliberal Democratic Party (DP) (Bond 2000, Marais 2000, McDonald and Smith 2002).

This ideological transformation is not total, however. There are still some bureaucrats, politicians and other members of the ruling elite, who believe that basic municipal services should be delivered by the state and should be heavily subsidised. But the paradigmatic shift to privatisation and cost recovery has been profound. Virtually every political party in the country has expressed explicit support for cost recovery in policy documents – most notably the ANC and the Democratic Alliance (DA)[1] – while implicit support from other quarters is evident in the silence that has met the introduction of aggressive cost-recovery measures in the legislatures and councils of the country.

Most South African municipalities are still a long way from meeting these cost-recovery goals – with payment rates in some areas as low 21 per cent of billings[2] – but the desire for full cost recovery is clear. In the meantime, it is *fuller* cost recovery that the South African government is after, with "cost reflexive" pricing being the preferred nomenclature.

Take, for example, the directive in the Municipal Systems Act (RSA 2000a) – the omnibus legislation that deals with municipal services throughout the country – that service delivery should be "cost reflexive" (s74.2.d). The same applies to policies for specific services such as electricity, water and sanitation. In the Draft White Paper on Energy Policy (RSA 1998b, 7), it is stated that "government policy is to ... encourage energy prices to be as cost-reflective as possible." In the White Paper on Water and Sanitation (RSA 1994, 19), it is argued that "government may subsidise the cost of construction of basic minimum services but not the operating, maintenance or replacement costs". The subsequent National Sanitation Policy White Paper (RSA 1996, 4) states: "Sanitation systems must be sustainable. ... payment by the user is essential to ensure this".

Some policy documents make it clear that *full* cost recovery is the objective. The White Paper on Water Policy (RSA 1997, 4) proposed that in order to "promote the efficient use of water, the policy will be to charge users for the full financial costs of providing access to water, including infrastructure development and catchment management activities".

It must be noted, however, that in each of these policy documents, attention is paid to questions of equity in the form of indigency clauses, progressive block tariffs and, most recently, "free services" for an initial block of consumption. After stating that government will "charge users for the full financial costs of providing access to water", for example, the White Paper on Water Policy (RSA 1997, 4) goes on to state that in order to "promote equitable access to water for basic needs, provision will also be made for some or all of these charges to be waived".

The National Water Act (RSA 1998c, s5.1) takes the equity issue further:

> *The Minister may from time to time, after public consultation, establish a pricing strategy which may differentiate among geographical areas, categories of water users or individual water users. The achievement of social equity is one of the considerations in setting differentiated charges. Water-use charges are to be used to fund the direct and related costs of water resource management, development and use, and may also be used to achieve an equitable and efficient allocation of water.*

---

[1] The Democratic Alliance (New National Party and Democratic Party) election manifesto for the 2000 local government elections, for example, states that "Increased [local government] income will be obtained from: expanding consumption-based user charging; recovery of outstanding rates and other debts; ensuring that all persons and organisations liable for rates, levies or other charges are properly billed; professional and tight credit control." The document goes on to state that "Municipal services delivered to households or used by households will be charged at cost, minus agreed-to rebates, plus a minimal surcharge sufficient to enable the accumulation of reserves for maintenance of equipment and facilities" and the party intends to "create a culture of payment for all services consumed above the lifeline level, inter alia by strictly collecting all arrears and debt" (Democratic Alliance 2000, 35, 39, 25).

[2] For example, for seven months at the end of 2001, residents of Khayelitsha in Cape Town paid 21 per cent of the amounts charged to them (*Cape Argus*, 20 February, 2002, "Khayelitsha is city's top debt headache" by Moses Mthetheleli MacKay).

Similarly, the Municipal Systems Act (RSA 2000a, s97.1.c) states that tariffs for municipal services can be differentiated if based on indigency (i.e. poverty).

In other words, cost-recovery policy in South Africa has explicit equity considerations, and distinguishes itself in this respect from more orthodox cost-recovery models based on simplistic downward-sloping marginal cost curves.

But, as noted above, progressive block tariffs, indigent policies and even free blocks of services are not necessarily inconsistent with full cost recovery. The difference is where price points are placed *vis-à-vis* levels of consumption and at what point on the consumption scale consumers are expected to pay towards the full cost of service delivery. As we shall see below, the manner in which block tariffs, free services and indigency policies have been introduced in South Africa has only marginally protected the poor but disproportionately benefited the rich. Within the neoliberal state, such measures are constrained by being part of a broader cost-recovery model and are intended to alleviate some of the hardest edges of this model, not replace it.

Another sign of the move toward cost recovery in South Africa is the rapid and extensive introduction of meters – particularly prepaid meters – for volumetric services. Even communal water stands are being metered using prepaid systems in many municipalities, while in some areas communal taps are being replaced with yard taps or in-house connections (with significant connection fees of up to several thousand Rands).

But the most visible feature of the move to cost recovery in South Africa comes in the form of punitive measures for non-payment of service bills. Service cutoffs, attachment of assets and evictions from households are now common throughout the country, and receive considerable media attention. Research undertaken for this book (see McDonald, Chapter 8 this volume), suggests that as many as 10 million South Africans have had their water cut off and 10 million have had their electricity cut off since the end of apartheid. Furthermore, some two million people have been evicted from their homes for non-payment of service bills. Legislatively, the Municipal Systems Act grants local authorities this power, most notably the right to "seize property" for non-payment of services (s104.1.f).

The Rationale for Cost Recovery

The following sections provide a theoretical overview of the fiscal, moral, environmental, and commercial arguments used by those who support cost-recovery measures, and highlights how these arguments have been adopted in the South African context.

Fiscal arguments

The single most important reason given for cost recovery is the need to "balance the books". Cost recovery, as the World Bank (1998, 44) is wont to say, is "a matter of good public fiscal practice", allowing governments to reduce tax burdens and thereby attract and retain human and financial capital. Cost recovery in lower-income areas, it is argued, reduces the need for cross-subsidisation from industry and higher-income households, making a country or a municipality a more financially attractive place to locate to. These competitive pressures are often most explicit at national level, but are becoming increasingly common at municipal level as well. Cities and towns are increasingly competing with each other for investment while struggling to deal with the downloading of responsibilities and cutbacks in intergovernmental transfers.

It is also argued that cost recovery is necessary to sustain services on a long-term basis. Without cost recovery, the argument goes, the state will not have the funds to invest in future service and infrastructure upgrades and extensions. Cost recovery is seen as "pro-poor" because it provides the fiscal basis for further service improvements and expansion: "When a public-sector utility does not recover the costs of providing a service, it is often unable to extend the system – leaving poorer, marginal areas unconnected to the grid" (Brook and Locussol 2002, 37).

The South African government adopts the same basic line of argument, stating in the Water Supply and Sanitation Policy White Paper (RSA 1994, 23) that if government does not recover operating and maintenance costs there will be a "reduction in finances available for the development of basic services for those citizens who have nothing. It is therefore not equitable for any community to expect not to have to pay for the recurring costs of its services. It is not the government who is paying for its free services but the unserved."

These micro-economic policies are reinforced at the macro level with the fiscally conservative Growth, Employment and Redistribution (GEAR) framework. Introduced by the ANC national government in 1996 without any consultation with its labour or civic allies, GEAR's effect on cost recovery has been profound. Firstly, it has resulted in significant decreases in intergovernmental transfers from national to local government, resulting in an 85 per cent decrease (in real terms) between 1991 and 1997, and further decreases of up to 55 per cent between 1997 and 2000 (Finance and Fiscal Commission 1997; Unicity Commission 2000). Moreover, the amount of funding from central government is so low that it will take decades to address the backlogs. In fiscal 2000, the total value of transfers to local government across South Africa was only R3 billion. Projections of the capital costs required to address service backlogs are in the order of R45 billion to R89 billion (depending on the level of service provided), with government-sponsored operating costs adding many billions more (RSA 1995, 2000c).

National government has also put caps on rates increases that local government is able to levy on (wealthy) property owners. The Draft Local Government Property Rates Bill (RSA 2000b, Chapter 2, s4–5), for example, states that local governments cannot apply taxes at local level which threaten its own tax-reducing, fiscally conservative strategy, as evidenced by the following quotations:

> A municipality may not ... exercise its power to levy rates on property in a way that would materially and unreasonably prejudice national economic policies, economic activities across its boundaries, or the national mobility of goods, services, capital or labour.

> The Minister, with the concurrence of the Minister of Finance, may by notice in the Gazette, set a limit on the amount of the rate that municipalities may levy on property; or the percentage by which a rate on property may be increased annually.

With approximately 90 per cent of all local government revenues being generated locally (of which approximately 25 per cent come from property rates), these caps mean that local government is unable to increase its own revenue pools significantly through progressive taxation. Little wonder, then, that local authorities have begun to push for fuller cost recovery as a way to finance and expand service delivery.

Competition for investment is also a critical factor here. As South Africa and its larger cities vie for increasingly mobile and fickle flows of private capital, municipal governments are under pressure to reduce tax and tariff rates in order to make it cheaper for firms to operate. As a result, there are pressures to minimise (if not eliminate and even reverse) cross-subsidisation measures in commercial, industrial and high-income areas.

Consider the following. The Durban Chamber of Commerce and Industry "has in recent years expressed the concern of its members regarding the increasing cost of doing business in the Durban Unicity area. The cost of water is one of the major components of the total infrastructural cost, over which our members have no control ... The prime concern of the Chamber is ensuring that the trading environment in the Unicity area contributes to the national and international competitiveness of its members in both commerce and industry." The Chamber goes on to complain that the "expensive rural water schemes" in the newly formed Unicity have "exacerbated the financial implications of possible solutions [i.e., put pressure on business to help pay for the costs of these water extensions]" and says that it will work to maintain "acceptable" bulk water tariffs (Anon. 2002).

Another revealing quote comes from the former Director General of the Department of Constitutional Development (the person in charge of all infrastructure development in the country): "If we increase the price of electricity to users like Alusaf [a major aluminium exporter], their products will become uncompetitive."[3]

In other words, if a country/city wants to be internationally competitive in terms of attracting private capital, it must reduce subsidies (at least for the poor), and boost its cost recovery efforts.

Moral arguments

Another set of arguments used to justify cost recovery are moral in nature. The first of these revolves around liberal notions of rights and responsibilities. If people have the "right" to a service like water, they also have the "responsibility" to pay for it.

The South African Constitution and Bill of Rights are classic expressions of this thesis. "Everyone has the right," for example, "to have access to sufficient food and water" (Bill of Rights, 1996, s27.1.b). All South Africans would also appear to have the right to services that protect their basic health and well-being, such as refuse removal and sanitation, as captured in the Bill of Rights environment clause (s24): "Everyone has the right to an environment that is not harmful to their health or well-being; and to have the environment protected, for the benefit of present and future generations, through reasonable legislative and other measures that prevent pollution and ecological degradation (for more on this point see Glazewski 2002). The right to electricity is more difficult to ascertain, but the Department of Minerals and Energy's Draft White Paper on the Energy Policy of the Republic of South Africa (RSA 1998b, 3), does argue that "Energy should ... be available to all citizens at an affordable cost."

But these rights are met with obligations. The Department of Water Affairs and Forestry, for example, has taken out half-page newspaper advertisements titled "Knowing your water and sanitation rights and obligations", in which it is clearly stated that one obligation is "paying your bills for services rendered".[4] According to the Municipal Systems Act (RSA 2000a, s5.2.6), this obligation applies across the board, with residents having the "duty" to pay for all of their municipal services.

Considerable efforts have gone into enforcing this message of civic responsibility in South Africa, and tying it to a broader notion of civic and personal development. These goals are perhaps best exemplified by the Masakhane ("let's build together") campaign. Introduced with much fanfare in 1995 by then-president Nelson Mandela, the campaign has focused largely on convincing (low-income) consumers to pay their bills for water, electricity and other municipal services. But the ANC has also been at pains to point out that Masakhane is about more than bill payments. It is seen as a broad political vision that makes service payments part of a larger societal transformation: "The true essence of Masakhane [is] mass involvement in the transformation process" (ANC 1997).

A related argument is to be found in the burgeoning "willingness to pay" literature. The rationale here is that most people – low-income households included – accept their civic responsibility to pay the full cost of service delivery, and are happy to do so as long as the services are reliable, affordable, and of good quality (see, for example, Jiminez 1987; Whittington, Briscoe and Mu 1990; Whittington, Lauria and Mu 1991; Alberini and Krupnick 2000).

---

[3] Chippy Olver as quoted in the *Mail & Guardian*, 22 November , 1996.
[4] See *Business Day*, 7 March , 2002.

Finally, it is argued that only by paying the full cost of a good or a service can one appreciate its true "value". Receiving a service for free, or having it heavily subsidised, distorts not only its exchange value but its use value as well. According to the World Bank (1999, 44) only "a fee reflecting the costs will encourage users to correctly value the service they receive". Charging a fee will "help reverse the 'entitlement mentality' that has been the historical result of subsidising public services".

The notion that a service such as water could have a use value without an exchange value – i.e. a right without a (financial) responsibility – is an alien one to the commodity-oriented cost-recovery literature. This final point takes on a didactic tone in South Africa, with private capital and apartheid-era municipal bureaucrats keen to inculcate market values in township dwellers and rural Africans.

Environmental arguments

These moral arguments are extended to the environmental arena. Subsidisation, it is argued, promotes wasteful consumption of environmentally sensitive services such as water, electricity and refuse collection because the "correct value" is not reflected in the price. There is, therefore, little financial incentive to limit consumption. In other words, subsidies promote waste, while cost recovery promotes conservation.

The World Bank (1994, 83) has the following to say about the environmental benefits of cost recovery on electricity:

> *Efforts to mitigate environmental impacts through consumer investments in energy saving are hampered by low consumer prices and subsidies. On average, developing countries use 20 per cent more electricity than they would if users paid the incremental cost of supply. Once economic pricing is established, governments are able to promote the use of more energy-efficient technologies.*

The argument that prices are the best or, indeed, the only way to shape human behaviour is central to all (neo)liberal tropes, from Adam Smith onwards. Without price incentives and market institutions, humans behave in self-maximising and destructive ways (the "tragedy of the commons" thesis). Proper pricing, on the other hand, creates a moral and economic framework for environmental sustainability by appealing to our own self-interest.

The World Bank (1994, 81) argues that these price incentives should be structured in the form of rising block tariffs (in order to curb over-use by the rich). With downward-sloping cost curves for many services, this is in fact the *only* way that conservation can be achieved through pricing mechanisms. In reality, however, the World Bank (and the South African government) do not always promote sufficiently progressive block tariffs with prices that would really make a difference to consumption at the upper end. This is especially true of commercial agriculture and industry in South Africa, which have been amongst the most inefficient users of water and electricity, and flagrant producers of waste, in the world.[5]

Commercialisation argument

Much is also made of the link between cost recovery and commercialisation. The argument that cost recovery promotes efficiency, accountability and transparency by providing easy-to-understand performance indicators is based on two premises: a financial surplus means success; a deficit means failure. Subsidies, by contrast, obscure the bottom line, making it difficult to evaluate service performance in a given sector, and contributing to bureaucratic sloth, mismanagement and fraud.

---

[5] For example, South Africa, with a miniscule percentage of global industrial production, produces some two per cent of the world's greenhouse gas emissions, much of which is generated by coal-fired electricity generators and consumed in large (and cheap) quantities by industry (Eberhard and Van Horen 1995). See also McDonald (2002).

This introduction of business principles is a key part of the neoliberal transformation of municipal services. Broadly defined as the "commercialisation" of services, these principles apply equally to publicly owned, ringfenced service units (i.e. corporatisation), as well as to public-private partnerships and outright privatisation.

The stated rationale here is that finances are the only true and reliable indicator of service performance (just as they are the only true indicator of a service's "value"). Cost recovery, it is argued, forces managers to think continuously about the bottom line, engenders creativity, forces transparency, and provides an incentive to improve service delivery constantly through performance-based salaries. This is a system where the evaluation and remuneration of managers is determined by financial results.

But cost recovery must also be seen as a crucial step in the privatisation of municipal services. For without full (or close to full) cost recovery in the public sector, there is little chance of furthering the cause of privatisation. No private firm is interested in purchasing a public utility that only collects 50 per cent of its costs in revenue (unless it can obtain subsidies from the state to make up the difference, which is not uncommon).

Addressing a UNDP/World Bank workshop on financing water delivery, Mike Muller, the Director General of the Department of Water Affairs and Forestry (DWAF) in South Africa, had the following to say about the relationship between cost recovery and privatisation:

> I must be blunt. There are many who believe and/or hope that the private sector may make money available for basic levels of service in poor communities. But we must remember, the private sector cannot (and should not) be bankrupted; it is there to make a profit. So we should not imagine that private-sector involvement is somehow going to make it possible for the poor to get what they cannot afford to pay for – at least not directly (1999, 4).

In other words, the private sector will not (and "should not") provide services to the poor at below cost. Cost recovery is paramount, and services will only be provided by the private sector to those who can pay, or will be provided at a level that people can afford (e.g. communal water taps and pit latrines).

Having said that, it would be incorrect to conflate cost recovery with privatisation. "Cost reflexive" service providers can remain public and still satisfy the fiscal restraint objectives of neoliberalism. It could even be argued in the current South African context that public-sector service managers are more aggressive than their private-sector counterparts when it comes to cost recovery. Given their desire to prove themselves as being "business minded", and the incentive of remunerations based on cost-effective performance, many municipal managers are keen to demonstrate that they can be as conscious of the bottom line as any private-sector manager. The public sector also tends to service more low-income areas due to "cherry-picking" in the private sector, and therefore has to deal with the more difficult cost-recovery cases, making its efforts more visible.

Problems with Cost Recovery in South Africa

I have alluded to a number of concerns with cost recovery thus far, but turn now to a more explicit critique of how it has been applied in South Africa. The discussion is broken into two parts. The first describes a series of practical concerns with cost recovery and highlights the inequitable manner in which it has been applied. South African cost-recovery policy and legislation makes a rhetorical commitment to equity, but when it comes to implementation it has been anything but. In highlighting these concerns, I also anticipate some of the short- to medium-term arguments being made in the final chapter of this book on "reformist alternatives" to cost recovery – quick and important ways of alleviating some of the most regressive aspects of cost recovery as it is currently practised.

The final section looks at the larger theoretical question of commodification and the distorting effect this has on our ability to develop systems of production and consumption of essential goods and services beyond the dictates of the market.

Historically unfair

Perhaps the single most compelling argument against full cost recovery in South Africa is the fact that it was not practised under apartheid. As noted earlier, white South Africans and industry benefited enormously in social and economic terms from heavily subsidised municipal services. Now that apartheid has officially ended, black South Africans are expected to pay their own way, with scarcely a mention of the fact that this has not always been state practice. The ahistorical nature of policy development and the hard-hitting tone of the Masakhane campaign reek of hypocrisy in this respect, with the biggest beneficiaries of the formerly subsidised system – white ratepayers and industry – being the most vociferous advocates of a user-pays system.

Continued subsidies for the rich

Inequality in cost recovery is not just an historical concern, however. There are clear and significant examples of ongoing pricing biases in favour of suburban residents and industry. There are, for example, enormously different tariffs for electricity in South Africa, with rural (African) households paying on average 48c per kilowatt hour (kWh), while suburbanites pay an average of only 23c. Township residents will often pay more for electricity than their suburban counterparts do, despite being in the same city. Residents of Soweto, Johannesburg, for example, were paying about 30 per cent more per kWh than were residents in the nearby wealthy area of Sandton (Fiil-Flynn 2001).

Industry benefits the most in this regard. To illustrate, average electricity prices for the manufacturing and mining sectors in South Africa are in the order of 12c per kWh, while deals are negotiated with large consumers (e.g. Alusaf) for prices as low as 3.5c per kWh (Fiil-Flynn 2001, 4). In fact, South African industry enjoys the lowest industrial charges for electricity in the world.[6]

Part of the reason for these price differences is that capital costs in most suburban and industrial areas are sunk and fully amortised, while in township and (especially) rural African areas, prices reflect the full capital cost of new infrastructure development and upgrading. In other words, suburbs and industry continue to benefit from the racially skewed investments of apartheid because of a pricing structure that has largely written off their fixed costs. There are competitive reasons at play here as well, with the South African government keen to keep industry globally competitive, even if this means subsidising its electricity at below cost.

There are also hidden subsidies for suburbs and industry. One of the most significant is the ongoing skewed nature of municipal spending and resource distribution. Recent research by the Municipal Services Project has shown enormous differences in resources available for service delivery in suburbs and industrial areas compared to townships. In Cape Town, for example, discrepancies of five, ten and even one hundred-fold were not uncommon in the water and waste management sectors (McDonald and Smith 2002), with similar results in the waste management sector in Johannesburg (Barchiesi 2001). In effect, township residents are paying the same (or higher) per-unit prices for a given service as are suburban residents, while in practice receiving considerably lower resource allocations.

---

[6] *Business Day*, 25 April, 2001.

Voluntarism as a form of cost recovery

Another form of inequality is found in the guise of voluntarism. Using the argument that low-income households/neighbourhoods are unable to afford the full cost of a particular service (or a particular level of service), municipalities will often ask local residents to contribute their labour on a volunteer basis so as to lower the costs of service delivery. Not only are there hidden health and social costs associated with picking refuse off the street, cleaning sewers, digging ditches, and so on, there are also gender, race and class dimensions to this form of cost recovery which make it little more than a neo-apartheid strategy of cost recovery. Take, for example, the following quote from a rural dweller:

> The RDP [Reconstruction and Development Programme established by the ANC in 1994] is ridiculing our mothers. Our mothers are made to dig trenches. It is called employment. Whereas you walk right around this South Africa and you never find a white woman digging a trench. The dignity of our mothers is taken because they have to dig trenches, while they have to feed their babies, cook for their loved ones (cited in Budlender 1998, 21).

Progressive block tariffs?

Despite the lip service paid to rising block tariffs for water and electricity, few municipalities in South Africa have introduced and enforced them in a meaningful way. Most block tariffs rise steeply in the first one or two blocks after the "lifeline" or free block, penalising those at the lower end of consumption while tapering off or even decreasing at the top end. Some municipal tariff structures are regressive from the start, with prices decreasing as consumption increases (see Ruiters, this volume, for a description of this phenomenon in the Eastern Cape).

But even where tariff structures are rising, they are unlikely to make any significant difference to the consumption patterns of well-to-do suburbanites as they are currently structured. In Cape Town, for example, which has one of the most progressive water-tariff structures in the country, a household will pay only R212.40 for consuming 60kl of water per month – an enormous amount of water (used for watering gardens, filling swimming-pools, and washing cars), but hardly a budget-breaking expense for the typical middle- to upper-income suburban family with monthly household earnings of R6 000 or more. Meanwhile, a household in the townships consuming 20kl of water per month would be paying R36.40 – a considerably lower payment in absolute terms but one that is likely to be much higher in proportional terms given typical household incomes in the townships of R500 per month or less.[7] In fact, it is not uncommon for low-income households to spend 25 to 40 per cent of their incomes on basic municipal services (see Chapter 8, this volume).

Block tariffs in South Africa must be considerably more progressive if they are to play an effective role in cross-subsidisation and conservation. They will also need to be more consistent across (and within) municipalities in order to avoid capital flight to places where tariffs for industry and high-income households are low.

Free services?

A related problem is the issue of "free services". This concept was initially developed by the national office of the ANC and used in the lead-up to the local government elections of December 2000. It was subsequently adopted by the Democratic Alliance as part of its election campaign the same year. The free services policy is a variation on block tariffs with the initial block of consumption in water (six kilolitres) and electricity (50kWh) provided free of charge on a per-household, per-month basis.

---

[7] Figures taken from the following tariff structure: the city does not charge for the first block of water (0 to 6kl), while the second block (7 to 20kl) is charged at R2.60/kl, the third block (21 to 40kl) at R4.10/kl, the fourth block (41 to 60kl) at R5.50/kl and the final block (61kl+) at R7.00/kl (City of Cape Town 2001).

Although potentially progressive, and an important step forward in the cost-recovery debates in South Africa, free services in practice would appear to have made little difference to the lives of the urban and rural poor since being introduced in mid-2001. First, there is the problem of the quantity of free services being offered. With respect to electricity, the 50 free kWh per household per month being offered by ANC-controlled municipalities (20kWh by DA-controlled municipalities) will provide some financial relief, but this amount of electricity will only run a light bulb and a few small appliances for a month (one kilowatt hour will light a 100-watt light bulb for ten hours). Moreover, 50 per cent of rural families are not on the electricity grid, which means that, for some time to come, millions of low-income households will not benefit at all.

The promise of 6kl of water per household per month also offers little financial respite. Many low-income households use considerably more than six kilolitres because of the relatively high average number of occupants per household and also because of the old and leaky apartheid-era infrastructure. Rapid tariff increases after this free block can mean that poor families end up paying more, not less, for water than they did under the old tariff structures. Those accustomed to paying a "flat rate" for services have seen dramatic price increases for both water and electricity (more than 400 per cent for the cost of electricity in some cases in Soweto, despite a 15 per cent decrease in the average real price of electricity since 1994 (Fiil-Flynn 2001)).

The 6kl figure is based on an average household of eight people and works out to 25 litres per person per day. This is at the bottom end of the World Health Organisation's (WHO) recommended daily minimum – with estimates of 50 litres being more common in the health literature – and is well below the 50 to 60 litres per day called for in the ANC's original Reconstruction and Development Programme (RDP) as a medium-term service delivery goal. To put this in perspective, the average bathtub takes 200 litres to fill, while the average toilet uses 10 to 15 litres per flush – a situation made worse by the fact that water (and energy) saving devices have never been a serious part of service delivery strategies in South Africa.

The fact that many low-income households comprise more than eight people heightens the problem, as does the fact that for many people this water is only delivered to a communal, metered standpipe within 200 metres of the recipient's household (as part of the "basic level" of services envisioned by the ANC). With violence and rape a serious problem in many low-income areas, these communal standpipes can be both inconvenient and unsafe, particularly after dark.

Another concern with the use of the household as a unit of measurement for free water and electricity is its intrinsic bias against low-income families. For example, a young couple with two incomes and no dependants living in a home in the suburbs receives the same amount of free water as a single, unemployed mother with seven dependants living in a run-down council house or shack in the townships. In many municipalities (e.g. Durban), households are not means-tested to see if they qualify for the free service (using the rationale that the administrative cost of these tests would outweigh the savings). The result of this is that some middle- and upper-income South African households are benefiting more from the provision of free lifeline services than are poor households. This is not to suggest that individual means-tests should be used to determine which households should have access to free services – a potentially degrading and divisive procedure separating the very poor from the even poorer – but it does highlight the inherently inequitable feature of basing free services on a per-household basis.

Finally, there is the problem of delivery. Although free water and electricity were to have been implemented across the country on 1 July, 2001, implementation delays have been widespread. This is particularly the case in rural areas. There have also been disputes over what level of government should cover the costs of free services. In the case of electricity, unresolved negotiations between the parastatal ESKOM and national government over the subsidisation of the free 50kWh has resulted in lengthy delays for free electricity in Soweto and other township and rural areas.

Moreover, many households are not receiving free blocks of water and electricity because they are in arrears, and there are widespread reports of continuing cutoffs of water and electricity despite the free services policy. The Department of Provincial and Local Government (RSA 2002, 30–1) reported that more than 296 000 disconnections of electricity and 133 000 disconnections of water took place in the last quarter of 2001 – most of which would have been low-income households. This at a time when "free services" promises had been in effect for several months. Still, these figures do not tell the whole story. Data are incomplete, with not all municipalities reporting and no statistics forthcoming from ESKOM which cut off as many as 20 000 households a month in Soweto in early 2001 (Fiil-Flynn 2001).

Narrow accounting methods

Even if block tariffs were more progressive, municipal resources more equitably distributed, and free services more accessible, neoliberal cost-recovery models (South Africa's included) are fundamentally flawed in their narrow accounting methods. Only direct financial costs are included in the cost recovery analysis, leaving out many of the less tangible but equally important cost and benefits of service delivery such as gender equity, public health and safety, and the environment. As a result, pricing structures tend to overcharge the poor (for whom lower prices would generate considerable private- and public-good benefits), and undercharge the well-to-do (who have never paid the *real* social and environmental costs of their hedonistic consumption patterns in South Africa). To account for all of these social and environmental costs would dramatically alter the cost recovery equation.

One of the reasons this is not done is that these social and environmental costs are very difficult to quantify. What kind of monetary value, for example, does one attach to a valley that has been flooded out by a new dam, or the loss of dignity associated with service cutoffs? These are real costs, nonetheless, and must be taken into account.

Other costs, such as public health epidemics, are more easily measured. A recent study has shown that the cost of dealing with all diarrhoea-related illnesses in South Africa in 1995 (much of which was a direct result of poor water and sanitation services and no doubt exacerbated by water cutoffs), was R3.4 billion in direct medical costs and R26 billion in lost economic production. This is more than the total amount needed to provide water infrastructure to everyone in the country for a ten-year period (Moodley 2000).

And yet, even these relatively easy-to-measure costs are ignored in the drive for cost recovery in South Africa. One tragic example is the cholera outbreak that began in mid-2000. As Deedat and Cottle argue (see Chapter 2, this volume), it was the introduction of cost-recovery efforts on water in rural KwaZulu-Natal that precipitated (or at least exacerbated) the cholera crisis. Households that could not afford the new connection fees and volumetric charges for water were forced to use contaminated ponds and rivers for bathing and drinking. The outbreak has been the worst in South Africa's history and has led to over 100 000 infections, and close to 300 deaths. Ironically, the state is now spending tens of millions of Rands dealing with the epidemic, many times more than it was costing the provincial government to provide free (unmetered) communal tap water prior to the cost-recovery measures.

Ringfencing is partly to blame here as service managers focus on their own narrow sectoral bottom lines – uninterested or uninformed about the implications of their decisions on other sectors. There is a fundamental contradiction here between the drive to ringfence a service so it can better isolate its own micro costs and the need to understand the broader macro-economic costs and benefits of a particular service (e.g. public health).

Nor can one forget the fact that national and municipal governments are under increasing pressure to keep operating costs as low as possible for footloose international capital. To include the true cost of gender equity, environmental sustainability and spatial desegregation into water and electricity tariffs would undoubtedly put South Africa and its cities at a competitive disadvantage. Instead, government has made it clear in its 1998 White Paper on electricity that prices to industry must not be affected by the (true) costs and benefits of a household electrification programme: "Cross-subsidies should have minimal impact on the price of electricity to consumers in the productive sectors of the economy" (RSA 1998b, 12).

Harsh measures

Another concern with the way that cost recovery is being implemented in South Africa is the harsh way in which it is enforced: letters threatening legal action, cutoffs, evictions, intimidation and even overt violence. In some cases, private companies (e.g. the so-called "red ants" of Johannesburg's townships) are hired to remove not only the furniture, but the physical structure of the dwelling itself. As people desperately resist, they are subject to significant physical abuse and intimidation. Tear gas, rubber bullets and real bullets are used against anti-eviction protestors, as happened in the township of Tafelsig, Cape Town, in September 2001. Members of the Soweto Electricity Crisis Committee in Johannesburg were shot at in April 2002 as they protested against cutoffs in front of the mayor's house.[8] Some families have returned from work to discover their homes auctioned for non-payment of services, and their belongings on the street (Deedat, Pape and Qotole 2001). In other cases, people have had services cut for non-payment of bills totalling thousands of rands, received as a result of defective piping, faulty meters, and/or incorrect meter-readings.[9]

More subtle forms of injustice and insult include: pensioners waiting for hours on end in the heat and cold to pay their bills at under-staffed municipal offices, and receiving rude service when they do finally get to speak to someone; a lack of flexibility when it comes to payment schedules despite (low) fixed incomes; being told that you should be used to living without water and can get by a little longer.

These are not merely isolated incidents. As noted earlier, cutoffs and evictions have been widespread in the country, with millions of people being subjected to either a water or an electricity cutoff, or an eviction from their home for non-payment of service bills. Not all of these incidents have been violent, but the emotional impact is extreme. The fact that ESKOM, the main electricity provider, reported a 37 per cent increase in profits to R2.56 billion in 2001 adds insult to injury.[10]

There are also the insidious injustices of prepaid meters. Far from being the friends of the poor, prepaid meters merely conceal the extent of service cutoffs by having low-income households cut their own consumption at the point of purchase by buying only as much as they can afford. Although it is too early to know the full impact that this new technology may have, if the experience in the UK of prepaid meters is anything to go by (Drakeford 1998), it is very likely that they will yield yet another layer of inequity in South Africa.

Finally, despite the fact that large commercial and industrial consumers are often the most delinquent, and largest, payment defaulters, low-income households bear the brunt of cost-recovery efforts. In the City of Cape Town, businesses and industry make up just under a third of the R2.1 billion outstanding in service payments.[11] Newlands cricket ground alone has been allowed to run a deficit of some R4 million in service arrears.

---

[8] See also Desai (2002), for examples in Durban.

[9] See also Fiil-Flynn (2001), for examples in Soweto.

[10] "Cost Cutting Helps Eskom Profit up 37 per cent", *Cape Times*, 7 March, 2002.

[11] "Council Takes Aggressive Action to Claim Arrears", *Cape Argus*, 26 February, 2002.

There has even been a proposal by the city to offer tax rebates to the stadium.[12] Meanwhile, low-income families have been evicted from their homes in the city's townships for arrears of only R1 500 and some have received threats of eviction for arrears as low as R250.[13]

Unconstitutional?

It is ironic that there are such strong moral overtones to the cost-recovery agenda, and such morally bankrupt means of implementation. In fact, service cutoffs and household evictions are very possibly unconstitutional. Although the Bill of Rights does not provide for equity based on income (see Introduction, this volume), it does provide the right to a "healthy and safe environment", as well as "access to adequate housing", under which access to basic municipal services would seem to apply. The landmark Grootboom case in the Constitutional Court in May 2000 would appear to have set a precedent for socio-economic or "second-generation" rights as enshrined in the Constitution (access to housing in this case), and could be used in future court challenges against service cutoffs and evictions.

One international indication of the potential for this constitutional/legislative change is found in the United Kingdom. Water cutoffs to residential homes, schools and other essential public buildings have been outlawed since 1999 after a rash of cutoffs took place following the privatisation of water services. It has also been ruled that self-imposed cutoffs through the use of prepaid meters is illegal, and that it is the responsibility of the water supplier to ensure water provision even if the household is unable to pay for prepaid consumption (Drakeford 1998).

Blindly ideological

It is also worth noting that much of the cost recovery efforts to date in South Africa have been driven by a blind ideological faith in neoliberalism. There has been no thorough analysis of the costs and benefits of cost recovery, and no dedicated effort to explore alternatives (aside from the politically expedient decision to offer "free" water and electricity in the run-up to local elections in December 2000). Nor has there been sufficient effort to restructure and redistribute existing municipal resources which remain highly skewed along racial lines and are inefficiently deployed. Local government has been virtually silent on the dramatic cutbacks in intergovernmental transfers as well, effectively accepting its fate of unfunded mandates, and has been pushing hard to collect the full cost of municipal services without challenging the state for a larger slice of the national budget. The DA in Cape Town did threaten to make this an issue in the lead-up to the December 2000 local elections, but did not follow up on it, no doubt because of its own commitment to macro-economic restraint at national level.

Municipalities, especially the large metropolitan ones, also seem blindly committed to the notion of being globally competitive. Barely a report from any city in the country is released without some reference to being "world class" and "a good place to invest."

But it is the lack of monitoring and evaluation of cost recovery that is perhaps most disturbing of all. This book represents the first concerted effort in South Africa to measure and evaluate the impacts of cost recovery, and provides the only comprehensive set of quantitative and qualitative data available. The Department of Constitutional Development, now the Department of Provincial and Local Government (DPLG), did run a tracking programme in the mid-1990s called Project Viability which included some questions for municipalities about the number of cutoffs they had undertaken each

---

[12] *Gemini News*, 22 February, 2002.

[13] In a revealing Letter to the Editor of the *Cape Argus* on 13 March, 2002, George D van Schalkwyk, the Interim Manager: Revenue and Debt Management for the City of Cape Town, wrote (in response to a previous letter in the paper): "The alleged threat of evictions for water accounts of R100 is incorrect; only accounts exceeding R250 were handed to the attorneys".

[14] For an analysis of Cape Town, see McDonald and Smith (2002).

quarter. Unfortunately, reporting rates of municipalities were as low as 30 per cent, and the programme stopped after a few years.

The DPLG has begun to collect this raw data once again – starting in mid-2001 – but has not made it available to the public through its website as it did with earlier Project Viability data. The results cited earlier (more than 296 000 electricity disconnections and 133 000 water disconnections in the last quarter of 2001) are included in this book only because we managed to get access to a leaked version of the report. The data are also incomplete, with only 88 per cent of municipalities reporting, and there are inconsistencies in data presentation. In the end, it is not certain that cost recovery advocates in the government understand, or even know about, the implications of the disconnection policies.

Nevertheless, bureaucrats and politicians accept the mantra of balanced budgets, ringfencing, and commercialisation, and forge ahead with a neoliberal agenda while listening intently to advisors from the World Bank and other like-minded donor institutions, paying millions of Rands to consultants from the private sector to help them with their cost-recovery plans.

Decommodification

Many of the concerns cited here can be mitigated to a greater or lesser extent by remedial policies and actions of local and national government: more progressive tariff structures; a better distribution of existing municipal resources; more flexibility in payment schedules and/or writing off of arrears; more holistic accounting methods; larger quantities and a wider range of "free" services; new legislation banning water cutoffs to residential housing and public buildings; a dedicated commitment to collecting and analysing data on the impact of cost recovery. Although complicated, these and other measures could be enacted in South Africa and would make a significant difference to the lives of millions of people in the short to medium term (see, Pape, this volume, for a more detailed discussion).

But as difficult as it would be to introduce these reformist policy measures in South Africa, it is the longer-term question of "decommodification" (i.e. removing "price" altogether as a determinant in the production and consumption of services like water and electricity) that will prove to be much more intractable. Decommodification is a call that is being heard with increasing frequency in South Africa and in the anti-neoliberal literature more generally (e.g. Barlow and Clarke 2002; IFG 2002). The rationale is that societies the world over have determined (and to some extent continue to determine) resource distribution by means other than exchange value, making decisions based on notions of "the commons", shared cultural values, etc. Although not unproblematic in themselves (e.g. gender relations can be unequal in "traditional" cultures), these noncommodified systems of production and distribution provide powerful alternatives to the neoliberal cost-recovery framework.

Are they feasible in South Africa? One immediate concern is what would be done with rich households and industry. Would these consumers also be given access to "free" water and electricity? Would their "shared cultural values" fit with those of low-income families? What would be the power relationships between multinational corporations and households when it came to determining distribution of water on a basis other than price? Clearly there are some very real concerns here that would require an enormous shift in institutional decision-making, political culture, and so on.

Partial decommodification (of, say, water and electricity) is not going to resolve these tensions either. The problem is that these services still function within a larger market economy which is constantly (re)inventing new products and needs, requiring ever-increasing volumes of supply and putting constant upward market-driven pressure on their use and allocation. The domestic use of water and electricity, therefore, cannot be separated from the broader production and consumption cycles of capitalism and the role of prices in determining what gets produced and for whom.

Decommodification is an all-or-nothing proposition that takes us to the heart of the market economy, built as it is on the transformation of "things" (with a "use value") into products (with an "exchange value") through the use of wage labour. To challenge this transformation process and the impact it has on growth and the allocation of resources is to challenge the very foundations of capitalism itself (Harvey 1982).

A massive proposition indeed, and one that takes us far from the seemingly technical challenges of a more equitable pricing system. These are essential considerations, nonetheless, as South Africa grapples with the question of what makes for a fair and sustainable system of producing and consuming basic municipal services.

Acknowledgements

I would like to thank the following people for their comments on an earlier draft of this chapter: Peter McInnes, John Pape, John Williams, Patrick Bond, Laila Smith, Alex Loftus.

Bibliography

Ahmad, J. (1995). "Funding the Metropolitan Areas of South Africa". *Finance and Development*, September.

Alberini, A. and Krupnick, A. J. (2000). "Cost-of-Illness and Willingness-to-Pay Estimates of the Benefits of Improved Air Quality: Evidence from Taiwan". *Land Economics* 76(1), February.

ANC [African National Congress]. (1997). Supplement to *Mayibuye: The Journal of the ANC*, October.

Anon. (2002). "Water Costs Increases". *Chamber Digest: Official Newsletter of the Durban Chamber of Commerce and Industry* 3, 16 February.

Arimah, B.C. (1996). "Willingness to Pay for Improved Environmental Sanitation in a Nigerian City". *Journal of Environmental Management 48*, October.

Barchiesi, F. (2001). "The Commercialisation of Waste Management in South Africa". *Occasional Papers Series No. 3*, Cape Town: Municipal Services Project.

Barlow, M. and Clarke, T. (2002). *Blue Gold: The Battle Against Corporate Theft of the World's Water*. Toronto: Stoddart Press.

Bond, P. (2000). *Elite Transition: From Apartheid to Neoliberalism in South Africa*. Durban: University of Natal Press.

Brook, P.J. and Locussol, A. (2002). "Easing Tariff Increases: Financing the Transition to Cost-Covering Water Tariffs in Guinea," in Brook, P.J. and Smith, S.M. (eds.). *Contracting for Public Services: Output-Based Aid and its Applications*. Washington D.C.: World Bank.

Budlender, D. (1998). *The People's Voices: National Speak Out on Poverty Hearings, March to June 1998*. Commission on Gender Equality, South African Human Rights Commission, and South African NGO Coalition, Johannesburg.

Business Day, 7 March, 2002.

Business Day, 25 April, 2001.

City of Cape Town (2001). Water and Sanitation Tariffs – 2001/2002 Budget Year, Executive Committee Memo, 22 May. Mimeo.

Cape Argus, 20 February, 2002.

Cape Argus, 26 February, 2002.

Cape Argus, 13 March, 2002.

Cape Times, 7 March, 2002.

DA [Democratic Alliance]. (2000). *For ALL The People*. Local Government Manifesto, December.

Deedat, H., Pape, J. and Qotole, M. (2001). "Block Tariffs or Blocked Access? The Greater Hermanus Water Conservation Programme". *Municipal Services Project Occasional Papers Series*, 5. Cape Town.

Dinar, A. (ed.). (2000). *The Political Economy of Water Pricing Reforms*. New York: Oxford University Press.

Desai, A. (2001). *The Poor of Chatsworth: Race, Class and Social Movements in Post-Apartheid South Africa*. Durban: Madiba Publishers.

Drakeford, M. (1998). "Water Regulation and Pre-payment Meters". *Journal of Law and Society*, 25 (4), December.

Eberhard, A. and Van Horen, C. (1995). *Poverty and Power: Energy and the South African State*. Johannesburg: Pluto Press.

Fiil-Flynn, M. (2001). "The Electricity Crisis in Soweto," *Municipal Services Project Occasional Papers Series,* 4. Cape Town.

Financial and Fiscal Commission (1997). "Local Government in a System of Inter-governmental Fiscal Relations in South Africa: A Discussion Document" Midrand: Mimeo.

Gemini News, 22 February, 2002.

Glazewski, J. (2002). "Rule of Law: Opportunities for Environmental Justice in the New Democratic Legal Order" in McDonald D.A. (ed.). *Environmental Justice in South Africa*. Athens: Ohio University Press.

Harvey, D. (1982). *The Limits to Capital*. Oxford: Basil Blackwell

Hui, E.C.M. "Willingness to Pay for Better Housing in Hong Kong: Theory and Evidence". *Urban Studies* 36(2), February.

IFG [International Forum on Globalisation]. (2002). "A Better World is Possible: Alternatives to Economic Globalization – Report Summary". San Fransisco: IFG.

Jiminez, E. (1987). *Pricing Policy in the Social Sectors: Cost Recovery for Education and Health in Developing Countries*. Baltimore: Johns Hopkins University Press.

Mail & Guardian, 22 November, 1996

Marais, H. (2000). *The Limits to Change*. Cape Town: Juta Press.

McDonald, D.A. (ed.), (2002). *Environmental Justice in South Africa.*Athens: Ohio University Press.

McDonald, D. A. and Smith, L. (2002). "Privatising Cape Town: Service Delivery and Policy Reforms Since 1996". *Municipal Services Project Occasional Papers Series, 7*, Cape Town.

Moodley, S. (2000). "Investigating Total Economic Burden: South Africa's Diarrhoeal Disease Burden in 1995". Group for Environmental Monitoring, Johannesburg.

Muller, M. (1999). "From Where Does the Money Come for Basic Levels of Service for Water Provision?" Paper presented at the *Regional Workshop on Financing Community Water Supply and Sanitation White River, Mpumalanga, South Africa, 26* November to 2 December.

Renzetti, S. (2000). "An Empirical Perspective on Water Pricing Reforms". In Dinar, A (ed.). *The Political Economy of Water Pricing Reforms.* New York: Oxford University Press.

RSA [Republic of South Africa]. (1994). Water Supply and Sanitation Policy White Paper. Cape Town: Government Printers.

— (1995). Municipal Infrastructure Investment Framework, Ministry in the Office of the President and the Department of National Housing, 12 June Cape Town: Government Printers.

— (1996). National Sanitation Policy White Paper. Pretoria: Government Printers.

— (1997). White Paper on Water Policy. Pretoria: Government Printers.

— (1998a). Municipal Structures Act, No. 117. Pretoria: Government Printers.

— (1998b). Department of Minerals and Energy, Draft White Paper on the Energy Policy of the Republic of South Africa. Pretoria: Government Printers.

— (1998c). National Water Act, 36 of 1998. Pretoria: Government Printers.

— (2000a). Local Government: Municipal Systems Act of 2000. Pretoria: Government Printers.

— (2000b). Draft: Local Government: Property Rates Bill. Pretoria: Government Printers.

— (2000c). Draft: Municipal Infrastructure Investment Framework (MIIF), Department of Provincial and Local Government, February.

— (2002) Department of Provincial and Local Government, Quarterly Monitoring of Municipal Finances and Related Activities, Summary of Questionnaires for Quarter Ended 31 December 2001. Pretoria: Government Printers.

Unicity Commission (2000). "Building a Unified City for the 21st Century: A Summary of Proposed Service Delivery and Institutional Change for the Term of Office of the New City of Cape Town". Cape Town.

Whittington, D., Briscoe, J. and Mu, X. (1990). "Estimating the Willingness to Pay for Water Services in Developing Countries: A Case Study of the Use of Contingent Valuation Surveys in Southern Haiti". *Economic Development and Cultural Change* 38, January.

Whittington, D., Lauria, D.T. and Mu, X. (1991). "A Study of Water Vending and Willingness to Pay for Water in Onitsha, Nigeria". *World Development* 19, February/March.

World Bank. (1994). *World Development Report: Infrastructure for Development.* New York: Oxford University Press.

— (1999). *Urban Property Rights Project Appraisal Document*, Report No. 18245 PE, 15 July, Poverty Reduction and Economic Management Unit.

— Latin America and the Caribbean Region, accessed on 8 May 2002, at http://www-wds.worldbank.org/servlet/WDS_IBank_Servlet?pcont=details&eid=000009265_39 80901093233.

People and Service Delivery

A skin disease called *"kwasa-kwasa"*, said to be caused by polluted river water, is afflicting infants and children of Soweto-on-Sea and Veeplaas in the Eastern Cape. Clinics in the area devote much of their time to the treatment of children with this skin disease. Similo Wonci of the Zwide Health and Welfare Forum says people often dump dead animals and domestic waste into the Chatty River. This combines with toxic industrial waste ejected from the Swartkops salt lakes.

Some residents have also been found keeping pigs and grazing other animals on this marshy area, which is also used as a playground by children. Some of the pupils of the Soweto-on-Sea Primary School are alleged to frequent the area after school to play.

Wonci said they were alarmed to discover that children swim at a spot just a few metres from where the pigs are kept and where the toxic industrial waste was dumped.

The erstwhile Port Elizabeth Municipality cleansing division, which previously collected refuse and guarded against the pollution of the Chatty River, contracted this function out to Umzamo Waste.

Umzamo has been responsible for the cleaning of Soweto-on-Sea since 1996. Municipal environmental health officer Lulama Snyman said they were not satisfied with the performance of Umzamo Waste. Since the company had taken over, a problem of littering had emerged in Soweto with dumping of domestic waste and dead animals in open fields and the river. Snyman says according to recent tests the polluted water was causing the spread of a skin disease among children and muscle and joint pains amongst older people.

Umzamo Waste chairperson Mbulelo Nikwa denies these allegations. He says they collected refuse in every street on a regular basis. However, his company was not responsible for the cleaning of the Chatty River. This was the function of the municipality, he said.

(Adapted from City Press, 20 May, 2001)

Debt, Disconnection and Privatisation

The Case of Fort Beaufort, Queenstown and Stutterheim

by Greg Ruiters[1]

Since 1994, when the African National Congress (ANC) came into power, much has been made of the progress in water and electricity connections to the poor in South Africa. Yet the daily reality of disconnections and social exclusion remains under-explored and a one-sided view of progress in service delivery has emerged that ignores qualitative changes in the entire field of local politics brought about by privatisation. In the last seven years, large-scale disconnections of water and electricity for non-payment of services have become a standard feature of all local municipal politics. For example, in the winter of June 1998, an estimated 90 000 South African homes had their electricity cut off, with only 42 000 subsequently reconnected (DCD 1998). Taken over a year this rate suggests that more than 500 000 homes may have been disconnected in 1998. In many cases, these mass disconnections have fuelled left-wing local politics, inner council splits (between politicians themselves, and between politicians and bureaucrats) and new social movements.

This chapter examines the record of privatised municipal services debt and related service disconnections in three Eastern Cape towns. Fort Beaufort, Queenstown and Stutterheim were among the first municipalities in South Africa to experiment with having their water and sanitation services handed over to private companies in long-term contracts. Under these arrangements, municipal services were run as public-private partnerships, a policy that subsequently became a central thrust of the ANC's solution to service delivery problems in South Africa. In terms of these contracts (signed between 1992 and 1995), a territorial monopoly was transferred to the private company, which became the sole provider of water services within these three municipalities. The municipalities had to pay the company a predetermined fixed fee each month and a variable fee depending on the volume of water sold to consumers. The fixed monthly

[1] The author acknowledges the support of the International Dissertation Field Research Fellowship of the Social Sciences Research Council (New York), the Washington Explorers Club, and the kind assistance of councillors and other interviewees in Fort Beaufort, Queenstown and Stutterheim.

payment rose every year, linked to inflation, and had to be paid by the council, even if water consumption declined or consumers boycotted payments.

This chapter argues that the policy of cost recovery, and the commodification of basic municipal services associated with these contracts, has pitted local bureaucrats and politicians against communities, and destroyed reciprocity between citizens and the local representatives of the state. Cutoffs of water, electricity and streetlights have become part of the arsenal of weapons the state wields against the poor in a low-intensity class war between desperate consumers and embattled local authorities. Councillors have been charged with policing neoliberal austerity at local level, testing their credibility and putting their positions in jeopardy. Witness the following ultimatum laid down by the Acting Municipal Manager of Queenstown:

> If people do not pay rates and services accounts, there will be no option than to reduce services. The extreme would be to cut salaries of councillors and municipal employees (The Representative, 12 January, 2001).

In the first part of this chapter, I offer a brief introduction to privatised services, the background to the company operating the water and sanitation systems and the aims of privatisation. In part two, I show the size of tariff increases in the 1990s, the racial inequalities in tariffs, and changes in tariff systems. Finally, I look at the magnitude of consumer services debt and service cutoffs in all three towns as a result of cost-recovery efforts.

The French Water Company and Depoliticised Services

Water and Sanitation Services South Africa (WSSA), previously called Aqua-Gold (AG), originated as a French-South African company. Formed in 1986 as a subsidiary of the Goldstein Group, and based in Natal, the firm had its first contracts with the bantustan government of KwaZulu. The company gradually built up a large number of service con-tracts with other homeland governments (specifically Bophuthatswana and KaNgwane), and various mining companies (Aqua-Gold 1991, 1). Aqua-Gold, in partnership with Group Five, also absorbed Everite Holdings (a pipe manufacturer) in 1992, thereby extending vertical integration and consolidating monopoly power in the water industry. The combined leverage of several large firms thus lay behind Aqua-Gold.

Aqua-Gold changed its name to Water and Sanitation Services South Africa (Pty) Ltd (WSSA) – a wholly owned subsidiary of Lyonnaise Water Southern Africa (linked to the large French multinational Lyonnaise des Eaux). Between 1992 and 1995, in the dying days of apartheid, WSSA took over three Eastern Cape towns' water and sanitation systems in what were called "delegated management contracts". By 2001, the French transnational company could boast another three million Johannesburg water-users, about half a million connections, water and wastewater networks of about 8 000km in length, and at least 1 500 more workers, pushing the total number of people served to over 5.2 million or 13 per cent of South Africa's population.[2]

WSSA had promised to "manage" the highly politicised relationship with "customers" and unions, implement "effective consumer management", and ensure that customers were "willing and able to pay for services, while maximising revenue collec-tion". Privatisation was sold as a cheaper way of running the municipality and governing recalcitrant communities and workers under the rubric of "customer management." In effect, a new political strategy was being forged.

WSSA's success came from its combinations with other firms and an active strategy of winning government backing. By 1996, it could boast in its annual report: "Whilst

---

[2] For details see www.suez.fr/finance2/english/news/detail.php?id=516&pg=arch. Add to this the numbers of people in at least a dozen towns served by other private companies such as Vivendi, Biwater and SAUR, and the proportion of people in South Africa served by private companies is even larger. WSSA is also a shareholder in Amanz' Abantu, the programme-implementing agent for rural schemes in the Eastern Cape (www.g5.co.za/WSSA.html).

these are early days in winning their acceptance, we now have the support of the government. We helped draw guidelines on private-sector management of water and sanitation services and are now helping with a regulatory framework" (Everite 1996). In its newsletter a year earlier, WSSA announced:

> Water and Sanitation Services South Africa has poised itself to playing an active and meaningful role in ensuring that the Government achieves its mission. This will include the direct delivery of services as and when called upon to do so by various municipalities and local councils; and the implementation of customer management programs to ensure that communities also play a part towards the delivery of quality services by paying for services (1995a).

In 1996, so as to ensure a bright future for French capital in South Africa, the French Minister of Trade, Yves Galland, accompanied by 31 business-people (including executives from Lyonnaise), met President Mandela, Deputy President Mbeki and three ministers, and declared that French business in South Africa should double in three years. He also brought more than R155 million in aid to help South Africa buy equipment from France. As Ambert, the Suez Lyonnaise director at the time, put it: "We are in the starting blocks, waiting to get work, or at least to bid for projects" (*Financial Mail*, 26 April, 1996).

WSSA has also been extremely active in promoting the concept of delegated management to municipal officials around the country, holding regular seminars in different centres on how delegated management can work with water concession projects. It has also made an effort to win the approval and support of the unions involved in the municipal sector, such as the South African Municipal Workers' Union (SAMWU), although the latter has been fiercely resistant.

The Queenstown contract was signed in 1992 for a 25-year period and was the first of its kind in South Africa. Previous agreements held by WSSA (or AG) were short-duration service contracts held mostly with bantustan governments. WSSA and Queenstown's white, and later ANC-led, municipal councils promoted themselves as the pioneers of the delegated management contract in South Africa. The "French way" was adopted by Stutterheim in 1993, and by Fort Beaufort in 1994.

Selling Privatisation as a Political Package

When WSSA met with Fort Beaufort officials in 1994 it was still under apartheid control. With Fort Beaufort, the company used a range of tactics to sell the privatisation option. First, there was the panic strategy: "Fort Beaufort is facing a health crisis," WSSA warned, "all local authorities face demanding consumers, a payments crisis and militant unions". Water is "too politicised [and] ... municipal officials face an increasing work-load," they argued (WSSA 1995b).

Second, the company assured that it could implement "an integrated approach to addressing the *predicament facing Local Councils throughout South Africa* of meeting the expectation of the consumer in respect of provision of affordable and acceptable standards versus the ability and willingness to pay" (WSSA 1995b, emphasis added).

Third, WSSA claimed that it "provides the town with an additional ability to address the challenges facing the town in the changing times and in catering for future requirements well into the next century". This was also referred to as reducing government "overstretch", and of great benefit if government capacity was weak (Kerf and Smith 1996, 8). Privatisation was sold as a way of adding to government capacity. WSSA would "free the municipalities from arduous and time-consuming work" so that they could "devote their creative attention fully to the development of the region and the community" (WSSA 1995b, 33).

Fourth, the main economic reasons given for privatisation were: to save the town money (Fort Beaufort: eight per cent in savings; Queenstown: 19 per cent); to provide "world-class" technical and organisational services at lower than usual municipal cost; to provide a stable cost structure for services; to perk up technologies to enhance "customers' willingness to pay"; to advise the council and to assist in planning for the town in a long-term partnership "to help communit(ies) realise their full potential" (WSSA 1995b). The company predicted that, over time, the towns would profit, with rising consumption volumes, reduced unit costs, reduced water losses and predictable costs. These municipalities would have better local economic prospects and could save time on enervating contact with workers. Privatisation by the multinational corporation offered a new vision for local governance, a new "structured coherence", a new configuration of forces, and a transformation of municipal-citizen relations.

Finally, the company insisted that it would use wide-ranging techniques to "manage" customers:

> It is essential that the management of the service is not influenced by the politics of the day. This can only be achieved by delegating the management of this function to the private sector, a reality proven over 100 years of international experience (WSSA 1995b, 20).[3]

"Customers" would become "aware" (through money discipline and disconnections) of the value of water. To marketise water would require WSSA to:

> Implement community-awareness programs; assist the authority in the development of socio-economic strategies to be applied for the current and future provision of services and the payment, therefore, by the community including liaison with the relevant community representative bodies, other than service departments (WSSA 1995b).

WSSA said that it would "carry out the necessary socio-economic analyses and present recommendations to the Authority" (WSSA 1995b, 20).

When making proposals for customer management, WSSA suggested that it and the municipal authority would jointly fund promotional material, newsletters, brochures, handouts and bulletins essential for the success of the programme. In Queenstown, for example, a provisional sum of R182 000 for the first year and R108 000 for the second year's propaganda was suggested (WSSA 1995c, 25). The economic "benefits of effective customer management" are described as "spectacular", with an "increased revenue of R500 000 per annum" predicted in Fort Beaufort's case. WSSA would charge only half this amount to provide customer management, making a handsome profit for the municipality (WSSA 1999).

By customer management, the company sought the "restoration of community acceptance and support for regular payment for services provided" (WSSA 1995c). In the 1994 proposals to Fort Beaufort, WSSA had ambitiously promised to "manage" the highly politicised relationship with the "customers" and unions, implement "effective consumer management" and ensure that customers were "willing and able to pay for services, while maximising revenue collection" (WSSA 1995b, 1). Customer management required an updated customer database, meter reading, receipt and enquiry centres and associated billing systems (WSSA 1995c).

Fort Beaufort's Privatised Water and Sanitation

"Normalising" tariffs in Fort Beaufort

Another major component of the privatisation scheme was the "normalisation" of tariffs. Consider Fort Beaufort as an example. From 1992 to 1993, before amalgamation and privatisation, residents of Bhofolo, the black township, were charged R10,60 for all services

---

[3] Consider that even when delivered by the welfare state or by nationalised enterprises, the World Bank always sought to stress that these services were non-political and had to be run like businesses (see Payer 1982).

(which, at this time, were limited to communal standpipes for water and refuse collection), but few residents paid this as organised community boycotts were still ongoing as a form of political protest against apartheid structures. These rates had been set by the Cape Provincial Administration (CPA) and the Bhofolo Town Council (an "independent" black local authority). There was a *de facto* decommodification through boycotts of payments and the state did not cut off basic services for fear of political reprisals.

In 1994, the services boycotts were called off after the ANC came to power. In 1995, Bhofolo and the formerly whites-only municipality of Fort Beaufort were unified financially and politically into a "transitional local authority" (TLC). A 300 per cent increase on service rates was announced for township residents in the first joint TLC budget (June 1995) to "normalise" charges. Bhofolo, following government instructions, had written off all service debt dated before 31 January, 1994. When, in late 1995, Bhofolo residents were suddenly presented with statements for 1994–95 services arrears based on massively hiked tariffs, there was significant community backlash.

From river access and a few communal standpipes in the 1950s, to public taps in the 1980s, Bhofolo infrastructure had only "improved" to unmetered yard taps and the bucket sanitation system (on which more will be said below) by the 1990s. By 2002, Bhofolo residents still had no indoor piped water or wastewater disposal. By contrast, whites had "first-world" services and up to 1996 were charged on a *declining* block tariff for water (the first 10kl at R2,23 per kl; the next at R1,54 per kl). However, in 1996–97 the rate structure changed to uniform rates for the whole town (see Table 2.1). By this new criterion of formal equality, township dwellers had their new R28 per month flat rate for their bundle of services raised by another 100 per cent to R60 per month in July 1996. Thus, from 1994 to 1996 townships faced a massive 600 per cent increase in service charges.

Table 2.1: Tariffs before and after privatisation, Fort Beaufort (in Rands)					
	1994/95	1995/96	1996/97	1997/98	1998/99
Basic Water (10kl)	6,10	6,10	22,30	27,00	27,80
Sewerage	–	10,13	30,39	35,00	–
Bucket	–	10,13	19,00	22,00	22,60
Electricity	–	4,50	prepaid	prepaid	prepaid
Refuse	4,50	6,50	20,00	23,00	23,70
All services – township flat rates	10,60	28,00	60,00	72,00	74,00

Source: Fort Beaufort TLC Minutes for June and July of each year in the table.

In 1997–98, the principle of formal equality was revised somewhat: rising block tariffs were imposed so that water usage of less than 10kl per month would be charged at a flat rate of R27 (or R2,70 per kl). This meant an increase of 50c per kl, or 22 per cent. Consumption between 11 and 40kl incurred a R2,90 charge per unit. At 41 to 60kl, one would pay R3 and at 61 to 80kl, payment per unit was set at R3,10. The flat-rate was a fixed sum, so even if a household was away, or used only five kilolitres, it would still incur the flat-rate charge. Black users in Bhofolo without meters could thus be overcharged, if they used less than ten kilolitres. To make matters worse, the rising block tariffs, as is evident, were on a very gradual incline. Town users, who used four to six times more water than township residents, paid a nominal 25c more per kilolitre than poor users (about R3/kl in total). The overall difference was nominal: no more than a loaf of bread.

A Tug of War in Fort Beaufort

At the time of privatisation in October 1995, Bhofolo residents paid R10 per month for having sanitary pails (buckets) emptied once a week. Later, this increased to R19, and then in 1997–98 residents paid R22 for a poorly-run 19th-century bucket system. Black residents in 1995–96 paid the same tariff for bucket sanitation as (predominately white) suburbanites who received full, water-borne sewerage. In 1997 black residents still paid *two-thirds* of the amount suburbanites paid with full water-borne sewerage.

But by December 1995, the council had only collected 10.3 per cent on monthly bills (R25 288 out of R241 469) based on a new flat rate of R28 (Fort Beaufort TLC 1995). With such low collection rates and the pressure of fixed WSSA charges, a further hike of flat-rate tariffs to R60 (a more-than 100 per cent increase) was not long in coming. Most residents declared that they could not pay:

> On the advice of some councillors, residents [said they] are prepared to pay the old flat rate of R28, but not the new flat rate of R60. [But] the 1996–7 budget was based on 2 600 flat rates of R60 each, and if residents are allowed to pay R28,60 there would be a shortfall of R705 000 for the year on flat rates only (Fort Beaufort TLC, 1996, 6–7).

Council resolved to give consumers three months' grace on electricity arrears, resolving that the names of those unwilling to pay the new flat rate be forwarded to council. Residents had discussed this with councillors in ward meetings. Council also resolved that the new R55 tanker fee for emptying septic tanks (only found in a few coloured and African homes) be waived and the same fee for water-borne sewerage (R30) be charged (Fort Beaufort TLC 1996, 7). Prepaid electricity meters also created hardship:

> The installation of prepaid meters results in financial difficulties for some consumers, as they have to pay in advance for electricity from the date of installation, plus having to pay the last monthly account for consumption registered on the old metering system (Fort Beaufort TLC, 1996d).

Higher Connection Charges In Fort Beaufort

As it was desperate for cash, connection fees seemed an easy way for the Fort Beaufort council to raise money (and thus meet its payment obligation to WSSA). From May 1996, therefore, a 100 per cent hike in water connection fees from R310 to R648 (which is more than a month's income for most Fort Beaufort families) was imposed. Contrast this with a much smaller hike in more complex sewerage connections in suburban areas from R360 to R496.

There was swelling disenchantment with these price increases. The direct role of WSSA in these increases cannot be determined since council set these tariffs. But from 1995 onwards, the council did not derive a cent in profit from its water revenue. In other words, all increases went directly to paying off WSSA charges. WSSA charges also accounted for the lion's share of water account expenses. Stuck with the non-negotiable contract charges, council was under pressure.

By 1997, the total service package (water, bucket-sewerage and refuse collection) for Bhofolo residents was fixed at R72 without rates charges (R10) and prepaid electricity (usually R60 to R70 per month). The water and bucket service alone accounted for almost 10 per cent of household income (in the Fort Beaufort case). If electricity and rates were added, the total payment to the municipality was over R150 or 30 per cent of a typical township household income.

A year later, by 1998, matters were still no better. The Tripartite Alliance (ANC, South African Communist Party and the Congress of South African Trade Unions, plus the South African National Civics Organisation) suggested a "tripartite sliding scale linked to household income to avoid the financial collapse of the council" (Fort Beaufort TLC 1998). ANC Councillor Mana argued for the sliding scale and proposed its approval by council. It was to be tested for three months, despite the town treasurer's firm warning that "the council cannot take a risk like that ... because the council's finances will not catch up in time if the sliding scale is proven wrong" (Fort Beaufort TLC, 1998).

Significantly, Fort Beaufort had tariffs at the time that were higher than non-privatised towns. For 30kl of water, for example, the country average was R82, whereas in Fort Beaufort residents paid over R90. In a small town comparable to Fort Beaufort, such as Reddersburg, residents paid R62 for 30kl. (Department of Finance 2000).

By the year 2000, the situation of households had worsened: close to 1 670 households had applied for indigence grants. Squatters were disqualified, since according to the Fort Beaufort TLC "the money to fund the indigence scheme was not enough and squatters only paid R20 per month". The maximum subsidy per household was R44 per month.

Fort Beaufort Consumer's Debt Crisis

By February 2000, Fort Beaufort consumers owed the municipality R13 million. By June 2000, services debts were at R15 million. Then, within a single month, it jumped a further 12 per cent to R17 million (Fort Beaufort TLC 2000b). Signs of this crisis were already evident in late–1995, in the months the contract was negotiated, when bankers indicated overdraft facilities were being withdrawn. By February 1996, the treasurer reported only 12 per cent payment rates in Bhofolo, and 15 per cent in "coloured" Newtown (Fort Beaufort TLC 1996a, 4). Considering the absolute level of poverty in the township (typical household earnings of less than R600 per month, with an average of seven to eight persons per home, and 50 per cent unemployment rate), to pay over 30 per cent of household income for services (as opposed to the previous two per cent of income under earlier rate structures) was beyond the capacity of most households, already burdened by other debts. The declining number of high-use consumers (since whites were leaving town) caused revenue to ebb further.

In 1999, consumer arrears neared R11 million (see Table 2.2). Council published a less onerous sliding scale of payments for arrears, hoping to induce payment, but with little effect. A few examples of debt may suffice. In Bhofolo, Extension 28, households owed R140 000, or an average of R5 000 each, to the council. In Bhofolo, Mpolweni and New Tinis extensions, 45 families alone owed R181 000, or R4 000 per household. In Hillside, debts ranged from R2 000 to R9 000 per household (Fort Beaufort TLC 2000a). These amounts added up to a full year's council revenue.

Arrangements were made for debtors to pay 30 per cent down on arrears (instead of the full amount). If the 30 per cent payment was not forthcoming residents would be barred from any electricity purchases via the prepaid system. Council would also sell rationed amounts of electricity. For example, a household with R1 000 debt would be limited to R100 per month in electricity. The council simply denied any electricity to those with water debt.

Table 2.2: Geography of Fort Beaufort consumers' debt 1998–1999 (Rand million)			
Sub-area		Accumulated Debt	% collection on billing
Town		2.6m	93%
Newtown		1.7m	57%
Hillside *		0.7m	7%
Bhofolo	New debt	4.2m	40%
	Old debt	1.9m	

Source: WSSA 2000a
* Hillside is a relatively new area with RDP housing with water-borne sewerage and a single inside house tap.

Stutterheim and Queenstown: Privatisation as "farming backwards"

Stutterheim Tariffs

In 1997, in Mlungisi (Stutterheim's black township), residents paid the following set rates for services: R22 flat rate for unmetered basic water supply (i.e. 10kl at a yard tap or R2,20 per kilolitre); for those with metered supply (white areas) a fixed amount of R16 (R6 less than the township poor) for that first 10kl and R1,80 per kilolitre above 11kl per month. But, said the Stutterheim TLC, the tariff does not "discriminate". The municipality rejected the idea of redistributive block tariffs and cross-subsidies, giving larger consumers cheaper prices (Stutterheim TLC 1997).

Electricity charges were also regressive with 31c per kilowatt hour (kWh) for consumers using less than 300kWh compared to only 25c for those using more than 300kWh. A new electricity connection cost R1 616 in Stutterheim but twice as much in outlying rural areas, (i.e. R3 419) (Stutterheim TLC 1998, 44).

Queenstown Tariff Structures

In Queenstown, the flat rate for services was raised by 150 per cent from R15 per month in 1995 (pre-privatisation) to flat rates of R38 per month after privatisation (R10 more than in Bhofolo). Households earning less than R1 300 per month could apply for a 40 per cent brebate. The municipality used the intergovernmental grant to make up the shortfall created by this rebate. In 1995–96, a storm erupted over uniform tariffs, especially rates, and white residents threatened to withhold payment (*The Representative*, 29 March, 1996).

Geography and Size of Water Debt: A Deepening Crisis

Consumer municipal debt is a large and growing problem across South Africa, insoluble in the present policy context, and has multiple consequences (whether municipalities are privatised or not). Project Viability (SAIRR 2000, 386), a national government monitoring agency established in 1995 to look into the liquidity of South Africa's municipalities from 1995–98, reported that for 283 core municipalities, outstanding consumer debts doubled from R6.5 billion in December 1996 to R11.3 billion in September 1998. By 1998, unpaid bills altogether represented a loss of 37 per cent of rates and service charges income. On average, only 71 per cent of residents in the surveyed municipalities were regular payers (1997–98). In the Eastern Cape province, municipal services debt was higher, at R1 005 million (10 per cent of national debt) (SAIRR 2000, 387). In black townships, 60 to 70 per cent of charges were unpaid during this period, but in higher-income suburban areas, payment levels were usually above 90 per cent.

But these averages disguise the class and racial geography of debt and disconnections. In response to non-payment, municipal authorities threaten, cajole and battle with residents, impose service cutbacks, reduce capital projects, spend less money on mainte-nance, and retrench parts of the workforce. When this fails, they take legal action and seize residents' property, cutting them off permanently. Most of those people against whom legal action is taken are the poorest of the poor (pensioners and the unemployed), whose accumulated arrears run to R8 000. Legal and interest charges often exceed the initial amounts owed. As Henk Bezuidenhout, Assistant Treasurer of the Fort Beaufort TLC, wrote: "The majority of debtors against whom legal action was taken are pensioners or unemployed. Some of these debtors are up to R8 000 in arrears, which is impossible to recover. [Only] R270 000 has been arranged to be recovered on arrears" (Fort Beaufort TLC 2000b).

Water debt is proportionately larger than debt on other accounts. Water sales and sewer and sanitation fees make up 16 to 17 per cent of a typical town's revenue (DCD 1998). But in Queenstown water accounts for 38 to 40 per cent of debt, indicating higher-than national-average figures and that consumers prioritise other municipal bills (electricity, rates) over water. In Queenstown, 55 per cent default on water bills, but only 20 per cent on electricity.[4] Municipal debt per head of population in South Africa in June 1998 was R301 (DCD 1998) whereas in Fort Beaufort and Queenstown debt was 20 per cent higher.

Queenstown's Debt Geography

Most income from trading services (water and electricity) historically did not come from townships since townships used only a third of the amounts of these services that white households used and flat rates were low. For example, a 1995 geographical breakdown of average monthly water usage and sales per connection in greater Queenstown reveals some important average figures: Queenstown: 45kl; Ezibeleni: 13kl; and Mlungisi: 15kl. This consumption translates into revenue on monthly billing as follows: Queens- town: R267 660 (4 230 connections at R63,20 each); Ezibeleni: R69 300 (4 620 connec- tions at a flat rate of R15 each); and Mlungisi: R77 121 (4 510 connections, at a flat rate of R17,10 each) (WSSA 1995c, 27).

Queenstown's white and coloured residents (4 230 connections between approxi- mately 17 000 people) account for almost twice the monthly revenue of black households (although coloureds used considerably less than whites since many live in similar poverty to Africans). A 50 per cent non-payment rate in a white middle-class area could therefore be as large as the combined townships' bill.

But the picture of the *geographical* sources of council revenue changed significantly in 1996, when township flat rates were hiked by 150 per cent (from R15 to R38). The shape of municipal revenue sources changed dramatically as black townships were now billed R346 940 with new monthly flat rates. This change, which we may call "post- apartheid normalisation", basically means that black households face new financial burdens with deracialisation.

Queenstown township consumer debt grew rapidly once flat rates increased. In 1994, at the time of the amalgamation of racially separate municipal authorities, 99 per cent of Queenstown residents paid their service bills (they had privatised water and sanitation since mid-1992), whereas the townships had very low payment rates of 15 to 19 per cent because of an on-off boycott of municipal service payments.[5] By 1995, once the ANC had taken power, and boycotts were officially ended, township payment levels rose to between 26 and 33 per cent and then to a steady mid-30 per cent (*The Representative*, 14 June, 1996). Payment rates have not improved since then and with the move to equalise tariffs this low non-payment level has translated into a huge revenue loss.

In 1997, Queenstown adopted a "drastic action plan" to collect part of the R26 million owed, putting council hawks in the driving seat. To add to its woes, Queenstown faced a substantial reduction in intergovernmental transfers that year. Instead of an anticipated R518 000 from national government, it would only get R207 000 per month (*The Repre- sentative*, 19 June, 1997). The town clerk (since 1999) confessed: "We are slipping away; at present we can only pay ESKOM and WSSA ... we are farming backwards. We collected R6 million via the drastic action plan, from 1997 onwards, but then debt climbed by R30 million" (*Daily Dispatch*, 18 March, 1999).

Desperate, council considered turning to the private sector by privatising billing and debt collections. But after considering the matter, much to WSSA's chagrin, Queenstown Council deferred the plan. By 1999, the alleged "culture of non-payment", historically

---

[4] In many cases, electricity is supplied on a prepaid basis, using prepaid cards inserted into meters installed in homes. The prepaid system disguises disconnections (and debt) since people self-disconnect by only buying as much as they can afford (if any). High payment levels of 80 per cent for electricity may reflect the fact that middle-class homes are now the only ones that do not use prepaid systems.

[5] Of R350 000 levied for two months (November and December 1994), residents paid only R52 000 (14.8 per cent). National government grants of R180 000 per month helped keep Mlungisi "afloat" in the past (*The Representative*, 3 February, 1995).

seen as a black problem, was no longer reserved for blacks: town areas owed R4.2 million; Mlungisi and Ezibeleni (12 000 households) owed R7.4 million (*Daily Dispatch*, 22 April, 1999). In town (commercial, white and coloured areas) per capita debt was R1 000, higher than that of townships (about R800). Non-payment was generalised – an even more crushing blow to WSSA who had hoped improvements would translate into higher payment levels. More alarmingly, council only recovered R79 540 with legal action for the month of February 1999. Proportionately, this was untenable since R150 000 was paid to attorneys to recover the amount.

Equally noteworthy is that racial polarisation *within* council and between communities was heightened. Queenstown Mayor Xoseni warned hawkish councillors who had distanced themselves from the council's carrot-and-stick approach to defaulters that they were: "living against the spirit of an agreement taken in 1994 to make services available to all areas. We are not going to allow ourselves to be used for polarisation and political animosity that is being fashioned here" (*Daily Dispatch*, 1 April, 1999).

By 21 May, 1999, the regional newspaper *Daily Dispatch* reported Queenstown debt at R35 million. Non-payment rates were highest for refuse, then water (50 to 55 per cent), followed by general rates (36 per cent) and electricity (20 per cent) (Palmer Development Group/ DBSA 1999).

Worsening Municipal Debt

Stutterheim also faced a worsening financial crisis and a rapid decline in collection ratios. By 1997, 45 per cent of the town's 4 468 households were not paying bills regularly, and Mlungisi had accumulated a debt of R2.1 million. Non-payment of services was dealt with ruthlessly. In 1997 the municipality cut off the water supply to 20 per cent of all black township households (Bond 2000, 163), whereas most other towns only cut electricity. In 1999 and 2000 matters worsened with 59 per cent of revenue due from Mlungisi unpaid (Stutterheim TLC 2000a).

In March 2000, the municipality's treasurer reported that Mlungisi's accumulated debt alone had doubled to R4.5 million (about the total annual manpower wage bill for the municipality, and also about equal to the town's total cash and savings) (Stutterheim 2000e). Total debt for the town over a one-year period rose from R5.3 million (in March 1999) to R6.4 million (in March 2000) (see Table 2.3).

Mlungisi's debt was much higher than the national average. But large doses of government grants mitigated the effects of the non-payment crisis. For example, in February 2000, Stutterheim had received R354 931 for remissions from local government (Stutterheim TLC 2000b) – i.e. up to R86 per household per month for those with incomes under R800 per month (Palmer Development Group 1998). During 1999, 77 per cent of Mlungisi residents got state-funded remissions. "Coloured" Amatolaville residents had 89 per cent of utility bills remitted. In reality, these remissions went into paying WSSA since many who were officially receiving remissions had their services cut.

Table 2.3: Water and sanitation debts in Mlungisi/Stutterheim (Rand thousands)							
	Mar 1999	May 1999	July 1999	Sept 1999	Nov 1999	Jan 2000	Mar 2000
Sanitation	1 046	1 087	1 126	1 193	1 244	1 182	1 362
Water	1 05	1 07	1 07	1 11	1 14	1 182	1 218

Source: Stutterheim 2000b.

Local Government and Commodified Neo-apartheid

Back to the Dark Ages: reduced street lighting and collective punishment

In Stutterheim, as elsewhere, politicians were brought in to persuade defaulters to pay. When this failed, the municipality introduced a new round of service cutoffs. These cuts in Mlungisi began selectively at first: from Monday to Thursday street and high-mast lighting would be switched off. Individual families in arrears were also denied refuse collection (Bond 2000,158-160).

By denying high-mast lighting and not collecting refuse, council meted out collective punishment in black townships that only served to harden antagonism. In the event, most of the high-mast lighting was not in working order and residents were used to very poor water service (low pressure, intermittence, etc.). Those cut off simply fetched water from their neighbours who were on the indigent grant, and whose bills in turn shot up.

In Queenstown, "white revenge" themes also surfaced: on 29 March 1996 white councillors had to explain to an angry, largely white audience at the Town Hall that steps were being taken against those who did not pay. The councillors explained that bulbs had been removed from two out of every three Ezibeleni streetlights, and that only every third street light worked in Mlungisi. Speaking to the audience, the councilor intoned:

> We have a simple choice to make: either we pay and Queenstown survives or the culture of non-payment continues with the immediate result that our town will sink into degradation and hardship (The Representative, 26 January, 1996).

The Queenstown council, on 25 April 1997, had granted 1 000 residents a special six-month grace period to pay off two years of debt. Special debt collectors were appointed who "indicated a high level of unemployment amongst residents ... who said it was impossible to pay. It is not only a Queenstown problem; it's throughout the province" (*The Representative*, 26 January, 1996).

A further punitive and exclusionary measure was the huge R1 425 reinstatement fee (more than twice the average monthly household income of black townships) to reconnect water and the R865 reconnection fee for electricity (*The Representative*, 26 January, 1996). Warnings also included the following:

> The cutting of the delivery of services will focus on areas where payment is low and will include reduced street lighting, taking residential meter readings once every two months, a cutoff list two days after payment is due, the removal of meters and connections and cutting off water; road maintenance to be scaled down; employers are to be asked to deduct service charges from employees' income, payable to the municipality; capital projects worth R6 680 220 have been frozen, including the upgrading of Ezibeleni roads and upgrading the sewer network in Mlungisi (The Representative, 26 January 1996).

Municipal Revanchism and Water Disconnections

Stutterheim was the first of the three municipalities being discussed here to resort to water cutoffs; Queenstown and Fort Beaufort Council held back until 2000, cutting only electricity when water bills were not paid on time. In a council notice that seemed to be addressed to black residents, the "consequences of not paying" were presented as follows:

> In Queenstown, by February 1999, the bankruptcy of council had resulted in a drop in quality of service and finally the discontinuation of services. This is unfair as the majority of consumers pay for their services, therefore in order to protect these consumers, it is necessary to take drastic steps in order to encourage consumers to pay for services already received.... Council is currently making use

of the legal system to recover debt that cannot be recovered by withdrawing certain services. The legal process involves legal letters, summonses and finally executions by the Sheriff. Legal costs are born by the defaulters and not the council. Services such as electricity are disconnected ... the council now retains the right to disconnect the electricity supply for non-payment of water, refuse, sewerage, etc. This will also influence consumers using prepaid metering systems, as the consumer will simply be BARRED from purchasing coupons if other services are not paid for (reconnection fees apply). Council will also make use of discontinuance of supply of water to defaulters for whatever is owed (sewerage, refuse basic charge, etc); this will be specially [sic] effective in areas where council does not supply electricity. Consumers disconnected will be monitored and any tampering with disconnected service will lead to extensive fines ranging from R750 to R2 000. If the volume of debt financed by council still increases the council will have no other recourse but to consider means of reducing costs e.g. switching off the high-mast lights.

In Queenstown by February 1999, 2 282 electricity meters were disconnected and only 571 reconnected. According to the head of the electricity department, "residents are breaking open electricity boxes and reconnecting themselves shortly after they have been disconnected by the municipality for not paying for services. After disconnecting some residents up to three consecutive times, the municipality has had to resort to removing electric cables" (*Daily Dispatch*, 18 March, 1999).

As of April, 1999, 8 000 households (or 62 per cent of township households in the Queenstown municipality) had reported to council offices to arrange to pay off their arrears, but many failed to keep to the arrangements. Thus, one month later the Queenstown council announced that a private armed security company, Gray Security (in which African Harvest, a black-empowerment company, is a shareholder) had tendered to cut off water services of errant residents (*Daily Dispatch*, 5 May, 1999).

Threats of water cuts now became real in Queenstown for the first time. The resort to water cutoffs was used to cajole households to pay at least 50 per cent of arrears on bills of R10 000 or more. Moreover, penalties of R865 were to be imposed for meter tampering or illegal connections for first offenders. Thereafter the permanent removal of services would follow.

To press the point, on 17 January, 2000, the council cut water supply to Cape College, Thabalethu School and all other schools on the opening day of classes. Electricity to schools had already been cut (*The Representative*, 2 February, 2000) with 700 children having to be sent home less than a week after schools re-opened (*The Representative*, 2 February, 2000). By 19 May, 2000, Nomzamo and Newvalle residents (new zones of Mlungisi) were physically clashing with municipal officials.

Back to the Bush: Sanitation Cuts

The most bizarre development during this three-year study was the almost year-long cutoff in 1999–2000 of the Fort Beaufort bucket system in "squatter areas". Only 11 640 pails were collected during this time whereas 16 000 to 17 000 had been collected each month in previous years. The Fort Beaufort Council was slow to cut debtors' services, but targeted a vulnerable and relatively marginal group, the squatters, to make its point. In so doing, many more people in townships were forced back to the bush while theft and illegal sales of buckets became common.

Back to Apartheid: Permanent Cuts

Even more disturbing are the four forms of permanent cutoffs of basic services. The first involves shutting off services by removing cables, pipes, etc. In some cases this involves reinstalling prepaid communal water standpipes in each street (a Queenstown plan, currently underway). The second increases reconnection fees to such high levels that very few can afford to reconnect. This has the effect of promoting a secondary market in illegal connections. One can pay a municipal worker or "freelancer" considerably less than what the municipality charges to get cables or pipes put back in.

The third insists that residents pay off huge amounts of debt (up to 50 per cent) first, before being considered for any services at all, thereby effecting a permanent cutoff. Many residents face huge bills that range from R500 to R20 000 and simply give up hope of ever paying off their debt. Thus, Councilor Kemp of Queenstown, in heated debate, questioned how "a woman earning R350 per month was allowed to incur municipal debt on her accounts of R7 000 before she was cut off". Another, Councillor Luppnow, feared that debt-collection fees would exceed the amounts recovered. Councilor Hoko (who doubles as a WSSA publicity officer) argued that "council urgently needs a proper system of credit control" (*Daily Dispatch*, 14 May, 1999).

The fourth and most insidious method of permanent cutoff is self-disconnection by prepaid meter. In 2000, Stutterheim planned to spend a quarter of a million rand in the first phase of prepaid metering (moving funds from street and stormwater upgrading). On 25 April, 2000, Conlog (a company partly owned by the ex-minister of defence, Joe Modise) had its tender for prepaid water metering in Stutterheim's black townships accepted. Phase one of this project was to cost R230 000.

Commodification and Invisibility Through Prepaid Meters

The international trend of turning water into a business requires extensive consumer metering, billing and harsh cost-recovery policies. In previous years, it was common for water to be priced as a levy or rate, based on property valuations. Installing water meters, replacing older ones, changing the technology of metering (computerisation) and the move to prepaid water meters is changing the nature of water services and the relationship between the state and the citizen.[6] Along with this, according to Coing (1997, 151):

> There are a number of plans to stamp out the practice of being illegally connected
> ... and in Argentina and Columbia a start has been made by publishing in the press
> the names of those found to be acting fraudulently.

The importance of the now-ubiquitous move to prepaid meters cannot be exaggerated. Prepaid metering is a new political technology since individuals end up self-disconnecting: no billing and meter reading is required, and domestic water consumption or lack thereof becomes statistically invisible. Prepayment is seen as an alternative to municipal disconnection when "customers" cannot afford to pay accounts. However, whereas municipal disconnection is a visible (and sometimes violent) physical process, self-disconnection is invisible and masks the extent to which people go without water supply. These transactions are not in the public domain and can be blamed on the individual sovereign consumer.

In Stutterheim, community standpipes and yard taps are first in line for prepaid meters. In the event of non-payment of rates or other charges, residents could be blocked from access to prepayment tokens or cards. It would cost R1 550 for a standpipe prepayment meter and R750 for a yard-tap meter. In addition, consumer tokens, vending units, management systems, security devices and training would be required (Stutterheim TLC 2000d). It was envisaged that black areas with high debts (i.e. Mlungisi) be targeted for prepaid water devices.

---

[6] In Argentina (1993) and Mexico, privatisation meant prioritising metering, and bringing order to "customer" databases. "The stage will include the constitution of an inventory of water users, instalments of water meters and of new methods of invoicing" (*Financial Times*, 18 March, 1993).

In Queenstown, prepaid meters are also on the cards. The WSSA (2000c) notes:

> *The TLC called for tenders to finance the purchase and installation of prepaid water meters. A tender offering two options for the supply and installation of these meters using "contractor finance" was submitted. To date no reply has been received.*

In Fort Beaufort (Fort Beaufort TLC 1997) the SANCO leaders, who address council on prepaid electricity meters, noted:

> *Pre-paid meters are being installed without ample notice residents expressed dissatisfaction over the fact that pre-paid meters are to be compulsory as they say they were not informed as such. Further, as this is a new system, the residents are very weary of it and believe that they are being tricked with regard to usage.*

In the UK, one in ten consumers with prepaid meters has gone without water for 24 hours, despite the safeguard of one week's supply on credit (not applicable in South Africa) (Herbert and Kempson 1995, 82).

Reasons for Non-payment

Increases in township water bills in the order of 300 per cent (after old townships were incorporated into white towns) in Fort Beaufort, and similar percentages in Stutterheim and Queenstown, were untenable. Water bills previously "invisible" became big-ticket items. Most township defaulters are on very low incomes (and qualify for extensive state subsidies on service charges). Many workers have lost jobs, especially in gold mining, historically a major employer of migrant workers from these towns. Almost 90 per cent of the township residents live on less than R600 per month. These poor households consist of at least six people, at least half being children, and there being two pensioners or sick persons. With consumption already low (under ten kilolitres per month) people cannot reduce consumption any further (as was suggested by WSSA [2000a]).

The blanket "culture of non-payment" to explain non-payment is an oversimplification since users discriminate and appear to juggle between utility bills. Users also seemed more than willing to approach council offices to reschedule debt when given proper support (for example, when candidate councillors accompanied/advised them). Communities may also see payment boycotts as a form of collective power given the overall worsening of their situation. The solidarity and latent strength of community feeling allows people to ignore the law and to explore survivalist options (i.e. obtaining services from neighbours) or popular, illegal options such as self-connections, "slowing" meters down, and tampering with prepaid meters.

With many municipalities on their knees financially, some communities have been able to get councils to backtrack and charge lower flat rates (Fort Beaufort, for example, agreed to charge informal settlements R20 instead of R80 per month for services). Communities feel that if they do not pay they may increase their bargaining power in the long run. Most councillors now fear that large tariff hikes will discourage payment.

Inadequate billing (in some cases no billing at all) and poor communication with consumers has exasperated residents. The harsh collective punishment meted out to communities by councillors such as switching off high-mast lights and plunging an entire township into darkness has fuelled hostility to council. Finally, incompetent council bureaucrats undermine a relationship of trust between citizens and government.

Reordering the Community and Community Resistance

By the late 1990s, old-style anti-apartheid resistance tactics were re-emerging, if only episodically, with stone-throwing in townships and violent confrontations between the local state and communities in many Eastern Cape towns. Queenstown figured prominently: in "Ezibeleni, a council vehicle was stoned after disconnections of electricity in the township" (*Daily Dispatch*, 27 February, 1998). More than 500 residents from newly established areas of Nomzamo and Newvalle marched on the council offices (*The Representative*, 25 February, 2000). They threatened "rolling mass action" against the municipality's policy of cutting of water and electricity. "We are particularly worried about the health risks involved in cutting the supply of water to the areas," they said. This was conflated with other problems: the "shocking state of disrepair of recently construct- ed houses, roads, absence of street lighting".

In the meantime, a new anti-ANC political group emerged. "After a week of unrest in the Condev area, and a large number of collective illegal connections," Xoseni, the ANC mayor of Queenstown, appealed to residents not to join the breakaway group from the ANC. He called them a "vigilante group deceiving the most vulnerable sector of our community and aiming to fulfil sinister political agendas" (*The Representative*, 19 May, 2000). As the local Queenstown newspaper noted, "Council removed electricity cables in Condev, warning of criminal syndicates responsible for illegal connections." The response of the authorities has thus been to criminalise collective actions such as illegal reconnections. Residents in turn threatened to "take action against municipal officials who are cutting off water supply" (*The Representative*, 19 May, 2000).

Conclusion

Through all of this turmoil, the WSSA showed remarkable tenacity in clinging onto its three contracts. In the context of massive unpaid utility bills, it optimistically pronounced that "[b]ased on our experience, we know that revenue can be gathered humanely and fairly and that the town can be put back on its feet in spite of the unemployment and poverty which is prevalent" (WSSA 2000b). Yet the situation did not improve and hostility towards the company mounted. In a report on the privatisation of water in Queenstown, residents remarked that "the situation is worse now, bills are higher and our services are being cut." Fully 71 per cent of households surveyed for the study said that the service had worsened or stayed the same but bills had become more expensive (Timms 2000, 20).

In the case of Fort Beaufort, the pressures became too great and have resulted in the nullification of the WSSA contract (only five years into the ten-year contract). The Mayor of Nkonkobe (the newly amalgamated municipality that includes the towns of Alice, Fort Beaufort, Middledrift and Seymour) expressed "joy and relief" after the Grahamstown High Court nullified the contract. According to a report in the *Daily Dispatch* (15 December, 2001), the municipality was paying R400 000 a month to WSSA and "the scrapping of the contract meant that the Nkonkobe Municipality would save R19 million".

The Court found the contract was invalid because it had not been published for comment by members of the public before signing and because approval for the contract from the provincial minister responsible for local government was never obtained. The Mayor of Nkonkobe said that the municipality "was not prepared to honour invalid contracts" and WSSA was given until 21 December, 2001 to vacate the municipal offices they were occupying.

The implications of this nullification for the two other WSSA contracts discussed in this chapter – and indeed all other private-sector municipal service contracts in the country – remain unclear. What is clear is the continuing inequalities of infrastructure and services in South Africa and how these have been exacerbated by the logic of the market. It is evident in the three cases outlined here, that enforced contract payments to WSSA were driving a brutal process of cost recovery, disconnection and reduced services for township debtors who were increasingly being blamed as a collective unit for non-payment. In desperation, councils imposed collective punishment alongside efforts to break consumer resistance by installing individual prepaid meters. Privatisation, rather than depoliticising water, has in fact re-politicised it. Municipalities are engaged in a revanchist war on largely black consumers, while whites become increasingly mobilised to block concessions to black communities. It is also clear that cost recovery, debt, disconnections and the intrusion of foreign private companies in local urban services have qualitatively changed the nature of municipal politics and denuded notions of citizenship. The Eastern Cape privatisation experiments have failed for both municipal authories and the communities they represent.

Bibliography

Aqua-Gold Services. (1991). *A Proposal for Queenstown Water and Sewage Systems*, Municipality Queenstown Privatisation Files, Vol. 1. June.

Bond, P. (2000). *Cities of Gold, Townships of Coal*. Trenton: Africa World Press.

Coing, H. (1997). "Transnationalization in Latin America". In D. Lorrain, and G. Stoker, (eds.). *The Privatisation of Urban Services in Europe*. London: Pinter

DCD [Department of Constitutional Development]. (1998). *Project Viability Report*. July.

Department of Finance. (2000). *Intergovernmental Fiscal Review*. 2000.

Everite PTY, LTD. (1996). *Annual Report*.

Fort Beaufort TLC. (1995). Minutes of Monthly Meeting, June and July.

— (1996). Minutes of Monthly Meeting, June and July.

— (1996a). Monthly Meeting of Fort Beaufort Transitional Local Council, Agenda, 25 March.

— (1996b). Minutes of Standing Financial Committee, 9 September.

— (1996c). Minutes of Monthly Meeting of the Standing Financial Committee, 11 March.

— (1997). Minutes of Monthly Meeting, June and July.

— (1997a). Minutes of Meeting with SANCO Deputation, 4 July.

— (1998). Minutes of Monthly Meeting, June and July.

— (2000a). Minutes of Fort Beaufort FMC, 4 October.

— (2000b). *Monthly Report of Assistant Treasurer*, 14 August.

Herbert, A. and Kempson, E. (1995). *Water Debt and Disconnections*. London: Policy Studies Institute.

Kerf, M. and Smith, W. (1996). *Privatising Africa's Infrastructure: Promise and Challenge*. World Bank Technical Paper No 337. Washington, D.C.: World Bank.

Palmer Development Group. (1998). *Introduction to Water Services Management in South Africa's Urban Areas*. Water Research Commission Report No TT 98/98.

Palmer Development Group/ DBSA [Development Bank of Southern Africa]. (1999). *Infrastructure Investment Guidelines – Queenstown Cases Study*.

Payer, C. (1982). *The World Bank*. New York: Monthly Review Press.

Saunders, P. (1995). "Consumers and Privatization: The Case of the Water Industry." In Morgan, P. (ed.). *Privatisation and the Welfare State*. Aldershot: Dartmouth Publishing.

SAIRR [South African Institute of Race Relations]. (1998). *Annual Review of The Institute Of Race Relations Survey*. Braamfontein: South African Institute of Race Relations.

South African Institute of Race Relations. (2000). *Annual Review of The Institute Of Race Relations Survey*. Braamfontein: South African Institute of Race Relations.

Stutterheim TLC. (1997). Notice from the town treasurer, concerning the cost of supplying services to consumers.

— (1998).

— (2000a). Minutes of Special Meeting of TLC, TLC Budget, 12 June.

— (2000b). *Treasurer's Monthly Report*, February.

— (2000c). Minutes of Monthly Meeting, 25 April; Memo to Town Clerk re tenders pre-paid meters, from treasurer, 18 April.

— (2000d). Minutes of Monthly Meeting, 25 April.

— (2000e). *Treasurer's Monthly Report*, March.

Timms, J. (2000). *A Case Study of Private, Public Partnership, Queenstown*. Water, Engineering and Development Centre, Loughborough University, Leicester.

WSSA. (1995a). WSSA *Newsletter*, Municipality Queenstown Privatisation Files, Vol. 8, May.

— (1995b). *Proposal for Management, Operation and Maintenance of Fort Beaufort Water and Sanitation Services*.

— (1995c). *Extension of Existing Contract for Supply of Water and Sanitation Services to Greater Queenstown*. Municipality Queenstown Privatisation Files, Vol. 7, item 136/3/32/1, January.

— (1999). *January Monthly Report to Queenstown*. Municipality Queenstown Privatisation Files, Vol. 9.

— (2000a). Letter to Fort Beaufort TLC, 3 April.

— (2000b). WSSA *Network Activities from January Monthly Report*, Queenstown.

— (2000c). *Monthly Report for January*, Municipality Queenstown Privatisation Files Vol. 9. Queenstown.

People and Service Delivery

Ask almost any resident of Soweto's Diepkloof and you'll be told that the neighbouring Mandelaville squatter camp was a squalid, over-crowded nest of crime. Ask anyone who lived inside Mandelaville and they'll tell you it was home.

For 12 years the two communities lived side by side — hating one another. In January the shantytown ceased to exist. While armed police looked on, men in red overalls pulled down the shacks. Children, oblivious to the drama around them, played happily in the streets as the adults, some carrying babies, piled their meagre belongings onto municipal trucks.

Those evicted gathered on the grounds of the nearby Diepkloof Hall to have their forms processed. Ahead lay a long trek out to Durban Roodeport Deep mine west of Johannesburg, where new state-funded housing awaited them. No-one complained of being late for work: most of the residents were unemployed and had lived there for years without visible means of subsistence. This alone had made them suspect in the eyes of neighbouring communities, who watched the evictions with undisguised relief.

Diepkloof residents have stronger roots in the city. They stay in brick houses and most of them are employed. Compared to their squatter neighbours, they live in relative comfort. They resent the presence of outsiders who retain strong ties to the countryside. To them, the removal of the Mandelaville eyesore has been long overdue...

The case of Mandelaville brings into sharp focus the challenges facing post-apartheid municipal authorities. The spectacle of an informal community being removed inevitably rekindles memories of brutal forced removals carried out by the apartheid police. That a black government must resort to removals is an irony of our times. On the one hand, the state has, through its Reconstruction and Development Programme, prioritised housing the poor. On the other, the housing ministry clearly can't cope with the huge influx of migrants to the city. Most of the evicted Mandelaville residents are first-generation migrants from the Eastern Cape, the poorest province in the country. They have come to Johannesburg in search of the elusive gold.

(excerpt from article by Thomas Thale, Johannesburg: Gateway to Africa website, http://www.goafrica.co.za/joburg/jan_2002/shacks.htm.)

3

"Massive Cutoffs"
Cost Recovery and Electricity Service in Diepkloof, Soweto
by Grace Khunou

Introduction

In post-apartheid South Africa, electricity has become an issue of great conflict in Soweto. At the centre of this conflict has been the policy of cost recovery. According to previous research done by the Municipal Services Project, cost-recovery measures led to the cutoffs in up to 20 000 households per month during early 2001 (Fiil-Flynn 2001, 2). These cutoffs precipitated considerable community action. The most notable resistance has come from the Soweto Electricity Crisis Committee (SECC). The SECC responded to cutoffs by launching Operation Khanyisa (light up) in certain parts of Soweto. Under this campaign SECC activists illegally reconnected households that had been cut off by ESKOM, the service provider in the area. Not all areas of Soweto have chosen the course of mobilisation and collective reconnections. Yet, nearly every part of the township has been touched by cost-recovery measures for electricity.

This paper explores the responses and attitudes of residents of Diepkloof, one of the oldest areas in Soweto. In particular, our research examines the extent to which cost-recovery measures have contributed to a diminished sense of citizenship and perceived lack of access to constitutional rights among people in Diepkloof. Such notions have a special importance in Soweto. The uprising led by the students of Soweto in 1976 was a turning point in the liberation struggle against apartheid. The achievement of full citizens' rights for the people of Soweto is a crucial barometer of the depth and sustainability of South African democracy.

The Content of the Service Delivery

Historical background

Diepkloof

Diepkloof is situated on the western side of Johannesburg. It lies to the east of Orlando township, south of the Soweto Highway and North of the Old Potchefstroom Road which passes the Chris Hani-Baragwanath hospital. Diepkloof covers an area of about 50 hectares within a valley between the Witwatersrand mine dumps and the hills seen along Old Potchefstroom Road.

Diepkloof was built by Harry Oppenheimer between 1954 and 1957 to accommodate the mine employees of his Anglo American Corporation. Previously these workers lived in Alexandra and Sophiatown. People who lived in these two areas were mostly from rural areas. According to Anglo American and the government of the day, the pattern of settlement in Alexandra and Sophiatown was not acceptable. Officials had concerns that the lack of proper servicing of the area and the unplanned nature of the development might lead to health hazards and other socio-economic problems.[1]

By the mid-50s the dye was cast. The Bantu Settlements Board entered into an agreement with Oppenheimer to lease employees' quarters for 99 years. Initial settlement was voluntary, but people were soon being forcibly relocated to Diepkloof.

From the outset, Diepkloof was divided into six zones. Following the pattern of apartheid development, people were grouped into six zones based on ethnicity. However, these zones have since become integrated because of marriages and movements from rural areas. A seventh zone was built later to accommodate the growing population. This zone is known as Diepkloof Extension.

Diepkloof contains both formal and informal housing. According to municipal data the population living in formal houses totals 164 514, with those living in back rooms numbering 32 477. In informal settlements such as Mandela Village there are 10 270 residents. The total population numbers 207 261.[2]

During the struggle against apartheid there was considerable militancy among community members. The formation of civic organisations and street committees reflected this political consciousness. At the level of immediate community issues, there was significant mobilisation to fight crime. For example there was a gangster from Orlando who used to harass and "jackroll"[3] schoolgirls. The community and students from different schools in Diepkloof came together to fight these crimes. But as Shubane (1991) has chronicled, there was a considerable spirit of resistance in greater Soweto after the apartheid regime declared a State of Emergency in 1985. Diepkloof was part of this upsurge. The community participated in the mass actions of the democratic movement, including strikes and stayaways in support of the Congress of South African Trade Unions (COSATU). During this period one of the key methods of resisting apartheid was non-payment for municipal services.

Since the first democratic elections in 1994, political mobilisation in Diepkloof has declined. Generally people supported the coming to power of the ANC and believed that an ANC-led government would redress the inequities of apartheid.

ESKOM

In South Africa there are two main service providers for electricity: the municipality and the parastatal company known as the Electricity Supply Commission or ESKOM. Soweto, including Diepkloof, falls under ESKOM. ESKOM, which was founded in 1923, took over electricity provision to Soweto from the municipality in 1993.

When ESKOM took over electricity provision in Diepkloof there were already significant arrears. ESKOM itself had just been commercialised and this added to the pressure on management to recover costs.

---

[1] This is the official version of why people were moved from Sophiatown and Alexandra. However, progressive historians have chronicled the destruction of Sophiatown in particular. For many of these commentators, Sophiatown was dismantled because it was a direct challenge to the racial segregation patterns of the apartheid state. For a detailed history of the event surrounding removals from Sophiatown, see Lodge (1983).

[2] The demographic data are from undated documents supplied to the author by the Diepkloof local authority.

[3] This term referred to forced removals and rape of girls from schools and the community at large. It used to happen during the mid-1980s. It was mainly done by gangsters.

After 1994, ESKOM, committing itself to the agenda of the Reconstruction and Development Programme (RDP), set itself a target of electrifying 1.75 million houses, schools and clinics nationally. The company also made an undertaking to bring down the real price of electricity.

Since that time, ESKOM has been at the focal point of the privatisation debate in South Africa. While urban and rural citizens have pressured for more access to electricity service, policy-makers have tried to find strategic equity partners to increase private-sector participation in the company. After many years of debate, this policy process culminated in the passage of the ESKOM Conversion Act in late 2001. Under the Act, ESKOM will be broken up into a number of smaller private entities in order to facilitate more competitive market structures for distribution. The Act maintains that transmission systems will still be government-owned, but run by small companies to further encourage competition. Critics such as COSATU, noting that with the introduction of commercialisation the budget for electricity has decreased from R1 billion to R600 million for 2001–2002, are concerned that the move towards privatisation will shift the focus to profit maximisation instead of "universal service delivery" (COSATU 2001).

As our research will show, the early stages of commercialisation have already placed enormous pressure on the low-income sections of the population.

Methodology

The purpose of this research was to explore the experience and attitudes of a number of people in the community. We did not intend to do a systematic survey but rather to use the insider knowledge of the researcher, a lifelong resident of Diepkloof, as a catalyst for accessing the range and depth of residents' views.

There was a conscious attempt to speak with people from the three main areas of Diepkloof: the formal houses in the working-class area (Zones 2 and 3), the formal houses in the more middle-class area (Diepkloof Extension), and the informal settlement known as Mandela Village. The expectation was that their different levels of income and electricity infrastructure would yield different views in terms of assessing existing service and suggesting improvements. Here we briefly describe these areas and their electricity service.

Zones 2 and 3

Zones 2 and 3 are working-class areas which include a large number of pensioners. The residences are largely the old municipal four-roomed units, known as "matchbox" houses. These have metered electricity connections. People are billed monthly for services. For most households in Zone 2 and Zone 3 affordability is the key issue with regard to electricity.

Diepkloof Extension

In terms of architecture, houses in Diepkloof Extension resemble many in the historically white suburbs. They are typically multi-bedroomed with inside bathrooms, full electricity service and large plots. For the most part, residents of Diepkloof Extension can afford the electricity tariffs levied by ESKOM. The Diepkloof Extension residents with whom we spoke generally had higher incomes and education levels than people living in the other areas of Diepkloof.

Mandela Village[4]

Mandela Village is an informal settlement. There is a high level of unemployment and a much lower per-household income than in Zones 2 and 3. There is no electricity provision from ESKOM in Mandela Village.

The interviews

Semi-structured interviews were used for households in Diepkloof Extension as well as in Zones 2 and 3.

Group interviews were used to get insight into the social relations, norms and values and different experiences of people of Mandela Village on lack of access to electricity and their opinions on the issue in general.

Altogether, 23 households were interviewed in Zones 2 and 3, and eight households in Diepkloof Extension. There were two focus groups of six people each in Mandela Village. There were also individual interviews with ESKOM management, community leaders and local-government officials.[5]

The Types of Cost-Recovery Measures put into Place

"Massive cutoffs" a cost-recovery measure by ESKOM

In April 2001, ESKOM initiated a crude cost-recovery project in Soweto that one company manager referred to as "massive cutoffs". This decision was affected from the ESKOM head office in Braamfontein, Johannesburg, via the greater Soweto branch. The Diepkloof branch of ESKOM argued that this project was not properly initiated and that it did not consider the problems experienced by the communities. Although the issue was later discussed internally, ESKOM continued with the cutoffs. Pricilla Maeda, Customer Services Assistant Officer of ESKOM Diepkloof, described the conflict within ESKOM over this issue as follows:

> At the moment the community is facing daily cutoffs, which is not only a problem for them, but it also represents a problem for ESKOM Diepkloof Branch. The problem is that we have built a relationship with our customers and we believe that such a relationship should be maintained and these measures will not maintain the relationship. The whole process is very frustrating for the customers and for us as the ones dealing with them on an everyday basis.

These problems were exacerbated by the lack of coordination between ESKOM'S Braamfontein and Soweto offices. For example, people who were cut off went to Diepkloof to make payments. They were then reconnected. However, when the next statement from Braamfontein arrived, the payment was not reflected, and so they were cut off again. According to Maeda:

> If the Diepkloof branch was running the project it would be run differently. It would take into consideration the fact that one customer was cut off last month and therefore avoid situations whereby people are targeted as if the idea is to make them victims. As a branch we take into consideration our customers' needs.

ESKOM Diepkloof acknowledged that the massive cutoffs were creating problems for communities. However, as much as ESKOM Soweto acknowledged the problems faced by community members, it still adhered to an overall approach of strict cost recovery. It argued that if consumers are unable to pay because of unemployment they

---

[4] Also sometimes referred to as Mandelaville. In late 2001 most of the residents of Mandela Village were forcibly removed to Durban Deep on the West Rand.

[5] A complete list of people interviewed appears in the bibliography section of this chapter. All quotes from individuals in this chapter are from these interviews, unless otherwise indicated.

should use less and therefore reduce their costs. And if they could not pay the reduced cost, they should be cut off. Pricilla Maeda put it succinctly:

You cannot run a business as if it is a welfare system (interview, 2001).

She further argued that the cutoffs project came about as a reaction to customers who were not honouring agreements reached in 1997 between ESKOM and residents who were in arrears. The agreements stipulated that a portion of the arrears accumulated as a result of the apartheid-era boycotts would be deducted According to Maeda, this was based on the condition that the current monthly account was paid in full as well as an extra R35 a month or so towards the remaining portion of their arrears. The agreement also stipulated that arrears should be paid off in five years. If the arrears were not paid off in the five-year period or if the current account was not paid in full every month, the agreement would be cancelled. Cancellation also meant that arrears deducted upon the signing of the agreement would be restored, and the "defaulters" electricity would be cut off.

The Impact of the Cost-Recovery Measures

The cost-recovery measures, largely related to the agreements, had a wide-ranging impact on the community. Respondents spoke of a number of problems which arose. A considerable number of respondents focused on the inefficient and inconsistent ways in which these agreements were implemented. Others believed that the cost-recovery measures reflected a much deeper political rift between themselves and the government they had elected.

Inefficiency and Inconsistency in Implementation

Our interviews indicated that many of the people who signed did not understand the terms to which they had agreed. For example, Mrs. Moche of Zone 2 Diepkloof, a pensioner who attended a meeting with ESKOM and signed the agreement, explained her situation like this:

When I signed with ESKOM they said I will pay R35 every month for my electricity, but now they say I owe them R12 000. Where do they think I will get this kind of money? They do not have the truth; they take us for a ride because we are old and poor; one day they say this the next day they say something else. What is happening?

Mrs. Moche's response explains why many pensioners interpreted the R35 payment as a continuation of the flat rate they had previously paid. Hence, they could not understand why their statements reflected different amounts each month.

Other residents complained that there was no apparent link between the meter reading and the amount for which they were billed. According to Shelly, a resident of Zone 3, after her circuit breaker was stolen and she reported the matter, a wooden circuit breaker was installed. This later burnt out, and she was without electricity for three weeks while waiting for ESKOM electricians to install a new one. Her next bill reflected that she had been charged for electricity consumption during this period. And this, despite the fact that there was no circuit-breaker installed, and also despite the fact that ESKOM did not have access to her meter as she locked her gate every morning when she left the house.

I do not understand how they know the amount of electricity I used, or do they have a central place where it reflects how much we use without checking our individual meters.

Other residents such as Mrs. Makhubedu of Zone 2 also showed incredulity as to how their bills were being calculated:

We are both pensioners with Mr. Makhubedu and we try our best to pay off what we owe, but it does not help. Especially with electricity I do not understand what is happening. We owe R8 000 to R9 000 of the old debt from the apartheid times.

According to our interviews, many of the residents dealt with their confusion by simply paying a flat rate every month, just as they had always done. The source of the problem, however, does not lie with residents alone. There are serious administrative problems within ESKOM which added to the confusion:

We usually experience problems with printers when our workers are in the field, which makes reading of the meters difficult because if there is this problem they are unable to offer statements. The other problem is that there are two billing systems: one is the reading of the meters, and then there is a posted bill, which is an estimated bill. The problem with this is that this estimated bill comes from Braamfontein and they are wrong 90 per cent of the time. This situation is frustrating to the customers because they do not know which one to take into consideration; they end up not paying their bills. This situation creates an environment where it seems as if there are two different ESKOMS operating (Maeda interview, 2001).

Although ESKOM acknowledged this problem, at the time of the research no measures had been put into place to rectify the situation. Furthermore, Pricilla Maeda's analysis of the billing fails to account for the fact that many meters simply were not read, either because they were broken, or because ESKOM fieldworkers could not always gain access to household meters.

But there is an additional problem related to the structure of billing. Most of the households in Diepkloof do not separate service fees from rent. They still argue that they pay rent even after they have been pronounced as owners of their houses. Therefore, the concept of paying for services is defined in their own way, a way which service providers do not consider.

When they said pensioners should come and sign I thought that there should be something wrong, or something for them to gain at the end. As a result I resorted to paying my arrears when I got my package from work. Thank God I did that; I would be cut off too if I did not do so. There is always something for them to gain. I knew that I could not trust them. (Mokoena, interview, 2001).

For Mr. Mokoena the solution to dealing with ESKOM was simply to use his accumulated savings to settle his arrears. But for many people, there is no package to square the accounts. For them, the problems with ESKOM are not simply about communication or understanding the billing system. There is the question of the affordability of a service which is seen as a basic necessity of life.

Affordability

Our interviewees generally showed a willingness to pay for services. However, they expressed serious doubts about their actual ability to pay. Ability to pay is constrained by socio-economic situation. A number of factors have contributed to this. Firstly, since 1994 there have been increased job losses, and the creation of flexible, insecure, low-paying jobs. As a result, many households depend on one income from an informal job or old-age pensioner.[6] This means that other than paying for services these people have to sacrifice certain things to survive.

According to research conducted in other parts of Soweto, this situation is the norm.

The main breadwinner is in more than 50 per cent of the cases unemployed or a pensioner, providing that the income in most of the surveyed households is very low.

---

[6] For a discussion of the unemloyment problem, see Makgetla (2001); for more on the issues of increasing flexibility and casualisation, see Kenny (2001) and Orr (2001).

Observation and cross-checks in the questionnaire show that more than 75 per cent
of the households live in modest or poor economic situations (Fiil-Flynn 2001).

My interviewees repeatedly mentioned similar economic conditions directly or indirectly. In particular, they expressed frustration that ESKOM did not seem to consider their situation when making arrangements to pay their bills. Elsie Thekiso of Zone 3 made this point:

> *Go ya ka gore omang ore o nale bokae – it depends who you are and how much money you have. I only go to ESKOM when I know I can pay what they ask me to. The way we are treated when we go to complain or try to ask for a deal because we are unable to pay it is really bad.*

Mr. and Mrs. Ntobong of Zone 3 expressed similar frustrations:

> *We are pensioners. As a result we can not afford the R250 they say we owe. We pay R100 every month. This is what we can afford. If we pay R250, it means we will not eat, my children won't go to school. Anyway R250, is too much; where do they think we get this much money?*

However, some middle-income earners in Diepkloof Extension responded differently. While also expressing difficulty in paying for electricity, the sources of financial pressure on Esther Makhama of Diepkloof Extension were not the same as those on Zone 2 and Zone 3 residents:

> *As compared to other needs I think electricity should be reasonable. This is so that it takes into consideration that people should eat or survive generally. We realise that inflation is too high, however we have been cut off because there is eight of us in the house. Myself and my husband are the only ones working. The real problem is that three of our children are in tertiary education and we pay their fees from our pockets and there is also a problem of finding work. If they could find work they would pay for their fees.*

Other residents of Extension showed similar concern about billing but responded at the level of administrative query rather than a broader questioning of ESKOM'S motives and general treatment of "customers". For example, Mrs. Mazibuko complained that:

> *We are not home during the day, and we do not cook every day because we work until late. The only time we are home is weekends and holidays. I do not under-stand why our electricity bill is so high; some months we even go and query it.*

But even when engaging with ESKOM on these issues, the people we interviewed in Diepkloof Extension tended to have a different perception of the company than those in Zones 2 and 3. Esther Makhama expressed general satisfaction with her treatment by ESKOM, an attitude not found in Zones 2 and 3:

> *I usually call ESKOM when I have problems with payment. Well, they are helpful; sometimes I do make an arrangement to pay later, then I go borrow money from friends or other people and then I am able to pay.*

A different view of consumption and cost: Mandela Village

Residents of Mandela Village presented a different view of consumption and cost. To some extent, respondents presented a pro-cost recovery view – that use should go hand in hand with paying. This different understanding could be based on the fact that they have had no direct experience as electricity users. Interviewees further argued that they do not want to "owe" ESKOM. Respondents expressed a preference for prepaid meters. They indicated that acceptance of prepaid meters was a way to show that they do not want to depend on the service providers without paying for their services.

But they recognised that they would only be able to buy prepaid cards once they found employment. They also noted that using coal and paraffin was too expensive. For them, however, alternative energy sources were more than an economic issue. Since they live in shacks which are built closely together, there is a constant threat of fire. As one anonymous resident put it:

Last year two zozos burned down because of the use of paraffin and candles. Paraffin and candles are also a problem for our children; it gets into their eyes and they can cause fires unintentionally when left by themselves. It was just luck that no-one was burned. During these periods we lose our furniture, clothes and other precious belongings. Mariga a tla le tlo rebala mo dipapapiring – winter is coming, you will be reading about us in the papers (interview, 2001).

Respondents in Mandela Village saw electricity not so much in economic terms but more as a tool for improving their lives. The use of electricity, they pointed out, would allow them to cook for their children, iron their clothes and be able to keep warm during cold nights. Most importantly they would feel safe leaving their children by themselves.

"Cutoffs"

In many households in Soweto, cost-recovery measures have ultimately led to cutoffs. A similar situation prevailed in Diepkloof. Of the 33 households interviewed, only seven had never been cut off. To implement cutoffs, ESKOM resorted to outsourcing the actual disconnections work. For most residents, cutoffs came without warning. The field-workers showed up with a letter and disconnected the electricity immediately. Very often, residents were not at home when this happened. They subsequently arrived only to find that they had been cut off. However, if someone is at home, cutoffs can occasionally be avoided through negotiation. Matete from Extension described such an occurence:

When this guy from ESKOM came to cut off, my mother was home and as a result the cutoff was avoided. We asked him to come back later and I was sent by my mother to go pay R500 on the spot. The ESKOM guy agreed, and when he came back later in the day he found that the bill had been paid and he did not cut us off.

Not everyone can afford Matete's response. Most of the people targeted are pensioners or have financial difficulties. And many of these people do not want to be seen disagreeing or fighting with the government. But still affordability remains an issue. Mr. Mokoena of Zone 3 argued:

As pensioners we do not love being in debt. We work hand in hand with the government. When they want us to pay we pay what we can afford.

Mrs. Aida Kingake of Zone 2 expressed a similar view:

This is our government so we can not disturb how it runs by not paying. But they should understand that as pensioners we pay what we can afford from this pension money. This money is also too little to accommodate all the costs we are facing.

Other residents who had experienced cutoffs were less sympathetic to the government's position. About half of the respondents defined or judged the cutoffs on a moral basis. They argued that they are targeted because they have no money and that this is wrong. They further point out that if their situation were different they would be treated with respect:

These people [ESKOM] think they have a right to come into our houses and tell us they will give us electricity. They took over from the government promising us manna from heaven. However, now that they have us in their hands they are cutting us off. I have never experienced such problems during the apartheid years. I think what they should do is come and take their wires out of my house because they think they can control me. I did not call ESKOM into my house; it had a deal with the municipality, not with me. (Mr. Ntobong, interview 2001).

Several respondents argued that cutoffs were an infringement of their basic rights. In their view, they were being targeted because they were poor and as poor people they had no rights.

> *What rights are you talking about, we do not have rights, none of us have rights. I mean if we did have rights, we would be treated with more respect. If ESKOM thinks he can just come and cut us off do you see rights and democracy in that? I don't. This democracy of theirs ends with the vote (democracy e ya bona efella ka go vota) (Mr. Ntobong, interview 2001).*

For Mr. Ntobong, democracy was linked to the ability to gain access to basic things. But some interviewees took the issue even further. They argued that rights for them meant access to a job so that they would be able to pay for their services. Ms. Elizabeth Thekiso of Zone 3 argued that:

> *If I had a job I would believe that there was democracy and rights. This would make my life easier; I would be able to pay and therefore, would not get cut off. However since I do not have a job I do not have rights, therefore ESKOM can just come in and cut me off.*

Even though Mrs. Buthelezi of Extension had not experienced a cutoff, she had a similar perception of the link between rights and ability to pay:

> *A lot of poor people are never in a position to realise their rights because they are unable to access these. I think democracy should allow for everyone access to basic needs and I consider electricity a basic need. Because not everybody has access, I think democracy in South Africa has a long way to go.*

Her views were particularly salient as she works as a nurse at Chris Hani– Baragwanath Hospital where she has seen many children burned from paraffin stoves and choked from the smoke of wood and coal fires:

> *Although people are not working they should be afforded a safe living environment. I mean we are in the year 2001 and people still die or get injured from smoke or fire caused by paraffin stoves and using "imbawulas" (braziers). I think technological developments should benefit everybody. At the end of the day all these are an increased cost to the state. This can be avoided by providing people with the most important things.*

As we have seen, residents' grievances about poor quality and lack of access to service delivery have taken on a number of forms. On one level, this amounts to grievances about administrative problems which seemingly could be solved by more efficient billing systems and perhaps some training in communications skills for ESKOM employees. But for a number of respondents the problem was much deeper. They associated attainment of their rights with access to service. Moreover, for some access to service also means access to the income to pay for the services.

The Response of the Community to the Cost-Recovery Measures

In the face of agreements and the "massive cutoffs" project, residents have responded in a number of ways. Here we will look at two general types of response. The first type of response is somewhat informal – illegal reconnections and violence directed at ESKOM. Then we will examine the extent to which making use of existing community-based structures like the South African National Civic Organisation (SANCO) has been an effective vehicle for citizens who want to regain access to services.

Illegal reconnections

A number of people responded to the cutoffs by illegally reconnecting themselves. The problems of restructuring within ESKOM have an impact on how these reconnections take place. ESKOM claims that the people reconnecting residents used to work for them as independent contractors and are now unemployed. But respondents said the situation is more complex.[7] Ms. and Mrs. Thekiso described the scenario for those opting for illegal connections:

> On this block everybody has been cutoff, but what happened is that the very ESKOM people who were supposed to do the cutoffs they come and tell us that if you give me R50 I will not disconnect you. Then what happens is they come to collect every month-end. There are those people who are vulnerable to these people. They give in to their demands. We said no to them, although we have an illegal connection we would rather pay the money we have to ESKOM. This is better than to pay thugs, this is because this does not help our situation, and they take the money and then the next day someone else will come claiming that they are also from ESKOM. In such a case what do you do, give another bribe? I think that is a waste and it is not fair because the people who do this are already employed.

Most of the respondents who had illegal reconnections did not worry about the implications that such action could have on them. Shelly argued that:

> If they find out I do not know, but I think I will deal with them. And if they take me to jail, well, I will go and I won't be the only one.

The respondents with illegal connections argued that they had no choice as coal was too expensive. Some argued that using coal was not an option since they do not own coal stoves, and that using "imbawula" was out of the question since it would endanger their lives and those of their children.

> We will agree to connect illegally because we are suffering, "re a sokola" but the problem with illegal connections is that these people from ESKOM will harass you wanting money every day (Rachel Nkhaphe, interview 2001).

Of all the respondents who had been cut off, only Mr. Ntobong who had been cut off for eight months would not hear of illegally reconnecting his electricity. The alternative fuel source for heating and lighting is a coal stove and candles. He is adamant that he will continue using coal despite the fact that it costs R26 a bag and he has to buy two bags every week.

Use of violence as a response to cutoffs

Pricilla Maeda (interview, 2001) from ESKOM pointed out that the Diepkloof community at times had resorted to the use of violence. She argued that a woman in Diepkloof burned an ESKOM fieldworker with boiling water. Another ESKOM worker who was supposed to carry out a cutoff was nearly shot by a man in Diepkloof.

The role of SANCO in dealing with service delivery issues

Before 1994, civic organisations were the structures most representative of the interests of township communities. Since 1994, however, there have been great shifts in SANCO and much debate about the role of such a body (Mayekiso 1996; Ngwane, interview 2001; Ndletyana 1998). In many communities, the key SANCO leadership has moved into government, leaving the structure seriously weakened. In other areas, SANCO has become indistinguishable from government and the ruling party. For Trevor Ngwane, leader of the SECC and a former councillor, SANCO no longer has much to offer communities. He argues that to be effective SANCO would need an independent political direction:

> SANCO does not have a real independent political direction. It is weak and its structures are built on non-existent politics. With weak politics nothing can be built.

---

[7] Almost all of the households interviewed in Zone 2 and Zone 3 had illegal connections at the time of the interview or earlier.

In Diepkloof such an independent direction would seem to be lacking. The chairperson of SANCO Diepkloof branch is ANC ward councillor Vuyisile Moedi. Rather than becoming an advocate for the community during its interaction with ESKOM, Moedi argued that community members are irresponsible and manipulative. In his view, they only approach SANCO when they have problems and even then they always present a one-sided story:

> We are dealing with manipulative people here. Affordability goes hand in hand with responsibility; it is like democracy. It cannot be business as usual for these people. For example, you find someone using a two-plate stove as a heater. This is irresponsible. It has an impact on cost. These people should change their consumption.

Oupa Serumola, the chairperson of the education desk for SANCO Diepkloof branch, is also critical of residents' attitude toward payment for services:

> We have changed the way we approach problems presented to us by the community. The thing is we realised that the community is manipulative. They give information which is misleading, sometimes to suit them. In situations where they have problems, we go out to their houses, but when we get to their houses we get a different situation from what they presented. Therefore our approach is that it is wrong for people to use services without paying.

> Unrealistic people in our community use up to R400 of electricity but they pay R100 at the end of the month. They then say they are unemployed; how do you have eight people unemployed in one household? As SANCO, we took a resolution that if they are unemployed they should take responsibility by using less electricity. It is a question of responsibility. As SANCO and as communities, we have a responsibility: we should account for what we use. Certain things we do not need, especially when we are not employed...

A number of residents expressed doubt concerning the extent to which SANCO would help them deal with their problems. Mr. Ntobong argued that:

> Just forget SANCO. A lot of people go to them, but what do they get? SANCO does not own electricity. If you owe OK you should talk to OK you cannot talk to Checkers. I do not think SANCO will help me. They are part of the government that is taking away our services.

Ms. Elizabeth Thekiso argued that SANCO members were not cooperative and that they had their own mandate. She said they told her she was a problem and wanted attention. She received help from other organisations like the Wits Law Clinic, when the local authority was trying to take her house after her husband died.

Hence, while SANCO remained the only broad-based structure which claimed to represent the interests of the community at large, the civic body had offered little assistance in responding to the effects of cost recovery. In fact, rather than showing sympathy or solidarity for those who had lost access to electricity for whatever reason, the leadership of SANCO placed the primary blame for service delivery problems on citizens who were "manipulative". Given this stance, without a substantial change in the local leadership, it is unlikely that SANCO will emerge as a "watchdog" over electricity issues for the community, much less an independent political force.

Analysis: from "Citizen" to "Consumer"

In 1993, the apartheid government handed over the provision of electricity in Soweto to ESKOM. At the time, ESKOM was just beginning its process of commercialisation. However, due to the militancy of Diepkloof residents at the time, it was unable to take any major steps in this direction. The community was firmly committed to a position of non-payment. But nearly a decade later, the commercialisation of ESKOM and the accompanying cost-recovery measures are part of the everyday reality for people in Diepkloof. This shift has major implications for notions of citizenship in a democratic South Africa. Ultimately, it has been frustrating for the community to use electricity. But this has been made worse by the fact that these problems are experienced within a democratic dispensation. Many of the respondents argue that when they were not paying for services during the struggle against apartheid, the situation was much better. They argue that now when they are trying their best to be in the "good books" of the service providers and with government in general, they are treated with "contempt".

According to the free-market notion of "consumer sovereignty", the consumer has power to influence the market through purchasing power, which is driven by individual tastes.[8] However, the findings of our research in Diepkloof show that consumer action cannot be divorced from the socio-economic context within which people live.

The transition to democracy in South Africa entails the advancement of citizenship rights, the increased provision of social security, and access to basic services for the previously excluded groups. These acknowledgments, as embodied in the constitution and the RDP, reflect the perspective on citizens' rights which is that citizenship cannot be built from purchase alone.[9]

Marshall (1963) has elaborated on such a conception of citizenship, linking it to decommodification. This principle underpins the concept of democratic welfare capitalism and inhibits the anti-egalitarian tendencies of the market. In this model, citizenship is not just about the right to vote. Rather, the state is designed to service the social needs of its citizens. According to this conception, the citizen is entitled to particular basic rights: a basic income grant, access to social goods such as health and education, a safe environment and access to heritage, etc.

Decommodification in this context would posit social services as a matter of right and not one dependent on, or exposed to, the market. This concept captures the fact that capitalism eroded the pre-capitalist forms of social protection of citizens with the intro-duction of the market. Therefore, individuals are forced to rely on the market for their survival irrespective of how much the market creates situations of low wages and unemployment.

In much of the world today, the move towards giving market provision preference to state provision is turning citizens into customers. The market does not examine the socio-economic background of individuals but values them in terms of their purchasing power.

In South Africa, therefore, the priorities of social citizenship or adhering to the country's constitutional provisions clash with the new economic dispensation accom-panying this transition which calls for fiscal discipline and reduced government spend-ing. These economic imperatives are derived from the Growth, Employment and Redistribution (GEAR) strategy, which is built on neoliberal principles. Democracy and the macro-economic strategy challenge the state on how to acknowledge citizenship rights. While the government prioritises reducing the budget deficit, there is an expressed commitment to making sure that all South Africans have access to basic social services.

The issue at stake is whether democracy can exist in the absence of social rights. Lack of access to social services leads to a negative definition of democracy. This was evidenced in the interviews where some respondents defined their rights as non-existent in conditions where they do not have employment. This further links democracy and citizens' rights to access to the market.

Apart from turning citizens into consumers, the reigning of the market further challenges democracy in South Africa. Since the market values citizens as individuals, there is an implicit acceptance of the notion that citizens do not pursue a common good.

---

[8] For more extensive discussion on the free market, particularly in the era of globalisation, see ILRIG (1997; 1999) and Bond (2000).

[9] For further discussion on this topic see Esping-Anderson (1990), Kultner (1996) and Amin & Hausher (1997).

As in "economic life", they pursue self-interest. But this view is challenged by the history of collective struggle in communities like Diepkloof. And in some areas during the post-1994 dispensation, individual resistance such as connecting illegally is being transformed into collective action, such as in the case of the SECC's Operation Khanyisa, which began just a few kilometres up the road from Diepkloof. While residents of Diepkloof may not yet have fully embraced the organised response of the SECC, unless cost-recovery measures are loosened, it is highly likely they will return to their historical profile of collective action.

What is disturbing is that rather than re-thinking the shift toward the market, the South Africa government is moving ahead toward more extensive privatisation. At the level of citizenship, such measures will further entwine rights with the ability to pay. This "trust" in the market shows an increasing lack of concern for the exclusion of the poor from basic services and participation in the new democracy.

Moreover, many residents themselves seem deeply suspicious of privatisation. For Mrs. Mogano of Zone 2:

> I think with privatisation things will be heavy for us. I think the government is the best to provide for us things to survive.

Mr. Ntobong:

> Private companies want one thing and one thing only, to make more money and more money. In the initial stage they will argue that they will sweep better than the municipality. However, after you give them the broom they do not do the job and then they start harassing you. I prefer the municipality, because they are not supposed to be working for more money but for the needs of the people. Furthermore, they are supposed to understand when you tell them you are unemployed and you cannot pay; not the private ones, they are not interested in why you cannot pay.

Sarah May from Zone 3 expressed similar sentiments:

> When I was still at school, I remember my economics. Private corporations work to make profit. You cannot make profit from water. People who are poor need water but they will not buy it so you will not make profit and you will be out because of competition.

For these residents, and many others we spoke to, further reliance on the market offers no solution either for effective delivery of services or for the realisation of democratic rights. Enhancing their rights means some form of economic empowerment, not surrender to the market. As Ms. Elsie Thekiso put it:

> If I had a job I would believe that there was democracy and rights. This would make my life easier; I would be able to pay and therefore would not get cut off. However since I do not have a job I do not have rights...

My research findings suggest that cost-recovery measures are increasingly placing pressure on residents in a number of ways. At a financial level, cost recovery has led to reduced access to services or even to cutoffs. Such measures pose a range of strains on daily household life, from increased costs or labour time in order to access alternative energy sources, to health hazards posed by fire and fumes.

Conclusion

My research findings suggest that cost-recovery measures are increasingly placing pressure on residents in a number of ways. At a financial level, cost recovery has led to reduced access to services or even to cutoffs. Such measures pose a range of strains on daily household life, from increased costs or labour time in order to access alternative energy sources, to health hazards posed by fire and fumes. Mr. Ntobong went so far as to characterise being an electricity consumer as almost like a brush with satanic forces:

> Having access to electricity in Diepkloof is like inviting the devil into your household to harass you.

While electricity providers are likely not evil incarnate, the experience of citizens of Soweto with ESKOM and the local authority does raise fundamental questions for the building of a democratic South Africa. The difficulties in accessing basic services like electricity raise issues of whether citizens' rights have actually been enhanced since 1994. Under the reign of cost recovery, residents are defined and treated first as customers before they are treated as citizens. Their ability to pay defines whether they will be treated with dignity and respect. Therefore, for many, democracy and rights ended when they cast their vote.

This paper has pointed out these problems and would conclude that to resolve these problems, community organisations are needed. At present in Diepkloof the only active social movement is SANCO. But given SANCO's close relationship with local government and its leaders' open advocacy of cost recovery, this one-time civic power seems unlikely to drive any campaign to improve service delivery for the most disenfranchised Diepkloof residents. Therefore it is important for communities to start organising in ways that enable them to function as "watchdogs" over local government and service providers. They should be in a position to criticise and even bring down any of their leaders who do not represent community interests. Fulfilling this task may ultimately require new forms of collective action and organisation, forms which may ultimately look very similar to or maybe even be very different from those that were seen in the 1970s and 1980s.

Bibliography

Amin, A. and Hausher, J. (1997). *Beyond Markets and Hierarchy: Governance and Social Complexity.* Glostershire: Edward Elgar.

Bond, P. (2000). *Cities of Gold, Townships of Coal: Essays on South Africa's New Urban Crisis.* Africa World Press, New Jersey.

COSATU [Congress of South African Trade Unions]. (2001). Submission on the ESKOM Conversion Bill, accessed at: http://www.cosatu.org.za/docs/2001/ESKO Mcob.htm

Esping-Anderson, G. (1990). *The Three Worlds of Welfare Capitalism.* Princeton: Princeton University Press.

Fiil-Flynn, M. (2001). "The Electricity Crisis in Soweto", Municipal Services Project Occasional Paper Series 4, Cape Town.

ILRIG [International Labour Resource and Information Group]. (1997). "Workers World News, The Globalisation Debate Continues". *Apartheid Debt, GEAR and Privatisation.* No 9/10.

ILRIG. (1999). *An Alternative View of Privatisation*. Cape Town: ILRIG.

Kenny, B. (2001). "We Are Nursing These Jobs: The Impact Of Labour Market Flexibility On South African Retail Sector Workers", in ILRIG (ed.). *Is There An Alternative? South African Workers Confronting Globalisation*. Cape Town: ILRIG.

Kultner, R. (1996). *Everything for Sale: the Virtues and Units of Markets*. New York: Knopf.

Lodge, T. (1993). "The Destruction of Sophiatown". In Bozzoli, B. (ed.) *Town and Countryside in the Transvaal*. Johannesburg: Ravan.

Makgetla, N. (2001). "So how bad is unemployment really?" *South African Labour Bulletin* 25(2).

Marshall, T. H. (1963). *Sociology at the Crossroads*. London: Heinemann.

Mayekiso, M. (1996). *Township Politics: Civic Struggles for a New South Africa*. New York: Monthly Review Press.

Miller, D. (1995). "Consumption as the Vanguard of History". In Routledge *Acknowledging Consumption: a Review of New Studies*, London: Routledge.

Ndletyana, M. (1998). Changing Role of Civic Organizations from Apartheid to the Post Apartheid Era: A case Study of the Alexandra Civic Organisation (ACO). Unpublished Masters Thesis, University of Witwatersrand, Johannesburg.

Orr, L. (2001). Women's work and globalisation trends: the South African picture. *Agenda* 48.

Shubane, K. (1991). "Soweto" in Lodge, T. and Nasson, B. *All, Here, and Now: Black Politics in South Africa in the 1980s*. New York: Ford Foundation.

Interviews

SANCO Diepkloof Branch
17 April, 2001
Oupa Serumola
Vuyisile Moedi

Focus Group (Mandela Village)
19 April, 2001
Group 1
Kufa Gladys
Morobeng
Tinyingo Louisa
Baloyi
Sikulu Zulu
Shadi Kungwane
Group 2
Thoko Sibisi
Lindi Dlamini
Neliswa Mandi
Dudu Dube
Julia Maroleng
Meisie Ramaru

20 April, 2001
Justice Zuma – Councillor Diepkloof Ward 27
21 April, 2001
Zone 3
Shelly
Mrs. Morwe
Johanna Mntambo
Gladys Photo
Pollena Phetoe
Mr. and Mrs. Ntobong

23 April, 2001
Zone 3 outline to Mandela Village
Mr. Mokoena
Elsie and Elizabeth Thekiso
Rachel Nkhaphe
Mpho Motswagae
Sarah May
Meisie
SANCO Zone 4 Community Meeting (Ward 29) – 6pm

24 April, 2001
Zone 2
Mrs. Dikgale
Mrs. S Moche
Lebogang Dilwane
Mrs. Sithole
Mrs. Mogano
Mrs. Makhubedu
Taxi Driver
Ms. Talakgale
Mr. Sithole – SANCO representative 4
Aida Kingake
Mrs. Khutha

3 May, 2001
Diepkloof Extension
Esther Makhama
Matete Magongoa
Mrs. Nkonyana
Mrs. Zondi
Mr. Hlabathini

10 May, 2001
Mrs. Mazibuko
Elizabeth Buthelezi
Itumeleng Dikgale

11 May, 2001
Trevor Ngwane – former ANC Councillor at Pimville
ESKOM Diepkloof Branch

3 May, 2001
Pricilla Maeda – Assistant Officer Customer Service ESKOM Diepkloof

People and Service Delivery

Mr Fakude has been residing in Odondolo in KwaZulu-Natal for years. He and his family are not originally from the area. They are one of many families who were allocated land (by the Induna) on which they could live. They are still treated as *"outsiders"* and are often neglected or not considered since they reside in *"no-man's land"*. Neither the Induna nor the municipality wants to take responsibility for the community on this land, especially when it involves decisions around services.

Mr Fakude has had to deal with this frustration for all the years, the worst of which has been the struggle around water. A couple of years ago, while the municipality was converting the electricity supply onto the prepaid system, his application for a prepaid electricity meter was accepted. However his application for the private connection to a yard tap was declined on financial grounds. The reason given by the municipality was that the costs for the infrastructure for this connection would be in the region of R800 and that since Mr Fakude was unemployed, their chances of recouping the cost for the infrastructure, let alone the service, was unlikely, and therefore not viable.

Access to water via the prepaid system for Mr Fakude was just as complex. According to the Induna, he, like all the other families living on *"no-man's land"*, was not part of the water project. Secondly, the location of the prepaid taps was too far away from where they lived. Lastly, the amount of water that they would be able to carry in relation to the distance they would need to travel was not worth the effort. He and his family have had to resort to the nearby river for their water needs. He and his family are aware of cholera; therefore no-one drinks water unless it is boiled. He adds that he welcomes the rainy months of the year, during which time he collects the rain in buckets. He prefers rainwater to the river.

4

Cost Recovery and Prepaid Water Meters and the Cholera Outbreak in KwaZulu-Natal

A case study in Madlebe

by Hameda Deedat and Eddie Cottle

Introducing the Case Study

On 19 August 2000, the worst cholera outbreak in the history of South Africa was reported in KwaZulu-Natal. Researcher David Hemson from the Social Policy Unit at the University of Durban Westville reported the estimated cholera figures to be about 5 000 cases with 33 confirmed deaths by 17 October, 2000 (Hemson 2000, 1). In February 2001, Chopra and Saunders commented on the severity of the situation and presented updated figures that reflected an escalation since the beginning of the outbreak: "The outbreak of the past five months has accounted for almost 30 000 cases and approximately 80 deaths..." (2001, 1). The *World Health Report* of 2001 figures for the cholera epidemic for the period August 2000 to April 2001 were 80 387 cases and 168 reported deaths in KwaZulu (Mugero 2001). In the lower Umfolozi district, which includes Madlebe, the World Health Organisation reported 18 436 cases for the same period and a total of 22 deaths (2001).

Cholera incidences in this area are not unusual. The outbreaks of the 1980s and 1990s have often been used as points of reference in evaluating the severity of the August 2000 outbreak. In fact, the 2000 outbreak was the worst in the history of the area. What makes it even more extraordinary is the fact that it occurred within the context of a purified water service. The installation of the service began in 1997. In 1994, the uThungulu Regional Council (URC) was appointed as the local authority responsible for service provision for certain rural areas, including Madlebe. The community put in a request to the URC for a purified-water service in the area. In keeping with current legislation on local government, the URC then appointed the uMthlathuze Water Board (MWB) implementing agent for this service.

The MWB accepted this responsibility. As a water service provider the MWB followed a policy of cost recovery (uMthlathuze 1998, 1–2). As the introduction to this volume has pointed out, cost recovery is in keeping with the South African government's macroeconomic policy, GEAR. According to GEAR, the delivery of a service must be self-sustaining. In the case of Madlebe, MWB decided to implement a prepaid water service under the assumption that it would increase, as well as regulate, access.

There was the expectation that this would also be self-sustaining since the "pay as you use" system camouflages infrastructural and administrative costs by attaching them to both the registration fee and the kilolitre/unit price. (Phil Berridge interview, 2001).

In 1997, the MWB began implementing a prepaid meter water service in Madlebe. The project was completed in August 2000, and the first cholera case from the area was reported on 19 August. The Provincial Department of Water Affairs and Forestry (DWAF) released a document, (2000, 2) which addressed the issue of cholera, how it spread, and how the outbreak became an epidemic. It confirmed the time of the outbreak to be August 2000 and acknowledged that the provincial Department of Health had declared cholera an epidemic in the area on 24 September, 2000.

At the time of the recorded outbreaks, allegations were made in Natal newspapers that the prepaid meter system was responsible for the scale of the outbreak. DWAF, who supported the project, conducted its own research into the outbreak and found that the water project was in fact "cholera free". In addition, in "Cholera Epidemic in Northern KZN", DWAF stated that an exposed "leaking pipeline" caused the infection (2000). DWAF further added that its findings did not support the allegations that the conversion of the communal taps to prepaid meters and the increase in service cutoffs in neighbouring Ngwelezane were related to the cholera outbreak. According to DWAF findings, the first cholera case was reported some ten kilometres away from the scheme in a place called Makholokholo in the Mzimela tribal authority.

It does, however, confirm that the Mthlathuze and Ntseleni Rivers and nearby streams were cholera-infested, and cholera cases were also reported downstream.

While DWAF and the MWB may deny that the prepaid meter water service in Madlebe had any responsibility for the cholera outbreak, and that the completion of the project and the cholera outbreak were coincidental, our research has led to a different conclusion. DWAF's investigation failed to address the issue of the prepaid meter system as a tool for cost recovery, and the impact it has had on the community of Madlebe. Despite its claim of a thorough investigation into the cause of the cholera outbreak, it fails to explain why people who had access to a "cholera-free" water system were drinking water from rivers.

Our research seeks to address this issue. We argue that the delivery of services under the framework of cost recovery leads not only to critical compromises on issues of equity, access and health, but also may actually increase overall expenditure.

Madlebe: historical background

Until 1994, South Africa was divided into four provinces (Cape Province, Natal, Orange Free State, Transvaal) and ten bantustans. KwaZulu was founded in 1972 as one of the bantustans. The KwaZulu bantustan consisted of small fragments of land scattered throughout the province of Natal. In 1994, Natal and KwaZulu were recombined to form KwaZulu-Natal province (KZN).

One of the many problems South Africa inherited from apartheid was a structure of race-based municipal boundaries. In 1999, in an attempt to address these inequalities of apartheid, new demarcation boundaries were drawn up in all nine new provinces. The new demarcations were formalised in KwaZulu-Natal through the local government elections which took place on 5 December, 2000. The province was divided into ten district municipalities, 46 local municipalities and one metropolitan municipality.

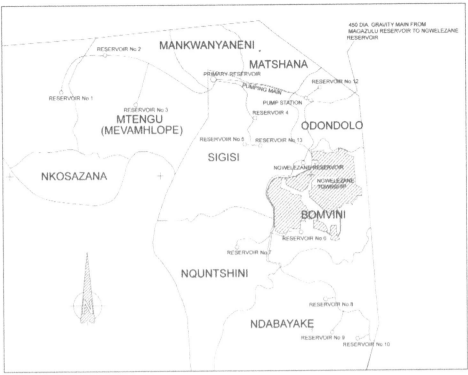

(Source: Knight Piesold)

Government envisaged that the new demarcation would ensure redistribution of resources via democratic and financially viable local authorities (*LGLB* 1999). Prior to this new demarcation, Madlebe fell under the jurisdiction of the Madlebe Tribal Authority, which was formerly part of the Lower uMfolozi Magisterial District. Today, there are two district councils for the area: uThungulu (DC27), and uMkhanyakude (DC28). Madlebe falls under the uThungulu District Council (MTAWSP Business Plan, 1996).

In 1997, the uThungulu region had an estimated population of 1 464 503, with 1 068 345 of those in the rural areas. Most of the population (91 per cent) lives in the former KwaZulu districts.These are rural areas with extensive poverty and low levels of service. The area is characterised by rapid urbanisation, with strong inward and outward migration between the former KwaZulu and Natal areas, as commuting and temporary labour migration continue to impact on the region.

Under the KwaZulu government, Madlebe did not receive proper health, sanitation or water services. Access to health services was mainly through mobile clinics that provided preventative healthcare. Although the Ngwelezane hospital and clinic existed as alternatives to the mobile clinics, the distances and poor roads made access difficult. 1994 marked the first real change in health services in this area through the introduction of free Primary Health Care (PHC) and improved infrastructure (mainly roads). This resulted in a greater intake at both the hospital and clinic. As a result of the new demarcation legislation, the Ngwelezane hospital is set to become the most utilised district hospital in the Madlebe area. Extensions so as to equip it with facilities capable of delivering specialised services such as radiology, orthopaedics and paediatrics are under way (Interview with medical official,[1] April 2001).

Incidents of cholera are common in this region, often reaching epidemic proportions. Tuberculosis, typhoid and gastro-enteritis are also rife. According to the latest HIV/AIDS statistics in South Africa, KwaZulu has the highest percentage of HIV/AIDS infection

---

[1] This person requested to remain anonymous.

(telephonic interview with Medical Research Council researcher[2], July 2001). According to the Department of Health website[3] this situation was unchanged in 2000, with the number of HIV cases increasing each year. In addition, 30 per cent of all pregnant mothers in KZN are HIV-positive (Telephonic interview with researcher at MRC in Cape Town, March 2002). Madlebe is no exception, and people who have HIV/AIDS are more vulnerable to infectious diseases such as cholera and tuberculosis (Interview with medical official[4] from Ngwelezane Hospital, April 2001).

Water and sanitation services in this area have always been very poor. Under the bantustan government, Madlebe relied on sparsely spread boreholes for water (Rylee 1990). However, for a rural area with a dense population, this did not suffice. As a result, nearby streams and the lower uMfolozi and uMthlathuze rivers served as the main water sources for the community.

This situation changed somewhat in 1982 with the installation of nine communal taps on the border of the newly established Ngwelezane Township. The taps were to serve as an interim measure to the Madlebe community during the 1982–1983 drought in KwaZulu. This region experienced a severe outbreak of cholera during this period. The communal taps remained the only purified-water service until 1997. MWB then introduced its cost recovery-based service with the installation of prepaid meters. There is no sanitation service in Madlebe – not even a bucket system. The community has to make do with the bush or the river banks. However, as of March 2001, the Department of Water Affairs and Forestry committed thousands of rands towards the construction of VIPs (Ventilated Improved Privy) as a measure to control cholera.[5]

Research Methodology

Since we were not familiar with rural KwaZulu-Natal, specific research methods were utilised to obtain information on the area. We found the streetscape technique very useful as it lends itself to both qualitative and quantitative aspects of research. Doing streetscapes is a simple method for gathering physical or visible data about an area. For example, as part of our streetscape, in each of the four areas we counted how many prepaid meters were installed, where they were located, and if they were in operation.

We also observed the community's daily routine for water collection. We noted:
- the gender and age of those fetching water;
- how much water was collected;
- the size and type of containers used;
- how the containers were carried (on their heads, in their hands, in a wheelbarrow, etc);
- how many people visited a tap at a given time; and
- what time of day most people went to the tap.

We also examined the infrastructural development of services in the area, its history and the current status of services. We gathered quantitative information on:
- the number of communal taps in each area;
- how many of these were on prepaid meters before March 2001; and
- the distance between taps.

After the observation period, we gathered further information thorough informal conversations held in the areas of Sigisi, Matshana, Nquntshini and Odondolo. Residents were asked to provide historical information on the kind of service or water access that was

---

[2] This person requested to remain anonymous.

[3] www.kzn.gov.za.

[4] This person requested to remain anonymous.

[5] Little progress appears to have been made on these. Although the implemetation of this program had begun early in 2001, by April there were no more than a handful visible.

there before the prepaid system, and how they felt about the change. These issues were explored in greater depth during the semi-structured interviews conducted at the nine communal taps, and during the household interviews.

The interviews

We decided to interview as many stakeholders as possible within the timeframe of the research: SAMWU, the communities affected in the area, community organisations, councillors and municipal officials. Our research was further complicated by the fact that neither of us spoke Zulu, the primary language in the area. We asked Dudu Khumalo, the SAMWU provincial water coordinator to assist us with interpretation. Each interview was guided by a semi-structured questionnaire with immediate translations for both the questions and the interviewees' responses. Both individual and group interviews were conducted, and all were recorded on tape.

Our first interview was conducted with Mr. Wilson Xaba, the leader of a community-based organisation (CBO) called *Shona Khona*, meaning "go to them". Mr. Xaba referred us to Ngwelezane residents who had experienced service cutoffs or who had no access to purified water. We interviewed 10 households in the township using the snowball method.

Interviews were conducted in the following rural areas: Bomvini, Ngobothi, Matshana, Sigisi, Nquntshini and Odondolo. In Bomvini, residents referred us to Mr. Madida, the local Induna. In the other areas, nine group interviews were conducted at the taps, mainly with women. Approximately 12 households close to the tap-stands were interviewed. A concerted effort was made to include at least one household where a family member had contracted cholera.

Apart from the community-based interviews, we also spoke with municipal officials. We wanted to evaluate the officials' level of understanding of the concept of cost recovery, and how this translated into their business plan. The issues of service cutoffs, credit control and indigence policy were central to these discussions.

We also went to key personnel in the two local water service providers: uMthlathuze Municipality, which services the urban area of Ngwelezane; and the uMthlathuze Water Board, which services Madlebe.

Background: Water Service Provision in Madlebe pre-1994.

As indicated above, the water service in Madlebe prior to 1994 amounted to no more than the occasional bore-hole and nine communal taps. Unpurified water sources such as the lower uMfolozi and Empangeni Rivers, nearby streams, and rainwater during the rainy season became the traditional water supply. Phil Berridge, the project manager for the uMthlathuze Water Board confirmed this in our interview with him:

> There were no historical water schemes in the area apart from the nine communal taps on the boundary of Ngwelezane. During problems such as cholera or droughts potable water was transported into the area to deal with the problem. There were also boreholes but no significant water schemes.[6]

The nine communal taps installed in 1982 were the community's first access to purified water. The next major change took place in 1993 when the water system was decentralised in KwaZulu. There was a separate budget for each locality. Also, each rural area had to do its own drilling for boreholes. In 1994, the Department of Water Affairs and Forestry assumed responsibility for water provision in Madlebe. A new local authority, the Transitional Local Council (TLC), was then established in the area.

National policy on service provision mandated uThungulu, a newly formed District Council, to take responsibility for the provision of "basic" services in the rural parts of Empangeni. Madlebe, which is directly adjacent to Ngwelezane, fell under the same

---

[6] All quotes in this chapter are from personal interviews, unless otherwise indicated. A complete list of those interviewed appears in the Bibliography section of the chapter.

TLC. The formation of this local authority resulted in a request from the community of Madlebe for a water service. Since Madlebe was both a rural area and high-risk area for cholera infections, this was "identified as a priority" (Berridge, interview, 2000).

The Phasing in of the Prepaid Water Service, 1997 to 2000

Although the uThungulu Rural Council (URC) was the body responsible for the provision of services to the rural areas, legislation such as the Local Government Transition Act of 1993 makes allowance for service providers to outsource the provision of services. This is most common for services such as water, electricity and sanitation. The URC chose this option and outsourced water to the uMthlathuze Water Board (MWB). The URC's role was thus redefined from service provider to "assurer" of the water services in this area.

In light of the absence of infrastructure in Madlebe, the task facing the MWB was a daunting one indeed. In the words of the MWB project manager Phil Berridge: " [the] MWB had recognised the need to design a water project that would ensure financial sustainability." Given the MWB's theoretical framework for service delivery, its decision to deliver a prepaid meter service was not surprising.

In 1996, the MWB submitted a business plan to DWAF with a request for financial assistance. According to Berridge, the project aimed to implement a water-provision scheme in Madlebe that would provide taps 200 metres apart and ensure at least 25 litres of water per person per day. Berridge argued that community participation was crucial in establishing such schemes:

> If the community feels ownership it will look after the project but if people are not part of the process and are not held responsible and accountable the project will fail. And they won't care if the project is looked after or fails.

For this reason, a Project Steering Committee (PSC) was established at the outset of the water project. The PSC consisted of the Induna (headman), the Nkosi (chief), and two representatives from each ward. The PSC discussed the MWB and its role in detail.

According to Berridge, the committee supported the idea that "the communities should look after their own water supply". The MWB then presented its business plan to the PSC and the community. This plan made it clear that the intention was to remove what Berridge called the "conflictual elements of the system". Prepaid meters were supposed to eliminate squabbles over costs and arrears.

The local authorities argued that cost recovery was necessary in this area because of the absence of industry or wealthy households as a source of cross-subsidy. As Berridge put it:

> It has to be determined, with cross-subsidisation, who's going to pay for it; it is not for free, somebody is going to pay for it. Well, you see it comes back to the cross-subsidisation story: until such time that we had to run this scheme we had no means of cross-subsidisation.

The costs considered were for the actual infrastructure. This was estimated at R3 000 for each household, calculated as follows:
- prepaid meter: R1 800;
- labour and piping: R1 200.

The charge or fee for a private connection was between R600 and R2 500, depending on the distance of the yard or house from any infrastructure. To recover the overall cost for supplying water (operational and maintenance), the charge for water per kilolitre was estimated at R12,50. The MWB was willing to reduce this to R10, i.e. one cent a litre, once the project received more support from the community. Berridge defended this charge of R10 once again, making reference to the demography of the area:

> R10 per 1kl sounds incredibly high when most people in the town are paying R2,30. In the town your water bill is R60 to R100 a month whereas their water bill

is R20 for 2kl. You must remember that the level of service is different; in the town people have a full-blown service. One should be careful about the figures one uses and saying that a R10 charge is too high and how can you be charging poor people so much. For the amount of water that they are getting and the fact that they have access, considering the fact they use between five and ten litres on average a day, they are getting it at 1c a litre.

They are not paying for overall water usage, they are paying for plus minus 1 litre of drinking water per day and plus minus three litres of water for cooking. It is physically impossible for them to carry 25 litres per person per day, because of the distances.

Hence for Berridge and the MWB as a whole, there was only one way to ensure an adequate supply to the area: by getting people to pay in advance through prepaid meters. The Project Steering Committee (PSC) supported the motivation for cost recovery as presented by the MWB. It agreed to the provision of a water service via the prepaid meter system, rather than a communal tap with a flat rate. In the words of the chair of the PSC, the Induna in Bomvini, Mr. Madida:

The prepaid was supported by the PSC; it came from us because there would be no wasting of water, we would not need to monitor the meter and have meter readers, we would not have to go around collecting money.

The system was to be operated through the use of a card. To obtain the card, each household had to register as a participant in the water project, and pay a R50 registration fee. Those who had money registered and bought the card, while those who did not shared the card with their neighbours and usually bought about 50 or 60 cents of water a day.

According to Berridge:

700 of the 2700 residents in the area had taken up the offer of the prepaid system and had bought coupons for it. R50 – every area has a ward committee – a R50 buy-in commitment to their own water supply, that is how they saw it. This was their idea. They had a similar system for bore-holes.

The Induna added that the PSC did not consider the need for an indigence policy.

For those who really cannot pay, well, they know that there is nothing for "mahala" (free). The community of Madlebe has to buy the water from the municipality who has to buy the water from uMthlathuze. That's how it goes and at the end of the day you have to pay.

The prepaid meters were then systematically installed throughout the region at the PSC's request. Meters were installed in each area in Madlebe, one at a time. The installation of the meters began in 1997 and was completed in August 2000. These are the details for the areas under investigation:

- Nquntshini was provided with a reservoir that serviced 19 prepaid meters, which were attached to 37 taps. 262 households with 2 081 residents were serviced by these taps.
- Matshana and Odondolo had one reservoir servicing 30 prepaid meters that were attached to 54 taps. 440 households with 3 311 residents were serviced by these taps.
- Sigisi had three reservoirs that serviced 25 prepaid meters attached to 52 taps. 301 households with 2 302 residents were serviced by these taps. (Berridge, interview, 2001).

The MWB also decided to use the nine communal taps as a means to train a number of community members to maintain the service. This job creation was an additional incentive for the community if its members agreed to the prepaid meters. Before 1996, the former Empangeni municipality was held liable for the water costs of the nine communal taps. The municipality viewed the implementation of these taps largely as a public health measure. Hence there was no pressure to collect user fees. But when the Transformation of Local Government Act introduced measures for more rigorous financial management and cost recovery, this situation could no longer continue (MWB 1996, 8). Berridge described the situation at the time:

> What happened after that is the taps remained and the taps just ran. In Ngwelezane, residents were required to pay a flat rate of R45 for water and electricity service. The eight taps were not accounted for and the residents around the taps, which was the residents under the Nkosi and the squatters, were accessing water from these taps – and in some instances they made personal connections to these taps and had water running up to their houses.

Empangeni Municipality then approached the MWB, as the water service agent in Madlebe, and requested that it incorporate the nine communal taps into its service. Since the MWB had become the recognised water service provider (WSP), it was now financially accountable for the water supplied through the nine communal taps. The MWB agreed, and at the end of 1998, the nine communal taps were converted to a prepaid metered system. The MWB also did a simultaneous upgrade of the infrastructure to improve the water pressure.

uMthlathuze then attempted to establish where these connections were by visiting households in the area. It tried to negotiate with residents to apply for a private connection. By the time the project was complete, some of the households with the private connections were unwilling and unable to pay. The MWB then gave them a six-month grace period after which the uMthlathuze municipality would be instructed to cut them off. Berridge related his experience of communicating the new policy to the community:

> I told them the municipality wanted the water to be cut off and that they were leaving me with no choice. They just said "ja-ja-ja" but did nothing.

This change in service authority had implications for those residents who had made connections from the communal taps to their homes. They would now need to obtain permission for the connections from the former Empangeni Municipality and would be charged R3,25 per kilolitre of water.

Eventually, this intensive application of the principles of cost recovery was initimately linked by community members to the cholera outbreak. It is to the community's perceptions of cholera and the cost-recovery measures imposed by the MWB that we now turn.

Voices from the Community

The discussion in this section will focus on the social, financial, infrastructural and health implications of the prepaid meters for the rural community of Madlebe. We will explore these largely through presenting comments from members of various communities on their water service and the cholera outbreak.

In Bomvini, a number of people spoke to us about the process which led to the installation of the prepaid metering system.

> Prior to the prepaid meters in this area we had free water via a communal system. The taps did not have meters and we got water free. They came to us about two years ago to tell us that they are going to put in prepaid meters because we are wasting water. We were not consulted as a community; they were just telling us, not discussing with us (Resident 1).

> For those houses with taps they put in meters first. Then after that they wanted to put in prepaid meters. We said no and then they cut our water. They said that the water belonged to the municipality; that is why they have to cut off the water. So we had no water unless you buy the card and use the prepaid system. We had taps before this! (Resident 2).

Induna Madida, who was one of those on the PSC who had supported the prepaid meters, now admits that two years down the line the meters have proved to be a problem.

There are still people who do not have cards and must still register, they don't have money so they share a card. It is a problem because you cannot get clean water without a card. We used to use spring water before this but now it is dry.

Generally, the interviewees were not satisfied with the prepaid meters. A number summed up the situation in the phrase "no money, no water". Some felt that "it was a good system" while the overwhelming majority said "it was fine in the beginning but if you have no money then it was not so good". One resident summarised the situation:

Only my father works so it is difficult to get water through the card and many people feel like this. We used to get the water from the communal tap down the road and it was free. When we don't have money we don't have water. There is no river so we stay without. We ask our neighbours for drinking water but that is all (Resident 1).

Respondents described a number of problems they had experienced. One interviewee, for example, said that she could only afford to buy water to drink because she had no work. Many of the respondents who were part of this group interview nodded their heads in agreement. Most people used purified water for drinking and cooking. Only a handful in the community could afford to buy water for bathing and then not every day. As a result of the prepaid meters a large number of women spoke of feeling humiliated because of problems of access to water. Many respondents described how they had to beg for water from their neighbours since they had no money. Many said even asking the neighbours had its own set of problems.

We tried to get water from other meters. Otherwise we go and ask for water in the township. Sometimes these people will say water is expensive and they cannot give water (Resident 1).

Other interviewees said that they could not bear the thought of continually asking for water and being belittled in the process. As a result of their desperate need for water, many residents then resorted to the more "traditional" unpurified sources of water, the rivers or streams.

Moreover, the prepaid system did not only create problems for those who could not afford to pay the tariffs. According to the information obtained via the interviews, infrastructural breakdown was common after the implementation of the prepaid water project in each area. In Sigisi, the respondents complained of persistent breakdowns in the system. In some instances the problem was the actual meter; in others it was a leaking pipe. There was the odd occasion when someone in the community had tampered with the meter and caused a failure in the system. But the general feeling was uncertainty or lack of confidence in the system:

Now they have taken out the meters because the meters kept on breaking down. Many times we go to sleep at night thinking that there is water and in the morning when you go to the meter with the card you find it does not work even after we have paid for the wate (Resident 1 from Ngobothi).

But the main problem was the length of time it took the MWB to attend to problems. In this rural area, telephones are rare. Hence, problems were communicated via word of mouth. This could take up to a week. It could take another two weeks to find the plumber, the project manager and get the tap operating again.

This prepaid meter has lots of problems. It takes weeks to fix a problem because there are only two people who have to take care of all the problems in all 12 wards (Resident 2).

The respondents reported that the community received no backup or alternative water supply when there were breaks in service. If people wanted to access purified water with prepaid cards, then the onus was on them to walk to the next available and functioning meter to get water.

During this time we don't have water and this is a problem. When there is no water we have to walk a long distance to another meter to see if it is working or otherwise we have to ask for water from the township. Even the communal taps are prepaid meters so there is nowhere else to get water (Resident 2).

The respondents also indicated that attempts were made via the Induna and PSC to get the MWB to attend to these faults more promptly, but without success. These comments by residents were supported by water consumption patterns of the nine communal taps, after the conversion to a prepaid meter system:

Table 4.1: Madlebe Communal tap stands consumption patterns April – December 1999 (kl/month)

Tap no.	April	May	June	July	August	September	October	November	December
1	1	477	234	240	169	298	193	268	210
2	1	250	283	230	104	160	123	124	216
3	1	300	104	0	0	1	119	25	0
4	1	255	45	181	61	78	107	82	123
5	1	96	15	21	35	93	33	15	17
6	1	372	153	173	106	191	312	508	101
7	1	349	350	0	0	21	152	114	184
8	1	399	410	0	0	0	0	0	0
9	1	0	0	0	0	0	0	0	0
TOTAL	9	2 498	1 594	845	475	842	1 039	1 136	851

Analysis of data from April to December 1999:
Only one kilolitre was consumed in April 1999 by all nine communal tap stands.
- Tap no. 3 had zero consumption from July to August and December.
- Tap no. 7 had zero consumption from July to August.
- Tap no. 8 had zero consumption from July to December.
- Tap no. 9 had zero consumption from May to December.
- Four taps indicate a zero reading at some point for the period of study.
- All taps consuming water except tap no. 6 indicate a tendency for a dramatic drop from May/June to December.
- Taps no. 1 and 6 have the highest consumption.[7]

The Cholera Outbreak

In further discussions, residents went on to describe the events that culminated in the worst cholera outbreak in the history of KwaZulu-Natal:

Sometime in August last year [2000], something happened to the meters. They were faulty, not one but all of them. We could not get water from anywhere. Those of us who had bought water on the cards, even we could not get water. Nobody came to explain to us what had happened. We did not get any warning. All we know is we had no water (Resident 3 from Ngobothi).

---

[7] As explained earlier in the report, in 1998 the nine communal taps on the border of Ngwelezane and Madlebe were converted to prepaid meters. However, since the water supplied to these taps was from the Empangeni Municipality, and the MWB would be billed for it, water consumption levels for these taps were metered. We were not able to obtain a reading of water consumption for these taps before the conversion, but what is evident from the above data is that there were either cutoffs in water supply, infra-structural failures or non-use of the prepaids. In the event of either of the above the result is reflected by the zero water consumption levels for the various taps. This information appears consistent with the details provided by members of the community in their accounts of the numerous infra-structural problems they have had. Many had said that it had resulted in cutoffs that lasted for lengthy periods.
Our overall assessment of the consumption patterns illustrated by the table is the following: most of the taps reflected little or no consumption at some time between May and December. This can most likely be attributed to the laying of infrastructure in the various areas.

It was bad; it took three weeks before the meters were working again and in the meantime we had no clean water. The boreholes were dry. We needed water to live. We had no choice but to get water from the rivers (Resident 2 from Matshana).

Another resident corroborated this:

Prior to 1994 we got water from the borehole; between 1996–1997 we got water from the prepaid meters. Two months ago we started getting water from water trucks. We don't know who has sent the trucks but they know it is because of the cholera. No-one is using the prepaid meters any more because there are taps now (Group interview in Ngobothi).

The prepaid stopped working, that is why we have this communal tap. The Deputy Mayor of Empangeni put the tank here and the truck fills the tank. The prepaid has been here since January 2000, and in December the meter was broken (Resident 3 from Sigisi).

The quotes above represent sentiments that were frequently reiterated by members of the community in their description of the water cutoff that occurred in August 2000.

Table 4.2: Madlebe Communal tap stands consumption patterns Jan – August 2000 (kl/month)								
Tap no.	Jan	Feb	March	April	May	June	July	August
1	259	220	231	196	227	187	94	142
2	178	12	65	55	75	51	52	59
3	120	44	74	48	63	37	74	183
4	86	27	23	64	44	46	60	94
5	15	23	55	15	50	21	0	0
6	430	943	930	780	800	0	81	97
7	154	115	144	50	93	56	0	0
8	0	3	0	0	0	0	0	0
9	0	832	236	202	0	0	0	0
TOTAL	1 242	2 219	1 758	1 410	1 352	398	361	575

Analysis of data from January to August 2000:
- Tap no. 5 had zero consumption in July and August.
- Tap no. 6's levels of consumption fell dramatically after May.
- Tap no. 6 had zero consumption in June.
- Tap no. 7 had zero consumption from July to August.
- Tap no. 8 had zero consumption in January and from March to August.
- Tap no. 9 had zero consumption in January and from May to August.
- Taps no. 1 and 6 have the highest consumption.
- Five taps indicate a zero reading at some point for the period of study.

All taps have an erratic consumption level which declines dramatically from June to August. The low levels of consumption for this period appear to correlate with the infra-structural problems experienced by the community during the construction phase of the water project. It presents evidence that the community was left to endure inconveniences as a result of the cutoffs in its water supply.

Hence, our oral evidence is corroborated by the consumption patterns in the communal standpipes from January to August, 2000.

The first case of cholera was reported on 19 August 2000. By December 2000, there were thousands, with approximately 20 deaths reported in Ngwelezane and Madlebe alone. Several residents made clear linkages between the breakdown in the system and the spread of cholera:

As soon as the prepaid came in people started to get sick and people could not get water. When we got the water from the taps it was a better system because no-one in this area got cholera. You have to buy this R50 card, then you had to pay R5 to charge the battery before you could use the meter and get water. We were told to go and buy this R50 card. In 1997 they put in the meters then you buy the R50 card and then you have to keep paying R50 to recharge the card to get water (Resident 4 from Ngobothi).

You know before the township was built the Madlebe community got water from a spring-hole but after the township was built this water was contaminated by problems with the sewerage works. This is where our problem started with cholera in Madlebe and it is still continuing under the prepaid system. It is since the whites came here with their talk of water and sanitation that cholera became a problem. (Induna Madida interview, 2001).

But the Induna also expressed a slightly different view of the origins of the cholera:

There are about 200 houses in Bomvini and some of the people here did have cholera, I am not sure how many. I don't know where the cholera came from. The people in this area had standpipes in their yards. Cholera must be something in the air that causes people to get sick.

As soon as the community realised that the contaminated water from the rivers and streams was the cause of the cholera, it appears people/community members had by now learnt from experience that the prepaid meter system was not all it was set out to be. They expressed quite explicitly their view that the prepaid was responsible for the cholera since it cut off their access to clean water.

Interviewees expressed frustration and anger with the system. Some interviewees admitted that residents had resorted to removing or breaking the meters:

We had problems with this meter since 1999, which is when they put it in our ward and our problems have continued ever since they introduced this new communal system. Because we had this problem all the time with the meter, people ended up breaking it because they had to get water (Resident 4 from Sigisi).

We had a lot of problems with this prepaid meter all the time so the people ended up breaking it because we had to get water. They could not get the card to work. Also the people did not come soon to fix the meter. It took three weeks before they fix it. And even if we had bought water with the card we still could not get water. We tried to get water from other meters otherwise we go and ask for water in the township (Resident 5 from Ngobothi).

That tap used to be a communal tap then at the end of 1999 they told us that they are putting in prepaid meters. By the end of 1999 that tap became prepaid. The tap is broken because perhaps people are unhappy. (Group interview from Sigisi).

They are unhappy because they do not have money and with no money they cannot get water. People were happy before with the communal tap. It may happen that people have cholera now because of the prepaid. By Christmas last year there was no water coming from this tap (Group interview from Sigisi).

Dissatisfaction was expressed most strongly when the respondents discussed the way in which their problems were taken up by the MWB. Their major grievances were the length of time it took to attend to their problems and the MWB's inability to provide them with an alternative supply of clean water during the breakdown of the system. They said that three weeks was an unacceptable waiting period for the resumption of their water supply, particularly when they had already paid for the water.

Financial Implications

Apart from the devastating health implications, the breakdown of the prepaid system and the outbreak of cholera also had serious financial implications for the area.

Money had to be spent in correcting the infrastructural problems in order to resume the service. However, since hundreds of cases of cholera were reported from this area, the MWB was under pressure from DWAF and the community to remove the meters, thereby changing the nature of the service.

The meters, which had cost in the range of R3 000 each, were now redundant. In addition, some of the meters had been removed and some irreparably damaged. The MWB was to reconvene the PSC and request its assistance with the financial administration of the flat-rate system. The financial costs to the MWB of the corrective measures were the following:

- cost of an investigation into the causes of failure to the system;
- cost of an additional financial audit of MWB income and expenditure;
- cost of implementing a system to curb the water losses owing to damages to infrastructure;
- cost of backup stock;
- cost of training of Water Service Provider staff; and
- cost of re-implementation and promoting awareness of the program.

The National Department of Water Affairs and Forestry could not turn a blind eye to the plight of the communities of Madlebe. The media coverage on the epidemic highlighted the fact that the prepaid water meters had resulted in a massive cutoff and government intervention was necessary.

In response, the provincial department of DWAF hired water trucks from Amanzi Water to provide the community of Madlebe with an alternative source of purified water. Fifty 25kl tanks were also put in the area to top up the supply and were refilled regularly. DWAF national then organised a programme for Water Week in March 2001 when Minister Ronnie Kasrils visited areas around South Africa, including Madlebe, to educate communities about water conservation, water purification and sanitation.

According to Mr. Mchunu from DWAF, the initial cost for water reticulation in Madlebe had increased from R14.8 million to R16 million, and then to R18 million as a result of the outbreak. In addition, the expenditure for actual water was originally to be covered by the PSC. In the end, DWAF also paid this expense, which according to Mchunu came to another R18 million. To address the sanitation problem which was directly related to the cholera outbreak, DWAF had contributed an initial R2 million for VIPs (Ventilated Improved Privy), and a further R837 000 to ensure the construction of 2 400 VIPs in Madlebe. By January 2002, 2 386 VIPs had been installed. (Mchunu, telephonic interview, 2002).

In Kasrils's speech of 19 March in Madlebe, he pledged thousands of rands towards the community's struggle to access basic water and sanitation. This was reiterated in his budget speech in May 2001:

My department will spend R100 million annually for the next three years to speed up water and sanitation provision in cholera prone communities. During this year 59 water and sanitation projects will be implemented in vulnerable areas. Efforts will be intensified, because the current winter lull could see a resurgence next summer (Kasrils 2001, 6).

In response, an agreement with the uThungulu Regional Council (URC), DWAF, Amanzi Water and the provincial Department of Health was drawn up. Dealing with the epidemic ultimately had major financial implications for DWAF. To begin with, DWAF had approved a budget of R35 million. This would cover the provision of emergency water and sanitation services, the hiring of trucks, the purchasing of purified water, and the purchasing of building material. The average cost of operating a single truck for a month, including weekends, was R30 000. The project made allowances for 30 trucks to be used throughout the infected areas. The total estimated cost for the trucks over the three-month period was R2 700 000 (Mchunu, personal interview, 2001). Private contractors were asked to tender for the construction of stands for the 5 000-litre water tanks.

The cost could not exceed R500 per stand and the contractor had to ensure that the labour for the building of the stands was sourced from the community. (DWAF 2001, 3–4).

Since the cholera outbreak had reached epidemic proportions, the Ngwelezane clinic and hospital found their financial resources strained. Treating cholera was expensive. It required more staff, longer working hours, medication and equipment.

The Ngwelezane hospital erected nursing stations in Matshana, Nquntshini and Sigisi, in order to relieve pressure on the hospital and clinic.

There was also expenditure on nurses doing health education with the community and handing out free bleach. Pamphlets to raise awareness of cholera, informing people how to avoid contracting it and how to treat it, were printed and distributed.[8]

Other health-related expenses linked to the cholera epidemic included:
- Sampling of water resources;
- Collection of daily statistics.

Hence, in addition to the human cost of disease and deaths, the outbreak led to increased expenses for one of South Africa's most cash-strapped provinces.

Prepaid meters, cost recovery and equality

Apart from the human and financial costs which are directly related to the cholera outbreak, cost recovery also contributed to the perpetuation of social inequality in KwaZulu-Natal.

A brief comparison of water tariffs between Madlebe and the historically white and affluent area of Empangeni will illustrate.

Historically, Madlebe had no water service in the area and therefore had no infra-structure. Empangeni, however, had a sophisticated water service with in-house connec-tions as early as the 1940s.

Post-1994, implementing a water service in Madlebe would automatically have cost more than in Empangeni since the infrastructure, maintenance and operational cost of the service had to be factored into the user fee. Hence, under the system of cost recovery applied in 2000, Madlebe residents paid R12,50 per kilolitre while Empangeni's charges were a mere R2,30 (*uMthlathuze Newsletter* March 2001, 2). This inequity was in line with a cost-recovery policy which stipulated that residents had to pay the full cost of providing a service, even when the costs of provision included financing infrastructure which was not created by the apartheid regime.

It was only in April 2001, with the introduction of a R20 flat rate, that this situation was reversed and Empangeni residents paid a higher tariff for water per kilolitre than did the community of Madlebe. The drop in tariffs in Madlebe was not, however, initiated by the MWB but was instead an effort from the national DWAF to deal with the cholera outbreak. The MWB's view on this was apparent in Berridge's comments about the future of water service delivery in the area:

Signing up households for R20 a month and no stipulation on the quantity is going to lead to problems. The main principle of success is that you need commitment and responsibility from the community. They need to feel that the project belongs to them. That places us in a hell of a quandary. You plan for years ahead and then you have this free water issue and bang, you have to plan all over again. Government will have to foot the bill. We had the people learning the process and just when they were getting used to the prepaid, they go and put them onto a flat

---

[8] Attempts have been made to ascertain the additional costs that were incurred by the Provincial Health Department, but were unsuccessful.

rate system. And even though the PSC will collect the money in each ward, they now require constant mentoring.

Conclusion

Our research found that three main issues linked cost recovery to the cholera outbreak in Madlebe:

Affordability

Affordability in the context of Madlebe had two meanings. For the MWB it meant a prepaid metered system that is affordable for it as a business, is financially sustainable and is in keeping with the principles of cost recovery.

For the community, affordability means and/or determines access. Those who had money had water. For the majority affordability meant "no money, no water". Only 700 residents out of the entire community were of the financial means to join the prepaid scheme and buy water.

Information

According to residents that were interviewed, many people in the community did not understand the system or why they had to pay money for water when it is a "gift from God". This lack of understanding was aptly illustrated in an earlier quote where a resident referred to the R5 she used to buy water as a fee to recharge the battery of the prepaid meter so that she could get water. What she did not know was that she was paying for the water and not the battery.

Maintenance

The intermittent breakdown in the water service because of infrastructural faults recurrent in the scheme did not appear to be a matter of concern for the MWB. In spite of continuous complaints by the community about the long waiting periods that cut off their water supply there was no attempt to provide an alternative water service or to reduce the incidents. Berridge's response to this question was:

> *These people have been without clean water for years. They are used to it. What is a couple of weeks to them?*

These faults in the system go a long way toward refuting DWAF and MWB claims that the water project was "cholera free". While the MWB's reservoirs and pipelines may have remained uncontaminated by cholera, the cost-recovery policy had created a situation where these reservoirs and pipelines were no longer the water sources for the community. We conclude, therefore, that the cost-recovery policy was instrumental in the outbreak of cholera culminating in an epidemic in Northern KwaZulu-Natal.

Aside from contributing to the cholera epidemic, the cost-recovery measures also contributed to an overall diminished quality of life for poor people in the area. By reducing access to purified water and imposing exporbitant tariffs on residents of Madlebe, the local authority and the MWB contributed to a perpetuation of the poverty and inequality which have been an integral part of the recent history of rural KwaZulu-Natal.

Afterword

When the president opened a village tap and served water to two elderly women, they raised their cups in happiness and cried, "Bye-bye cholera!" (Kasrils 2001, 3–4)

This speech was delivered on 15 May, 2001, and on 8 October 2001, a new report revealed that a 44-year-old man from the Inanda area North of Durban had died of cholera. The report also stated that his was the eleventh case that was reported to the Department of Health during that quarter. His death brought the total cholera deaths since August 2000 to 229 for the province. The total number of cases recorded stood at 105 762.

The Minister's recounting of women saying "Bye-bye cholera" seems to be lauding a premature farewell. In the case of Madlebe, the eradication of cholera is far from reality. Providing access or delivering a water service is not just for today or tomorrow or next week. It is supposed to be access for all forever, and this research report indicates that on this score cost recovery does not deliver.

Bibliography

Chopra, M. and Sanders, D. (2001). *Cholera: A wake-up call for South Africa's Development strategy. Business Day*, 23 February.

DWAF [Department of Water Affairs and Forestry] (2000). *Cholera risks from well serviced areas*. Water Quality Management and Cholera. http://sandmc.pwv.gov.za.

— (2001). *Cholera Epidemic in Northern KZN*. Report compiled by T. Mchunu, Principle Community Development Officer.

— (2001a). Media Statement on *Government's response to the outbreak of cholera*. 18 January, embargo 2pm.

— (2001b). Budget Speech, 15 May. *"Water for people for thousands of years" –Li Bing 250 BC*. Media Release.

Hemson, D. (2000). *Closing the Gap? Policy and Practice in Water and Sanitation*, Indicator, no.17 (4), December.

Local Government Law Bulletin (1999). Vol. 1 (1), April.

MTAWSP [Madlebe Tribal Authority Water Supply Project] (1996). *Business Plan*.

Mugero, C. (2001). *World Health Organisation Report: Review of cholera epidemic in South Africa, with focus on KwaZulu-Natal Province August 2000 – 11 April 2001 (8 months)*. Epidemiology and Health Indicator Unit, KwaZulu.

No author (2000). Cholera, Statistical Notes, 2, 14 (2000), Statistical Notes: Focus of the month Cholera.

No author (2001). *uMthlathuze News*, Official Newsletter of the uMthlathuze Local Municipality, March.

uMthlathuze Water Board (1998). *Business Plan*.

Interviews

Phil Berridge, 10 April 2001.
Medical official, 16 and 17 October 2001.
Telephonic interview with a researcher at MRC in Cape Town, 7 November 2001.
Medical official from Ngwelezane Hospital, 25 and 26 October 2001.
Mr. Mchunu, 23 January 2002.

People and Service Delivery

She's 68 years old, lives with her unemployed son and four grandchildren and does not know what rates are. But her two-roomed house, which she has tried to enlarge by adding two shacks, is being sold by the Cape Town Unicity to recover her rates arrears.

Last Thursday when millions of South Africans were celebrating Human Rights Day, Vuyelwa Skelemani was informed by the authorities her house was on sale because she owed R1 185,03 in arrears. She has lived in the house for 18 years and feels her only option if it is sold is to build a shack on land reserved for Urban Renewal Projects.

"What are rates? We were never told anything about rates. All I know is President Nelson Mandela gave me a title deed and told me I have to pay for water and electricity. And now they are talking about rates. It's not that I don't want to pay. I can't pay the whole amount they want at one time. I asked the young man wearing a tie at the Tygerberg municipal offices if I can pay the money in instalments but he refused. I get only R570 a month in pension to feed seven mouths and pay for electricity and clothes ... Where are we supposed to go? There is no rest on this earth, maybe things will be better in heaven."

Skelemani, like other Khayelitsha residents who have rates arrears, wants answers from her councillors who she thinks can turn things around. Councillor Hitler Mdodo sat in front of Skelemani unable to explain what would happen to her and her grandchildren.

"It's council policy for residents to pay for rates but the problem is that there is no indigent policy in place that assists unemployed residents ... Some people can barely afford supper but are expected to pay rates. We are talking about taking people off the streets, but on the other hand kicking them out of their houses back into the streets."

(Cape Times, 6 March, 2002)

Fortunately for Skelemani, after this story appeared in the media, a company came forward and paid her arrears.

5

"They are Killing us Alive"

A Case Study of the Impact of Cost Recovery on Service Provision in Makhaza Section, Khayelitsha

by Mthetho Xali

Introduction

In line with global trends, the Unicity Commission[1] of Cape Town placed financial sustainability at the core of its service-delivery strategy. Its final report emphasised "establishing a stronger relationship between city government and the public built on their respective responsibilities to deliver affordable services and to pay for those services" (n.d., 11). In its leaflet "Pay and stay – it's the right thing to do" the City of Cape Town states:

> *Action will be taken against those who do not pay – the Council will not hesitate to cut off services and take legal action where necessary. Residents who do not pay will be without electricity or water and will have to pay the additional costs of reconnection fees, lawyers' fees and legal costs. They could ultimately have their houses sold (if they are ratepayers) or be evicted (if they are tenants in a Council house) (2001).*

This punitive approach is broadly indicative of what has become known as cost recovery. Our research is aimed at understanding the impact of such measures, by focusing on Makhaza, a settlement within Khayelitsha. Makhaza came into existence in the early 1990s and at present has tarred roads, both brick houses and shacks, and serviced sites.[2]

Located some 30km from the central business district of Cape Town, Khayelitsha was created in 1983 as a residential area for "Africans" under the apartheid segregation policy. Estimates of the population range from 350 000 to 900 000 (Dyantyi and Frater n.d., 11), making it, potentially, the largest township in South Africa. Khayelitsha fell under the jurisdiction of the City of Tygerberg until December 2000, when the Cape Metropolitan Area or Unicity was established.

---

[1] The Unicity Commission was an interim structure formed in November 1999 to prepare a plan for the unification of the Cape Metropolitan Area after the second democratic local government elections in December 2000. One of the main tasks of the Commission was to develop a strategy for service delivery.

[2] Attempts to obtain figures for the total number of households in Makhaza from the council were not successful. According to Makhaza resident Soyiso Mtemekwana, there are about 16 000 households in Makhaza (interview, 2001). He told us he obtained these figures from the ward councillor at a community meeting.

Methodology

Our research included a number of different methods. We used a survey for individual households, semi-structured, focus-group interviews with residents, as well as individual interviews with community and local-government leaders. Here we will briefly review each method.

Survey

Our survey targeted households within Makhaza whose water and/or electricity had been cut off. A significant number of these residents responded to the cutoffs by mobilising and resisting the attempts at cost recovery.

Our survey questionnaire dealt with all issues related to service cuttoffs (water, electricity, and waste removal). The questionnaire was developed in English and then translated into Xhosa, which is the mother tongue of most residents in Makhaza.

Since issues of service delivery are sensitive and politically charged we employed research assistants from Makhaza itself to assist us in conducting the survey. Through the Alternative Information and Development Centre (AIDC), a non-governmental organisation with branches in Cape Town and Johannesburg, we made contact with Youth for Work activists in Makhaza. Youth for Work is a brainchild of the AIDC, and is actively involved in the resistance to water cutoffs. We employed a total of ten activists. The assistants were selected on their ability to read and understand English and their familiarity with issues related to service delivery.[3] Once we had completed selection, we organised two all-day research workshops for the assistants. In the first workshop we discussed research methods and the aims and objectives of our research in Makhaza. We also made a presentation on the concept and policy of cost recovery and discussed the issue with participants.

After the first workshop, we asked the research assistants to go back to the community and identify households from the different areas in Makhaza (Matthew Goniwe, Solomon Mahlangu, and Mayibuye) would be potential subjects for interviews.

Once they had identified households for interviews, the assistants came back for a second workshop. This was a more practical session where we reviewed the questionnaire and did a role-play exercise with the research assistants asking each other the questions. As a result of this process, some changes were made to the questionnaire as per the comments of the workshop participants.

In this workshop the group also decided on its mode of operation during the field work. They agreed that:

- They would work in groups of five. Each group would have a coordinator. Pumeza Mpupa and Soyiso Mtemekwana were chosen for these roles.

- They would meet as a group each day before they went to the households. Then the actual interviews would be done by people working in pairs.

- At the end of each day the ten people would meet again and discuss progress and difficulties. We (myself and Simphiwe Dada of AIDC) would attend these meetings to help monitor the progress of the survey and to deal with whatever problems the assistants experienced in the field.

- The research would be completed in one week.

A major problem the research assistants experienced was the suspicion of the respondents that the survey was being administered by the council. In most cases the research assistants were able to deal with these fears by ensuring people that the outcome of the research would assist the community in formulating responses to its problems of service delivery. On a few occasions, the research assisants were not successful in convincing people that the research had nothing to do with the council. In those instances other respondents had to be found. The research assistants completed 63 questionnaires.

---

[3] The research assistants were: Nokwanela Gqolana, Nonkuleko Keke, Pumeza Mpupa, Thenjiwe Zenani, Nombulelo Tetani, Bongiwe Mzalisi, Ncumisa Mayo, Siyanda Yose, Soyiso Mtemekwana, and Vuyiseka Lusiba.

Apart from the household surveys, we conducted a focus-group interview with 18 people. We used this opportunity mainly to take up certain issues that emerged in the survey questionnaire. The participants in the focus group had also experienced water cutoffs but had not participated in the household survey.

We also conducted semi-structured interviews with two representatives from the South African National Civics' Organisation (SANCO)[4], a local council official from the financial accounts department, and a local water engineer. Furthermore, we communicated telephonically with Archie Hearne, Tygerberg Chairperson of the South African Municipal Workers' Union (SAMWU), and one council official from the Tygerberg Administration financial accounts department.

Having briefly outlined our approach to the research, let us now turn to the political context of Cape Town in which the cost-recovery measures we were studying emerged.

The Context of Cost Recovery

The introduction to this volume has outlined the global and national political context within which the policy of cost recovery emerged. In addition to this, it is important to note the specific urban history of Cape Town which is the backdrop to the situation in Makhaza.

As noted earlier, the second local government elections coincided with the unification of a number of substructures under a single Cape Town Metropolitan Area. The Unicity Commission, tasked with elaborating a service delivery strategy, took its cue from the national trend.

The Cape Town Unicity's approach to municipal services adopted the spirit set out by Mohammed Valli Moosa, former National Minister of Provincial Affairs and Constitutional Development, and echoed by officials in the previous City of Cape Town administration: "Municipal services need to be run like a business, with clear cost centres and management held accountable for performance" (*Sunday Times* 16 June, 1998). For its part, the City of Cape Town viewed electricity and water as "major services that residents buy from the Council" (City of Cape Town 1999). In this scenario, social services become just like any other commodity that is bought and sold in the market place. Full payment for services is the core of this cost-recovery policy. Cost recovery ultimately seeks to recover operating costs, maintenance costs and infrastructure costs. Cost-recovery policy also promotes the provision of different types of services. Basic services are short-term measures, and refer to communal standpipes, roads with gravel, ventilated pit latrines, open stormwater drains, and mast lights. These services are designated for households with an income of less than R800 per month which accounts for approximately 20 per cent of South Africans. Intermediate services entail water provision through yard taps on site, simple water-borne sanitation, narrow paved roads with no curbs, open drains, and 30 amps of electricity with prepaid meters for the household (Ruiters 2001, 21). "Full services" refers to connected water supplies, full water-borne sanitation, paved roads with curbs, piped drains, and 60 amps of electricity (RDSN 2000,15). The state says: "services and infrastructure will be introduced in line with the affordability levels of affected communities" (Ruiters 2001, 21). A similar point is made in the Local Government White Paper that services should be "provided at levels which are affordable, and that municipalities are able to recover the costs of service delivery" (White Paper on Local Government 1998, 131).

The differentiation of services is also reflected in the tariff policy guidelines as outlined in the Municipal Systems Act of 2000. A tariff policy must reflect "the amount individual users pay for services ... in proportion to their use of that service" (RSA 2000, s74.2.b). "[p]oor household[s] must have access to at least basic services through – i) tariffs that cover only operating and maintenance costs; ii) special tariffs or lifeline tariffs for low levels of use or consumption of services or basic levels of service; or iii) any other direct or indirect method

---

[4] Civic organisations emerged in most communities in South Africa during the 1980s. By the early 1990s "civics" were considered the legitimate organisational voice in most black communities. However, after 1994, with the election of a legitimate government, the power and influence of civics declined. Nonetheless, in many communities, SANCO remains the only force which claims to represent the interests of residents.

of subsidisation of tariffs for poor households" (s74.2.c). "Tariffs must reflect the costs reasonably associated with rendering the service, including capital, operating, maintenance, administration and replacement costs and interest charges" (s74.2.d).

The Unicity Commission couched the differentiation of services in a needs-based language:

"Variations in needs and priorities must be recognised and service should be responsive to the particular needs of individuals, household and communities. ... As part of this approach, the Unicity will also need to ensure that the special needs of different categories of people, including the poor, the disabled, youth and the formal and informal business community, are addressed" (Unicity Commission n.d. 10).

The so-called special needs will be in addition to what the Unicity Commission calls guaranteed packages of service that "at least include water and sanitation, electricity, refuse removal and access to his/her residence" (n.d., 10). Access to special needs will be at a price, which means that only the rich benefit.

Differentiation of service will perpetuate the imbalance of service provision between a wealthy area like Constantia and a poor area like Makhaza. This might also mean that working-class communities like Makhaza will receive low-quality services – the "basic" service that municipalities, national government and their policy-makers think working-class communities can afford. Those who cannot afford to pay for this "basic" service will have to prove their poverty and hence eligibility for inclusion in an indigence scheme.

Research Findings

This section of the chapter covers the findings of the research. It covers key issues that emerged from the survey; from focus group discussions and structured interviews.

Personal Details of Respondents

Sixty-three members of the community participated in the survey. Of the 63 respondents, 43 were women and 20 were men.

Table 5.1: Household size of respondents	
Number of respondents	Size of household
7	1
5	2
9	3
11	4
10	5
8	6
3	7
7	8
1	10
2	12

The majority of the respondents were from households where no-one was employed. Table 5.2 shows the number of people employed in each respondent's household.

Table 5.2: Employment profile of respondents	
Number of respondents	Number of people employed
32	0
26	1
4	2
1	No answer

Of the 30 respondents who were from a household with at least one person employed, 17 had casual jobs, nine had part-time jobs, and only four respondents said that members of their family had full-time jobs.

Service Charges and Rates

Payment for water is based on meter readings. The sewerage fee is R16,80 per month. An additional "sewer availability" fee (for the maintenance of pipes) is R9,12. The fee for refuse collection (curbside) is R15. The council officials could not explain the basis on which the service charges were calculated. According to Ms. Tshika, Senior Finance Administrator, the council was still waiting for the necessary documentation needed to explain and breakdown the different tariffs (Tshika interview, 2001). Chris de Vries, a Senior Manager of the Tygerberg Administration, responded by saying that it costs money to provide services: "if you need petrol you pay for it; the same principle applies to the services" (De Vries interview, 2001).

The council issues monthly statements for service charges and rates. Rates are charged on an annual basis, determined by the size of the plot. Residents have the option of being billed on a monthly basis. Interest is charged on overdue accounts. Legal proceedings are initiated against those who do not pay rates regularly.

Water Cutoffs

In this section of the questionnaire we wanted to establish the following issues:
- why water cutoffs occur;
- the duration of water cutoffs and alternative sources of water;
- the reasons for non-payment; and
- attitude to payment of services.

Residents' attitude and response to water cutoffs

The main reason for water cutoffs was non-payment for services. The residents whose arrears were in excess of R3 000 were targeted to have their services cut off (Tshika interview, 2001). Council was unable or unwilling to supply accurate figures of affected households. De Vries told us that only 25 per cent of Khayelitsha households pay for services.

When we asked residents how much money they owed before their water was cut off, 50 said "more than R1 500," six said "between R1 000 and R1 500" and five said "between R500 and R1 000." Two did not answer. Forty-one respondents who showed us their statement of account owed more than R3 000.

Duration of water cutoffs and alternative sources of water

Of the 63 respondents, 22 were cut off for a week; 13 were cut off for more than a week; nine were cut off for a month, and 19 were cut off for more than a month. When cut off, they were forced to look for alternative sources of water. Of the 63, 56 got water from their neighbours. This was not without problems, however. Focus-group participants reported that neighbours were worried that the extra water given out would lead to higher monthly bills which would add to their arrears. Neighbours resorted to locking their toilets. Some participants in the focus group indicated a concern that if they allowed neighbours to access their taps, they would not be able to afford the bills.

Reasons for non-payment and attitude to payment of services

When asked why they were not paying for services, of the 63 respondents, 44 said it was because they were unemployed. Six respondents said they did not have enough money; four said they had low-paying jobs. Of the seven respondents who had gone to the council to explain their situation, six presented the same explanation – unemployment. Council official Ms. Tshika said that "ignorance" also played a part. The participants in the focus group also gave unemployment as the main reason for non-payment of services. One of the participants said that even though she went to the police station to make an affidavit that she was unemployed the council still cut her water off.

We also asked participants in the focus group for their attitude towards paying for services. They said that they were not opposed in principle to payment, but that since they were unemployed, they were unable to pay. They said the council should try to understand their situation. They also stated that they oppose payment based on meter reading. Respondents did say that they preferred a flat rate to the prepaid meter system, as this made it possible to budget effectively. The participants in the focus group suggested R10 per month as an affordable tariff for water. Some in the focus group argued that the community should demand the removal of meters. Other participants did not share this point of view, arguing that meters could be used to monitor how much water people used. Some who opposed the meters believed it would be a difficult demand to win from the council.

SANCO representatives had a different perspective on payment for services. They told us that "people must pay for the services". They informed us that they had embarked on actions in support of the Masakhane campaign.[5] In 1999, they organised transport for members of the community to various pay points. On that day, according to SANCO representatives, the council made "about R55 000".

When asked about those who could not afford to pay, SANCO representatives felt that the council should make arrangements for them. They said that the current council arrangement was not clear or effective, and had not "been communicated properly". They further stated that "the council does not have a proper way of reaching those who cannot pay". They told us that:

The council had asked those people who had difficulties with payments to come forward to make arrangement on how they want to pay. This had not benefited the community because those who went to the council to explain their difficulties were also affected by the cutoffs.

They also noted that the council should develop a strategy to monitor those who claimed to be unemployed. Council officials we spoke to said they were currently discussing the indigent policy. Water for those who could not afford to pay for services had already been reconnected. Council regarded such cases as "indigent: if consumption of water fell below 20kl a month" (Tshika interview, 2001). Ms. Tshika also told us that if an "indigent person or household uses more than the 20kl a month, the council does not regard such a person or household as indigent".

Focus-group participants were not aware of any indigence policy. They felt that the council simply expected everyone to pay for services.

Focus-group participants also felt that the council should try to improve the quality of services provided. A majority of the respondents in the survey had a negative assessment about the quality of services provided by the council. Seventeen said the quality of services overall was "poor"; 41 said it was "very poor". The other five respondents did not answer.

---

[5] Masakhane is the cost-recovery campaign that the South African government embarked upon to promote payment for services. It was announced by the former president, Nelson Mandela, in February 1995. The state spent R30 million on the Masakhane campaign in an attempt to recover the cost from the working-class communities (Bond 2000).

"They are Killing us Alive"

Attitude and response to water cutoffs

We asked the respondents whether they thought it was correct for the council to cut off water. Of the 63 respondents, 59 felt that it was not correct and four did not answer. This is what some of the respondents had to say about cut offs:

"Water is life, without it you die".

"It is not right, what are you going to drink, how are you going to cook, you are being killed".

"They are killing us alive".

"It is not correct because I cannot survive without water".

"No, I am suffering from TB and I must take tablets with water. I am also unemployed".

"It is not correct. I regard the action as the breaking of the law because water is the basis for life".

"Water is a human right".

"It is not right. We were supposed to be informed as the community, so that we can sit down with the council to discuss how payment should happen".

"It is not right, they are supposed to inform me. They don't care, they cut off your water even if you are not at home".

"This action shows that the council does not care about us".

"It is not correct, the council has not even fixed the leaking taps".

"No, they are not supposed to sell us water".

"No, we are unemployed".

"We are not working, we depend on water".

A similar question was posed to the focus group. Participants were in agreement that cutoffs were problematic. They complained that they were not notified by the council before water was cut off. They also said that the accounts were not easy to understand. This was further complicated by council's use of English instead of Xhosa. Of the 63 respondents 56 said the council never consulted them about their situation before cutting off their water, while seven said they were consulted. We also asked the participants in the focus group about the difficulties they experienced when their water was cut off. They mentioned that they could not use their toilets and that some of their neighbours refused to give them access to their toilets. In such cases, people were forced to relieve themselves in the bush. Many respondents complained of the difficulty of cooking with little or no water, especially since staple foods such as pap, mielie-meal and samp require lengthy boiling. Apart from practical difficulties, respondents also commented that water cutoffs diminished their dignity by making them request water from neighbours.

These difficulties led many community members to seek alternatives to requesting water from neighbours. Some went to council to explain their situation and made arrangements to pay. Of the 63 respondents, 22 arranged a monthly payment. Of these, 11 arranged to pay between R20 and R50, two between R50 and R100, six between R100 and R150 and three between R150 and R200.

The other members opted to reconnect water themselves. Of the 63 respondents, 23 said their water was reconnected by members of the community, 10 respondents said they reconnected their own water. The open-ended question asked the respondents if they had experienced any problems with service delivery: "has the community addressed such problems and if yes explain?" What emerged in their responses was that reconnection was a collective decision taken in a community meeting. We also asked the participants in the focus group about how community water reconnection happened. They told us that after the community's decision to reconnect water, they toyi-toyied around the township reconnecting water wherever they could. It also emerged in the focus group that the community marched to the pay-point offices to complain about the water cutoffs.

Focus-group participants also indicated that most people who tried to make arrangements with the council were given a minimum payment they could not afford. One woman informed us that she was asked to pay R300 to be reconnected. She said she could not afford such an amount. She decided to pay it over a certain period, but when she paid off the R300, she was told that she still owed a further R600. At that point she decided to join the community response to the cutoff and got someone to reconnect her water. A SANCO member we interviewed also told us that he had gone to the offices to make an arrangement to pay. His minimum payment, however, was set at R490. His offer to pay R300 (which was all he could afford) was refused.

The Tygerberg Admiminstration has specific guidelines for making an arrangement to pay off arrears. Should a resident default on an arranged monthly repayment scheme, the following penalties come into effect:

- For the first missed payment, there is a fine totalling ten per cent of the total debt. For example, if your arrears are R6 000 then you will be required to pay R600 over and above the current account, and the agreed monthly instalment.

- If you miss a second payment, your service will be disconnected, and the default fine is 20 per cent of your total debt, plus the monthly and arranged arrears amounts. In addition, a reconnection fee of R300 must be paid.

- If you miss a third payment your service will be disconnected and and the default fine is 30 per cent of your total debt, plus the monthly and arranged arrears amounts.

- If you miss a fourth payment, your service will be disconnected and you will be required to pay your TOTAL outstanding debt before reconnection.

At all stages when services are disconnected, consumption will be closely monitored to detect any tampering or illegal reconnections. Criminal charges will be laid against any debtor who illegally reconnects a supply (Tygerberg Administration 2001).

Electricity

Electricity is supplied to Makhaza by Phambili Nombane (PN). PN is a private consortium to which ESKOM outsources electricity for Khayelitsha. Phambili Nombane started as a joint venture in 1994 between ESKOM, Electricité de France (EDF) and Manchester Electricity Authority.[6]

Phambili Nombane aimed to provide electricity through "pay as you go" meters (Dyantyi and Frater n.d., 28). There are two amperage levels in Makhaza. The 9 000 houses electrified during 1994–95 are set at 60 amps and residents pay 42 cents per kilowatt hour. Those electrified after 1995 have 20-amp connections with kWh rates at 34 cents.

All electrified households have prepaid meter boxes. Electricity is purchased from 20 different vendors located throughout Khayelitsha. The vendors were established as part of the PN entrepreneurship development programme.

We asked respondents how much they spent on electricity a month.
Of the 63 respondents:

- 11 said they spent between R10 and R30;
- 16 said they spent between R30 and R50;
- 19 said they spent between R50 and R100;
- 15 said they spent between R100 and R150; and
- One respondent spent more than R150 per month.
- One respondent did not answer the question.

We also wanted to establish whether there are times when they do not buy electricity.
Of the 63 respondents:

- 48 said yes; and
- 14 said no.

Respondents were then asked what other form of energy they used; and
Of the 63 respondents:

- 53 said they use paraffin;
- Nine always buy electricity and do not use other forms of energy; and
- One respondent did not answer.

---

[6] The Manchester Electricity Authority subsequently pulled out of the partnership, leaving only ESKOM and EDF.

"They are Killing us Alive"

We also asked the respondents whether they experience any problems with electricity. Of the 63 respondents:

- 48 said yes;
- 14 said no; and
- One respondent did not answer.

A number of problems were cited:

- 33 said electricity switches off especially when it is windy and raining;
- eight said they had a problem with the main switch box;
- three said some of the plugs were not working;
- three said the cable outside was burnt; and
- one respondent said sometimes electricity is not available from the vendors that sell electricity coupons.

Focus-group participants also noted problems with PN electricity. Like those surveyed, they mentioned that when it is windy the electricity switches off. When that happens they lose some of their prepaid units. They also said that the price per unit was increasing.

Youth for Work activist, Soyiso Mtemekwana,[7] told us that in 1995 the community was getting 19.2 units for R5 and now they are only getting about 11 units. He said this increase was never negotiated with the community. The SANCO representatives also raised similar problems. They noted difficulties with vendors such as long queues and that of the four 24-hour vendors only one was in fact operational. Some residents went without electricity over weekends as vending equipment often broke down or vendors ran out of prepaid cards, etc.

Residents also complained that the supply of electricity was unstable, especially during inclement weather. Furthermore, after a power cut, residents of Khayelitsha, Harare and Monwabisi reported that the surge caused by the restoration of current damaged electrical appliances.

In Harare, *Vukani* newspaper reported that about 200 residents blamed Phambili Nombane for a power cut, which they claimed caused damage to their electrical appliances after the current was restored (*Vukani* 12 July, 2001).

PN's response through its community liaison manager, Mac Mndingi, was that "the weather conditions impact negatively on the distribution of electricity hence we sometimes experience unplanned power cuts". He further stated that "ESKOM, will not be liable for any damage to customers' appliances, damage is the full responsibility of the customers" (Epaphka Mbesi, "Power Cut in Harare: Residents blame Phambili Nombane For TV damage", *Vukani*, 12 July, 2001).The SANCO representative said they had approached Phambili Nombane about this problem but that the situation had not improved. The council also seemed reluctant to get involved, preferring to refer people to Phambili Nombane. In light of the poor service residents received from Phambili Nombane, the SANCO representative said that residents would prefer electricity to be provided by ESKOM.

Refuse Collection

In this section we wanted to establish the following issues:

- The type of refuse collection service provided;
- Problems with refuse collection; and
- Community responses on refuse collection issues.

Refuse collection takes place once a week. The council provides this service.

Problems with refuse collection

Of the 63 respondents:

- 39 said they had problems;
- 24 said they had no problems;

---

[7] Mtemekwana was also one of our research assistants.

- Of the 39, the following issues were mentioned: sometimes refuse removers damage the rubbish bins. The council expects residents to replace damaged bins at their own expense. Some respondents said that they did not have rubbish bins and were using black plastic rubbish bags;
- Some complained that refuse was not collected, or was collected very late; and
- In the last question of the questionnaire (Do you have any other comment that you would like to tell us about services in your area?), a number of respondents complained that the streets were not cleaned. They also complained that the 90-litre round bin is too small and becomes full before the day of collection. When it is full they are forced to dump the rubbish in open spaces. Some of the respondents complained that collection is done once a week. They said the council used to do refuse collection twice a week but later changed to once a week without consulting them. Some respondents suggested the council introduce the larger 240-litre bins used in other areas.

Participants in the focus group raised similar concerns. SANCO representatives noted that the streets were dirty. They argued that the council did not have enough staff to clean the streets. Johan Velem of SANCO argued that the council should hand over the cleaning of the streets to the community. Another representative had a different view. He argued that the council should employ more workers so that it could provide a proper service to the community. He felt that handing over refuse collection to the community could lead to privatisation. SANCO also said the once a week collection is problematic.

Street cleaning

As part of researching refuse collection, we also asked the interviewees about street cleaning. Of the 63 respondents:

- 12 said the council cleans the main street;
- Two said it cleans the main street and all other streets;
- Three said it only cleans all the streets inside the location; and
- 46 said the council does not clean the streets at all.[8]

Some of the respondents told us that some members of the community cleaned the streets on a voluntary basis. This was confirmed by a participant in the focus group and by a SANCO representative. The council allocates 10 sweepers for the whole of Makhaza.

Responses to Service Delivery Problems

Most of the responses dealt with how the community responded to water cutoffs. As noted before, the community had met and decided to reconnect the water supply themselves. Almost all the respondents, both individual and focus-group members, acknowledged this. One of the respondents noted that the community had not yet resolved the problem of refuse collection. Most respondents felt that the council should write off arrears, and negotiate with the community on the issue of payment for current services. Participants in the focus group also argued that the arrears should be scrapped. They noted that since most people were unemployed there was no way they would be able to pay the arrears. SANCO representatives had a different attitude to arrears. They argued that community members must approach the council, explain their situation, and negotiate to settle their debt. They also noted that the idea of scrapping debt is out of the question. They argued that Khayelitsha is part of the Cape Town Unicity, and that it cannot be expected to be treated differently from other areas.

In addition to scrapping arrears, some of the respondents said that the council should create jobs so that people would be able to pay for services. They also said the council should fix leaking taps as "they contribute to the high arrears". The participants in the focus groups also noted leaking taps as a problem. Residents told us that they have approached the council on this issue and that council response was that residents must bear responsibility for fixing

---

[8] The council workers only sweep in the main street.

the leaks. Since most of the leaks occur between the meter and the tap, the lost water is paid for by the residents. The community insists that the leaks started when the meters were installed, which is why they feel the council should take responsibility.

Quite a significant number of respondents (about 40) felt that the community should negotiate with the council on how to deal with the problems. Some of these respondents said if the council does not address their grievances, the community must embark on a "toyi-toyi". Only one respondent felt that the community should pay for services. Focus-group participants also argued that the community meet with the council, and that the council should not take unilateral decisions about provision of service, that "they must first consult with the community to hear its views". They also said that the council should meet with the community to try and understand why people do not pay for services.

The SANCO representatives had a different perspective on what the community should do about problems with service provision:

> We are avoiding toyi-toyi, it is not appropriate in the current period, it was appropriate when we were fighting against the apartheid regime. Toyi-toyi will not advance the interests of the community; it leads to the destruction of property. We prefer to meet with the community and also have discussions with the council on how to address our problems.

Youth for Work activists felt that the only way the community could solve problems with service provision was through struggle. They told us that they played a key role in the struggle against the water cutoffs, and that they had assisted the community to mobilise an effective resistance.

The focus group felt that the community should arrange a meeting to elect local representatives to take their needs to the council.

Analysis and Assessment of the Findings

Cost recovery measures:

Water cutoffs

Allegedly the main aim of cost recovery policy is to increase income and cut costs for the municipality. Yet, the cost recovery strategy of water cutoffs employed by the Tygerberg council has proven to be a costly excercise. Though he declined to give specific figures, Tygerberg official Chris de Vries said, "council spends thousands of rands attempting to do disconnections". The reason given by de Vries for the contracting out of cutoffs is that the council does not have internal resources. The other factor that might explain the contracting out of cutoffs is that the South African Municipal Workers' Union (SAMWU) has organised nearly all the workers in the water department. SAMWU has made a call on their members and the council workers to refuse to implement water cut offs. SAMWU's view is intended as a show of sympathy for working-class communities that cannot afford to pay for services.

Water meters

In pursuing cost recovery policy municipalities have initiated water meter reading, which costs money. Every household in Makhaza has water meters. When the council promotes water meter reading to working-class families, it says it will help them manage the amount of water they use. This is supposed to reduce the amount they pay for water. Through meters the council is able to give a specific price for the specific amount of water that is consumed by a particular household. However, the council's main motivation for installing the meters seems to be one of cost recovery. The council also argues that these meters are effective for monitoring the use of water. This is true, but for what purpose – in the neoliberal context the meters are mainly used to be able to give a price on the amount of water that has been used. The monitoring of consumption of water in different areas is possible without yard water meters. For example, in Khayelitsha, "District/Zonal meters have been installed to monitor consumption patterns in each area. These zonal meters also assist with the leakage investigation in these areas" (City of Tygerberg 2000).

With the installation of water meters the commodification of water is taken to a higher level. In the "Billing for Services" leaflet that the City of Cape Town sent to households, the authorities' counsel announced: "you have to pay for your water, which is delivered to your home by the council at high cost, so the less you use the less you are expected to pay" (n.d.). Those who do not have enough money to pay for water, particularly the working-class communities, are advised by the City of Cape Town to use less water.

Prepaid meters

The prepaid water system has not been implemented in Khayelitsha and according to the water engineer Mr. De Jager there are no plans to install prepaids. The engineer was critical of prepaid meters. He noted that they are too expensive to install and that it is doubtful that it will be possible to recover the costs of installation, noting the difficulties people in Khayelitsha have in paying for services. He further stated that "the council's duty is to provide water to the people and encourage them to save water". He argued that prepaid meters are appropriate for a private company – "if we were a private company we would go for a prepaid but we are not".[9]

The prepaid system has been implemented for electricity. Through this system the PN is able to charge users before they use electricity. The complexity of non-payment and issuing of statements is eliminated through this system. Under a prepaid system you pay and then you get the service. If you do not pay you self-disconnect from the system. The supporters of prepaids also argue that they "allow residents to monitor how much electricity they use and to budget for this without incurring arrears" (City of Cape Town, July 1999).

Most working-class families state clearly that they cannot afford pay more than R100 per month for electricity. Of the 63 respondents in Makhaza 46 respondents spend between R10 and R100 on electricity per month. Because of the limited access that the prepaid meter system encourages, working-class families use paraffin as an alternative source of energy. The notion that prepaid meters help to monitor and not incur arrears hides the real motivation why the prepaid system is implemented. The prepaid system is implemented to ensure that services are paid for before they are utilised. What is central in terms of this system is the recovering and cutting of costs, not the extension of services to the citizens. The cutting of costs is done by retrenching the staff that were responsible for issuing accounts. The council also does not have to hire collection agencies and lawyers to chase citizens with arrears. The main aim of the prepaid meter is to limit access to electricity, not to assist households to monitor electricity usage. When the red light next to the "buy card" inscription begins to flicker, the household is about to be disconnected from the system. The difference with this kind of disconnection is that the council (or PN in this case) does not have to send a worker or contract out the disconnection. This disconnection happens automatically when all units have been consumed.

The non-payment of electricity is not ruled out completely in the prepaid electricity system. Some in the community are able to fiddle with the system and access electricity without paying. Because of the possibility of accessing electricity without paying, Phambili Nombane has "instituted a highly effective monitoring system which picks up illegal electricity users and enables quick response" (Dyantyi and Frater: n.d., 28). Despite the so-called highly effective monitoring system, some members of the community are able to access electricity without paying. This we were able to gather through the research assistants we worked with in Makhaza.

---

[9] The City of Cape Town Unicity is planning to install prepaid meters for water services in all households. It is installing 170 meters in Klipheuwel near Malmesbury as part of a pilot project to test their effectiveness (*Sunday Times* 14 October, 2001).

"They are Killing us Alive"

Lawyers' letters and attachment of goods

According to Ms. Tshika, "residents that fail to pay for rates are handed over to the lawyers". Again this is a measure where the council spends money in order to squeeze payment from the poor. The lawyers are hired to pressurise the members of the community to pay for rates. If payment is not made, the resident is taken to court. The court then looks at the matter and issues a summons that facilitates the attachment of movable goods. Attached goods are subsequently auctioned. According to de Vries "After three years in which rates have been outstanding, movable property is attached" (*Cape Times* 6 March, 2001). While the attachment of movable goods has not yet happened in Makhaza, participants in the focus group said some members of the community had received letters from lawyers. This may be a first step toward attachment of personal goods. Early in March 2001, there were reports in the *Cape Times* newspaper that the Tygerberg Administration had attached the movable goods of several households in Khayelitsha (6 March, 2001).

The money raised from rates is used to pay for a range of public services such as the running of libraries, community halls, primary health clinics, fire services and cleansing, as well as road maintenance and traffic services. In other words the costs of providing public services are recovered through rates. In addition, costs are also recovered through service fees. For example, community members are expected to pay a fee to hire a community hall. Some of the services that are funded through rates have been privatised or are in the process of being privatised.

Impact of cost recovery

According to Bond (2000), cost-recovery administration incurs more expense than can be squeezed out of low-income people. He also argues that the consumption-related charges entail costly methods of collection which either lead to significant under-recovery of costs or significantly higher prices to consumers.

A participant in the focus group had this to say about her arrears: "At the moment I am owing the council more than R6 000; I must eat and I am unemployed. I do not think I will ever be able to pay my arrears. The council can do whatever they want to do."

While the council spent thousands of rands on cutoffs, there was no significant income. When we asked de Vries whether payment had improved after water cutoffs, he said that it had not. Tshika said immediately after the cutoffs quite a number of people came to make a payment arrangement. However, she was not able to give us even a rough estimate of how much improvement there had been in payment. She also noted that the increased payment for services did not last: "people stopped paying after few months". The reason payment did not improve after cutoffs is simple: people are unemployed and those who are employed are not earning enough money to be able to pay for services while being expected to settle a debt of more than R3 000.

The payment arrangements that the council encourages are insensitive. The amounts of payment required disregard the financial situation of the bulk of working-class families. For example, let us take the case of a resident who owes more than R3 000 and has failed to honour the payment arrangement as agreed with the council. According to the Tygerberg Administration guidelines, a payment arrangement will require such a resident to pay 10 per cent of the R3 000 (R300), plus monthly service charges that are more than R40 rands, plus whatever instalment arrangement she agreed to (let's say R45) and a reconnection fee of R115. In total the resident will be expected to pay not less than R500 to have access to water. The working-class families that are not paying and are in arrears as a result, did not pay because they could not afford to pay.

Such payment arrangements do not take into account the situation of those with arrears. Payment arrangements keep the poor in debt. To make matters worse, it emerged from our research thast there is an almost total lack of effective communication between the council and the community. The council appears to be insensitive to the fact that not all residents can read.

Limited access to social services

The consequence of this policy is that access to social services is based on money. When access to social services is defined in the same way as access to consumer goods that people buy in the capitalist market, the majority of those who do not have money will be denied access. This is what has happened to the people of Makhaza who could not pay for water – access was denied by the council, which cut the water supply off. It is because of the limited access to electricity, a product of commodification of electricity, that most working-class families still use paraffin as another form of energy.

Tensions and individualism

The water cutoffs also lead to unnecessary tensions and development of individualistic tendencies among the working-class communities. In Makhaza, it was shocking to hear from focus-group participants that some of their neighbours locked their toilets and that there was widespread reluctance to share access to taps. These individualistic tendencies are under-standable because people fear that they will end up paying more money for water and may themselves end up as victims of water cutoffs.

But this individualism is further problematic in that it does not address the root causes of the problem. The individualistic responses are short-term and are not sustainable given the fact that in Makhaza, as in most communities, employment opportunities are few. In most instances, jobs are being lost instead of created.[10]

Increased burden on working-class women

The cost recovery policy also increases the burden of social responsibility on working-class women. In most households it is women who must look for communal taps, schools or churches that can allow them access to their taps. It is women who have to be humiliated by requesting water from the neighbours who reluctantly allow them to use their taps. They have to waste their time walking to the alternative sources and standing in queues. Working-class women are most likely to end up taking responsibility for looking after those who become sick. There are other additional tasks that come with water cutoffs. One participant said "we are forced to take our children to the bush when they want to relieve themselves". Taking children to the bush to relieve themselves also puts the lives of working women at risk, given the high rate of rape in our society. It is women who will be expected to look for alternative forms of energy when access to electricity is limited by how much a family can afford – another additional task as a result of cost-recovery policy.

Health implications

Cost recovery measures also have disastrous health implications. These are largely due to limited access to clean water. Non-access to water results in unhygienic conditions that can lead to an increase in diseases such as diarrhoea. It is estimated that 43 000 people die from diarrhoeal diseases every year in South Africa.[11] According to McDonald (2002, 6): "the costs of dealing with all diarrhoea-related illnesses in South Africa (much of which are a direct result of poor water and sanitation services and no doubt exacerbated by wide-spread water cutoffs) is in the order of R3.4 billion per year in direct medical costs and R26 billion per year in lost economic production – more than the total amount that would be needed to provide water infrastructure to everyone in the country". What this implies is that while the state attempts to squeeze money from the poor through cost-recovery measures, it must spend billions of rands on the effects of cost recovery.

---

[10] Although we do not have specific job-loss figures for Makhaza, at a national level more than 500 000 jobs have been lost since the adoption of GEAR (*Workers World News* 21, 2001). These national trends, coupled with the employment profile of our respondents, indicates that the problems which result from unemployment and poverty are of considerable proportion in Makhaza.

[11] Figures from personal communication with Professor David Saunders, Director of School of Public Health, University of the Western Cape.

Limited access to electricity forces working-class families to use paraffin as an alternative source of energy. The use of paraffin has health risks like fumes and fire.[12] In the survey we did in Makhaza, out of 63 respondents, 53 said they use paraffin as another form of energy.

Undermining constitutional gains

In general, the policy of cost recovery undermines the human rights that the South African working class has achieved. According to the Bill of Rights, "Everyone has the right to have access to sufficient food and water." One respondent, in response to being asked the question of whether it is correct for the council to cut off water, said: "It is not correct. I regard the action as the breaking of the law because water is the basis of life".

The state is likely to misuse the Constitution's "within the available resources" clauses that go with some of the socio-economic rights in the Bill of Rights. This should be contested given the problematic way the government allocates its resources. For example the R43 billion arms deal approved by the state reflects problems with the way the state is allocating resources.[13] The continued payment of apartheid debt is also a waste of resources that could be used to deal with the plight of the poor. According to a Jubilee South leaflet, public funds should be rechanneled "away from debt service and ensuring that public funds be used primarily for people's welfare and basic services, and equitable and sustainable development" (1999). SAMWU, in its press statement of 4 November 1998 in support of a campaign to scrap the debt, stated that "The debt repayment does not benefit any section of the working class – rather, the R40 billion plus spent on servicing the debt each year merely serves to make apartheid's victims pay twice over for their suffering". The state allocated R46.5 billion for payment of debt in its budget for 2000–01 (Fair Share 2001).

Bond's contention that cost recovery in poor communities costs more to implement than it recovers, seems to be borne out by our research. The following are just some of the measures we have noted which are adding to the state's financial burdens: contracting out the water cutoffs; installing yard water meter reading and prepaid meters; hiring collections agencies and lawyers; and treating and coping with effects of water-borne diseases, as shown in the section under the cost recovery measures.

Community response to cost recovery

The people in Makhaza resisted the cost recovery measures, particularly the water cutoffs. The people that were affected came together and collectively decided to reopen water. The people of Makhaza, especially those affected by water cutoffs marched and toyi-toyied to the council pay points where the community voiced its rejection of cutoffs. They were not intimidated by the threats of the council that "Criminal charges will be laid against any debtor who illegally reconnects a supply". This militant response is understandable given the fact that water is viewed as a human right and essential to life. But there is also an economic aspect to the community's response. A large percentage of Makhaza residents are unemployed. Even those who do work must labour at part-time jobs; in almost all cases they do not earn enough to be able to pay for the services and settle their debts.

What is also significant about the Makhaza community response is that the coordination of its struggle happened outside the traditional civic organisation SANCO, and the existing political parties like ANC, PAC, UDM, and SACP etc. SANCO, did not support the struggle against the cutoffs.

The organisation that featured in the struggle against cutoffs was the relatively new youth organisation, Youth for Work. According to Youth for Work activist Soyiso Mtemekwana, the organisation, "actively supported the struggle of the community against water cutoffs".

The community resistance to water cutoffs was a success in that even the council decided to stop cutoffs. There have not been any reports of legal action against the reopening of water

---

[12] For details on the health risks of paraffin and wood, see Kenny (2002).

[13] The arms deal was signed in December 1999 with British, French, German, Italian, South African and Swedish firms. The main items in the deal were a number of naval vessels intended to protect South Africa's sea and borders from potential enemies.

by the community. When we asked Chris de Vries whether there were any plans to do water cutoffs, his response was that "we have stopped water cutoffs because people that do cutoffs were chased away by the community. People also just reconnect themselves". Of the 63 respondents 33 respondents had reconnected their water. Of the 87 736 cutoffs done between 1996 and early 2001 in Tygerberg, there were 52 670 "illegal" reconnections (McDonald and Smith 2002, 42). In Khayelitsha alone there were 14 355 water cutoffs between April 2000 and September 2000 (McDonald and Smith 2002, 41).

It is unlikely that the government will not act against people who are reconnecting themselves. The partial victory won by the people of Makhaza is going to be under attack from the state sooner or later. The Cape Town administration has already shown its vicious response to "illegal" connections. In many instances it sent in a contractor to rip out the water meter and remove a portion of the pipe from the ground, making it difficult for the household to reconnect "illegally" (McDonald and Smith 2002, 19). The Cape Town Unicity is currently implementing the harshest forms of cost recovery measures – evictions for service and rates arrears. The communities will have to think of creative ways of resisting these vicious attacks, if they are to sustain the victories they have made against the water cutoffs.

The community response has been militant and has succeeded in halting water cutoffs. Nonetheless, in order to sustain the struggle, organisation will have to be considerably tighter. For example, when people successfully resisted cutoffs and reopened water the struggle fizzled away without taking up other issues related to cutoffs. Hence, the community has raised the issue of the council repairing leaking taps. Neither has the general issue of arrears been taken up. The failure to take up other issues might be linked to the fact that no clear organisational expression emerged through the struggle against the cutoffs. Actions were ad hoc, not situated in the context of developing a medium- or long-term strategy.

Another shortcoming of the community's mobilitsation was the absence of any attempt to link up with SAMWU. Since SAMWU has adopted a position in opposition to water cutoffs, it would be a natural ally for those mobilising around this issue. Solidarity between community members and council workers could have been significant. For example, it would have been possible for council plumbers to train community activists to reconnect water so as to avoid creating further leakage. Instead of such solidarity, according to Tygerberg SAMWU Branch Chair Archie Hearne, the opposite happened. In some instances workers driving council vehicles became soft targets. Community members threw stones at the vehicles, apparently expressing hostility towards anything they associated with the council. This situation forced SAMWU to discuss the safety of its members with the council management.

Another issue which has not yet been addressed is the prepaid electricity meters. Despite the extensive cataloguing of problems with the prepaid system, no campaign has been organised around electricity. Even the increase in the price of electricity has not become a collective issue. Response to electricity issues remains at an individual level – tampering with boxes in order to gain free electricity. Similarly, the response to letters from lawyers also remains an individual one. Members of the community decide on their own either to ignore the letters or go to make an arrangement. The community response seems only to happen when the court gives permission to the council to attach movable goods. This happened in Ilitha Park and Mandela Park in Khayelitsha between September and December 2000. According to the spokesperson for the Tygerberg City Council's lawyers, the removal of "movable goods" was stopped last year when attempts to remove these were met with "chaos and stone throwing" (*Cape Times*, 6 March, 2001). According to participants in the focus group, to date there have been no attempts or explicit threats to attach movable goods in Makhaza.

Still, while much of the response remains at an individual level, it is significant. For example, the community has not heeded the call of the Masakhane campaign to pay for services. According to Chris de Vries, only about 25 per cent of people Khayelitsha are currently paying for services. While there has not been a a formal process whereby communities publicly agree to withhold payment, clearly non-payment is the dominant reality. From our research in Makhaza, the reasons behind this are far more likely to be affordability than the "culture of non-payment" which receives so much attention in the media.

"They are Killing us Alive"

Conclusion

Cost recovery policy is not sustainable. Even on its own financial terms, cost recovery leads to excessive spending in order to recover costs. Given the high unemployment rate amongst the South African working class, cost recovery is unlikely to succeed. But the problems with cost recovery are not only financial. There are other negative implications as well. For example, some cost recovery measures threaten the general health of the population. Ultimately this will mean that the state will have to spend money for those who become sick with water-borne diseases or due to smoke inhalation from paraffin or wood stoves.

Cost recovery also has important consequences in terms of building a democratic society. The methods the state pursues in implementing some aspects of cost recovery lead to lack of accountability. For example the outsourcing of electricity to Phambili Nombane makes it difficult for the community to hold the service provider accountable. When the council was approached by members of the community about the problems they were experiencing with electricity, the council's response referred people back to PN. The use of a prepaid system causes difficulties for the community in challenging PN. When a household does not have money to buy an electricity card and gets disconnected as a result, it becomes that household's individual problem. There is no-one within the council or the private service provider with whom individuals can negotiate. Furthermore, prepaid meters rule out boycotts of payment as a means of putting pressure on the service provider. In the case of prepaids, withholding payment is simply self-disconnection. The service provider bears no financial burden.

Ultimately, cost-recovery measures and the methods used to implement them represent an attack on working-class communities. Hence, if cost recovery continues or escalates, we are likely to see an increase in struggles against it and other neoliberal policies. Already we have seen the emergence of struggles in a number of working-class communities. People in Soweto are fighting against electricity cutoffs, the Tafelsig community is fighting against evictions and the Chatsworth community is resisting water cutoffs. Similar struggles in Nelspruit, Kathorus, Sebokeng, Upington, Topline, Grootdrink, Cilliers, Ahleit and Raaswaterand Hondel Klipbaai have taken place, though there has not been extensive media coverage of these struggles.

These initiatives are attempts to defend the working class against neoliberalism and are also the beginnings of the remobilisation of the working class. What is critical is that attempts be made to build alliances between the sectors that are at the receiving end of these policies. The critical sectors that need to build alliances with each other are the organised workers and working-class community initiatives formed during the current struggles. It is crucial to close the gap between the organised workers and community members so as to avoid what happened in Makhaza, where a potential ally (council workers) became the target of the angry community. The closing of the gap between these sectors is critical so that the community sector is not used by the council against the organised workers. Already there have been instances where the council was able to win the support of the community to outsource refuse collection in Khayelitsha[14].

When we started our study in Makhaza, the new City of Cape Town Unicity was putting in place mechanisms to implement the free lifeline of 6 000 litres of water per month per household and 20 kWh of free electricity.[15] Whether the implementation of "free services' will improve the plight of the poor communities remains to be seen. But even after the December 2000 elections, the Cape Town Unicity continued to carry out the harshest measures of cost recovery: service cutoffs and evictions. As long as these sorts of attacks on poor communities continue, it is doubtful that the promised lifelines will save the day. However, what is not doubtful is that the communities affected by cost recovery will continue to fight against the impact of these policies on their lives.

---

[14] For more information see Qotole, Xali, and Barchiesi (2001).

[15] After the 2000 elections, the Cape Town Unicity was ruled by the Democratic Alliance (DA). The DA implemented its own lifeline policy. For water, the lifeline was the same as the ANC's 6 000 litres per household per month. But for electricity the DA allocated only 20 kWh per month, less than the ANC's proposal of 50kWh.

Bibiography

Bond, P. (2000a). "Service Cutoffs: Financial Crisis or Political Choice". *Services for All:* Newsletter for the Municipal Service Project, September, Volume 1, Number 1.

Bond P. (2000b). *Cities of Gold, Townships of Coal: Essays on South Africa's New Urban Crisis*, Africa World Press.

Cape Times. 6 March, 2001.

City of Cape Town. (1999). "Paying for Services you use." Commitment to Cape Town, July.

— (n.d.), "Pay and Stay – It's the right thing to do".

— (n.d.), "Billing for Services". The Water Leaks Repair Project.

City of Tygerberg Water Service Department. (2001). Khayelitsha: Water Demand Management Strategy, Service Area: Coastal.

Dyantyi, R. and Fraterm W. (n.d.) "Local Economic Development Initiatives in Khayelitsha". In Case Studies on LED and Poverty, Department of Constitutional Development.

Fair Share. (2001). 2000 – 2001. *National Budget Handbook.* Cape Town: Fair Share.

Fick, G. (2000). "The importance of equality to the sphere of local government". AGENDA, 45.

Fiil-Flynn, M. (2001). "The Electricity Crisis In Soweto". MSP Occasional Papers Series No. 4. Cape Town, Municipal Services Project.

ILRIG. (2001). "GEAR: Five years is enough". *Workers World News*, September 2001, issue 21, Cape Town.

ILRIG. (1998). "An Alternative View of Globalisation". ILRIG Globalisation Series No.1, Cape Town.

Jubilee South (n.d.). Jubilee South for a debt-free millennium, information sheet, Cape Town.

Kenny, A. (2002). "Why electricity saves lives." FOCUS: Newsletter of the Helen Suzman Foundation, No. 25.

McDonald, D.A. (2002) ."No Money, No Service; South Africa's poorest citizens lose out under attempts to recover service costs for water and power". Alternatives Volume 28 Number 3.

— and Smith, L. (2002). "Privatizing Cape Town: Service Delivery and Policy Reforms Since 1996". MSP Occasional Papers Series No. 7. Cape Town, Municipal Services Project.

Qotole, M, Xali, M, and Barchiesi, F. (2001). "The Commercialisation of Waste Management in South Africa." Municipal Services Project Occasional Paper Series, No. 3, Cape Town, Municipal Services Project.

Republic of South Africa. (2000). Local Government Systems Act, Act No 32 of 2000, Pretoria: Government Printers.

Republic of South Africa. (1998). The White Paper on Local Government, Pretoria: Government Printers.

Ruiters, G. (2001). "After basic needs: social justice and water politics" *Debate: A journal of the South African left* Vol. 5.

RDSN [Rural Development Services Network]. (2000). "Water for All: Meeting basic water and sanitation": Discussion Document.

South African Health Review. (2000). Johannesburg: Health Systems Trust.

Sunday Times, 16 June 1998.

Sunday Times, 14 October 2001.

The Unicity Commission (n.d.). "Building A Unified City for the 21ST Century", Cape Town.

Tygerberg Administration (n.d.) "Debt Arrangement During "Period of Grace".

Van Niekerk, S. (2001). "A Commitment to Developmental Local Government". *New Agenda*, 2.

Vukani, 12 July, 2001.

Interviews

Individual Personal Interviews

Mr. De Jager, Engineer based in Khayelitsha council offices, 29 May 2001.

Soyiso Mtemakwana, Youth for Work Activist, 5 July 2001.

Michael Ngqoyiyana, SANCO Housing Department, Khayelitsha Local, 10 July 2001.

Johannes Velem, SANCO Safety Department, Khayelitsha Local, 10 July 2001.

Ms. Tshika – Senior Finance Administrator from financial account department based in Khayelitsha council offices, 17 July 2001.

Telephonic Interview

Chris de Vries, Senior manager in the financial account department of the Tygerberg administration, 20 August 2001.

Archie Hearne, SAMWU Tygerberg Chairperson, November 2001.

People and Service Delivery

Constantia is one of the wealthiest suburbs in South Africa. But not everyone who lives in Constantia has money. Workers employed in the area have a different experience of Constantia. For some, life has improved since 1994. Wilhma is employed at the Utisig wine farm. This property was put up for sale in 2001 for R97 million. Wilhma talks about her life on the farm:

I will say life is slightly better in comparison with when I grew up. You see today we have electric power here. Our houses are bigger compared to those in the olden days. We used to light candles but now that is a thing of the past. We have telephones which were installed. These things were not there when we grew up. It is only the whites who could have afforded such a luxury. But today we have running water, toilets which are flushing in our homes. We used to go behind the bush to answer "nature's call". Even the old houses are given a "facelift". Look around. You can see for yourself life is good here.

But for other workers, things have changed very little. Ivan and Raymond, employed at Groot Constantia, told a different story. Ivan, who came to Groot Constantia in 1988, says:

Since I came here... I have always encountered problems. I am a shop steward and I understand we are going to face problems. There is a contract which is circulating around. It has not arrived here yet but it is taking the last little right we have. But I must tell you I will fight it...This management doesn't care for us. Our demands are not met.

Raymond shares his views:

We are not treated equally on this farm. I remember one day when my daughter was left behind at school in Grassy Park. They gave me all sorts of problems. He refused to release me to go and look for my daughter. I had to leave without his permission. But what I realised was he had deducted a day as unpaid leave though I left an hour before my day was over.

Other workers complain of poor accommodation. Some even reported living in former animal quarters. While the average house in Constantia sells for R1,6 million, there are many for whom Constantia still spells poverty.

6

The Struggle Against Encroachment

Constantia and the Defence of White Privilege in the "New" South Africa

by John Pape

The good people of Constantia just need to take a drive around Cape Town to see how people in the rest of this city live.

Mike Richardson, Director of Finance, South Peninsula Administration

I'm gungho about Constantia.

Anthony Goldstein, Chairperson, Constantia Property Owners' Association

In the Western Cape there is perhaps no community which conjures up an image of relaxed opulence quite like Constantia. In a province where world-class wealth and world-class poverty sit side by side, Constantia soldiers on – idyllic, comfortable, able to advance its backward-looking development strategy with a forward-looking cohort of lawyers, consultants and ultra-conservative civic activists. To include the story of Constantia in our case study collection is to emphasise one point commonly made about post-1994 South Africa: the more things change, the more they remain the same.

In one sense, discussing service delivery in Constantia is addressing a non-issue. For the bulk of representatives the issue of services is, in the words of Anthony Goldstein, Chairperson of the Constantia Property-Owners' Association, "not a problem". Hence, the struggle in Constantia is not about improving service delivery. Rather, it is a struggle against encroachment, the encroachment of the needs of the rest of Cape Town on the world of Constantia. This is a struggle to protect a particular form of race and class privilege, and, in post-apartheid South Africa, protecting the privilege of Constantia is not always a simple affair. It requires resources, connections, mobilisation, and a profound ability to, as one resident put it, "put your head in the nearest available bit of sand". As we will see, central to the protection of privilege are notions of cost recovery and accountability. To encroach on the lives of present-day Constantia residents means holding them accountable for their privileged past and constructing a financial paradigm which recovers some of the costs incurred while constructing one of the few communities in South Africa which can legitimately claim to be devoid of service delivery problems.

In this paper, we will explore the struggle of the property-owners of Constantia against such an encroachment. We will look at this struggle from three angles. Firstly, we will examine the history of Constantia – how it has been constructed in order to shore up the anti-encroachment forces. Secondly, we will look at the ways in which the community is organised to fight its struggle – the structures and key players at the battle front. Thirdly, we will consider the actual development strategy that has emerged as the lynchpin in fighting off encroachment. And, finally, we will make some general comments about Constantia and its place in a democratic South Africa.

History of Constantia

Constantia is a residential area which includes slightly under 20 000 residents. Situated at the foot of Table Mountain, it occupies some of the most valuable land in Cape Town. Unlike other wealthy residential areas, Constantia has a carefully preserved under-industrialised, under-commercialised quaintness. There is a conscious effort to recreate the environment of an idyllic English manor – untouched by the crass modernity of the bright lights. Indeed, in contrast to its counterparts in residential wealth, Camps Bay or Sandton,[1] there are no luxury townhouses, no mega-shopping malls, not even a police or fire station. By choice, the property-owners have rejected ordinary urban features like street lighting, chain stores and cinemas. Constantia is wealthy, but it is a controlled wealth, a minimalist wealth, an icon of resistance to commercial and industrial activity. Yet ironically it is a community whose residents have earned their right to be property-owners by their success in the commercial and industrial world. Here, one has the right to be non-conformist, as long as one has the means to maintain the required standards of a "proper" non-conformity.

A drive through Constantia reveals much of this character. The plots range from 800 to 4 000 square metres – no living cheek to jowel with neighbours in this neck of the woods. Apart from big plots, Constantia is green, green, green. There are massive untouched public areas – forests, open veld, wooded hillsides – as well as many small- and medium-sized holdings primarily dedicated to wine grape production. To some extent these public areas remain pristine because of the area's demographics. Noticeably absent in Constantia are legions of uniformed school children or makeshift cricket games in local parks. This is a community where the wealthy elderly are the mainstream with the yuppies at the margins.

While the Pick 'n Pay supermarket situated in the understated Constantia Village Shopping Centre is a reminder that Constantia is part of South Africa, the other visible links are tenuous. There are no hawkers, there are very few kombi taxis, and very few black people in visible space. Not rural 18th-century England (as some might try to pretend) but a far cry from Crossroads or even Rondebosch. For students of urban strategies and development, Constantia is indeed a jewel of contradictory reaction. These contradictions are the result of an historical process driven by class-conscious agents – the current and past residents of Constantia. They have been key subjects in the social construction of a privileged community of a special type.

Constantia – Constructing a History

In one sense, the struggle against encroachment has been an attempt to create a brand called Constantia which is defined as a unique community with a unique contribution to make to South Africa. Part of the building of that brand is the careful construction of an official history of Constantia – a history the white landowners wrote.

---

[1] In a survey done by the Johannesburg-based consultancy, the Knowledge Factory, Constantia rated as the fourth-wealthiest suburb in South Africa in terms of average property value. With an average property price of R1 658 000, Constantia trailed only Dunkeld (Johannesburg 2 353 000), Llandudno (Cape Town 1 982 000), and Bishopscourt (Cape Town 1 978 000). However, with 3 134 households, Constantia had more than five times as many residences as the top three. Hence, Constantia represents the largest concentration of wealthy households in South Africa (Seery, 2002).

The official history of Constantia is episodic and selective, with just two main chapters. The first chapter is the "founding" of Constantia in 1685 when Simon van der Stel was given a grant for about 800 hectares of land. From there Constantia was subdivided and redistributed, with Hendrik Cloete ending up as the major lord of Constantia in the 1700s. Along the way, van der Stel, Cloete *et al.* managed to develop Constantia as a wine-producing area. Hence an important part of the official version of Constantia's history is the travels of the local home brew, *Vin de Constance*. This elegant drink has allegedly trekked across from the tables of King Louis Phillippe of France in 1833, to Napoleon in exile on St Helena. *Vin de Constance* even warranted mention in the world of literature, with direct references in the works of Dickens and Baudelaire. Jane Austen apparently recommended Constantia wine for "its healing powers on a disappointed heart" (Carew, 2001). Ultimately, the ancient history of Constantia is one of white settlement and development, followed by links to royalty. These images are periodically revived. For example, Klein Constantia wine estate owner Dugge Jooste celebrated his 75th birthday in August 2001 by opening a bottle of wine produced on his vineyard in 1791. According to newspaper accounts, although there was a fear that the brew had gone sour, the drink remained "sweet, yet crisp with a deliciously nutty flavour" (Carew, 2001).

The second chapter in the official version brings us into the 20th century and late apartheid South Africa. Here, as the story goes, Constantia became further renowned for two things. Firstly, it was an area where people allegedly opposed the crudeness of the National Party's apartheid plan. In the words of present-day councillor Joan Hemming, the National Party never "got its grips on" Constantia. She points with pride to the more than 80 per cent of Constantia who voted in favour of scrapping the Group Areas Act in a 1983 referendum.

Secondly, local-government operations during the late-apartheid Constantia Valley Local Authority (CVLA) were a model of good governance. Councillor Heming stressed that during those years, the CVLA was extremely frugal. For example, the Local Authority drew little by way of resources for capital expenditure. Through careful financial management and preservation of an ethos, it rejected urban frills such as street lights and pavements. This was a community that succeeded through effective governance, efficient allocation of resources, and hard work. Its efforts during the CVLA period led to the creation of a unique asset for the Western Cape: an idyllic community in the midst of South Africa's second-most important urban centre.

As attractive as this history is for tourist marketing and internal solidarity, it contains some glaring gaps. Firstly, while the residents of Constantia may not have voted to continue Group Areas in 1983, there was a context to this vote. According to Councillor Jonathan Hulley, the referendum was a response to a proposal from the municipal authorities to cut up part of nearby Tokai forest and turn it into a coloured township. The vote about segregation came in response to this proposal. Formally in the referendum, the residents of Constantia were voting as to whether they wanted segregation in the area or for it to be declared "open." Yet, there is a certain ambiguity to this declaration. Ultimately the referendum was perhaps not a general declaration of principle as much as it was a rejection of a plan to build a coloured township very close to Constantia. But regardless of the motives, the apartheid authorities did not take kindly to the residents' stance. Hulley says that the referendum became a "national event" with officials interpreting the vote as Constantia "sticking its nose up at government policy". But while the official version of Constantia history moves from van der Stel to the CVLA, the gaps in between are where the real story lies.

Noticeably absent from the official version of Constantia's history is the period of mass coloured residence (and even influence) from the early 1900s until the early 1960s. C.W. Pietersen (interview, 2001), a coloured man who was born in Constantia in 1928, recalls a community of several thousand coloured people and "less than a thousand whites" when he was growing up. He speaks of a bustling commercial Constantia where people of colour owned and operated market gardens and a number of other agricultural and commercial ventures. He points to a house just opposite the Constantia Village shopping centre as the home of the Imam for the area. His recollection is that even along the legendary Ladies Mile Road, few of the residents were white. Pietersen speaks nostalgically of a period of congenial relationship between whites and coloureds where the atmosphere was "a hundred per cent… There was never a fight amongst us."

But under apartheid and the Group Areas Act, Constantia changed. Firstly, more whites came in after World War II, as part of the government's efforts to recruit "Europeans". The genuine doomsday arrived in 1964 with the strict enforcement of the Group Areas Act. Constantia, like the more famous District Six and Sophiatown, underwent what today might be referred to as "restructuring". According to Pietersen thousands of people were moved out of Constantia to a range of locations on the Cape Flats.[2] He said the process began with the "touchables" – those who did not own property – and then finished with the "untouchables" – property-owners who were both removed and expropriated.

For those who have articulated the official version of Constantia's history, Pietersen and the several thousand other coloured residents who were removed have seemingly disappeared from the record book. But in 1990, as political thawing advanced, the former residents of Constantia found each other. In 1992 about 150 of them founded the Constantia Claimants' Association. Pietersen refers to them as the "courageous 150". Their aim was to reclaim the lands from which they were evicted by the apartheid state. For many of these people, some financial compensation and recognition of the injustice done to them is enough by way of reclamation. But Pietersen has a different orientation: "I prefer to go and live in Constantia and farm there again," he says.

Hence, while the official version of Constantia's history has forged ahead, a few dozen black people have been contesting the notion of Constantia as yet another example where white settlers have seemingly carved something out of nothing in Africa. The struggle of the Claimants' Assocation, has not been easy. George van der Ross, current Chairperson of the Claimants' Association, repeatedly emphasises that its demands are quite minimal. Of the 150 claimants, only about 30 were former landowners – the rest were tenants. The irony is that in a number of cases, according to van der Ross, once the coloured families were removed and their houses "flattened", no subsequent development has taken place. In such instances the response of the Claimants' Association is simple: "we don't see any reason why this land can't be given back ... there is no issue about it ... the title deeds are there."

But even in cases where land belonging to those who were removed has been developed, the Claimants' Association has found an alternative. According to van der Ross, "We have identified vacant state-owned land that can serve as alternative land ... we've identified sufficient land where tenants can be reintegrated into the area ... only state-owned land."

The association has been quite clear in its attitude toward the present situation. According to van der Ross when he spoke at a meeting of Constantia residents, he told them: "we don't want an adversarial relationship ... the present people are not responsible for forced removals ... we don't want to put you out of your homes."

Despite the considerable effort to go through the legal process, the claimants have found two clear-cut obstacles: government officials and Constantia residents. For their part, government officials have been trying to encourage the claimants to accept a lump-sum compensation payment rather than trying to obtain land. According to van der Ross, ex-landowners have been offered R40 000 each and former tenants R17 500. In the view of van der Ross, this sum is inadequate. He argues that it fails to take into account the difficulties those who were removed faced in re-establishing their livelihoods and also ignores the rise in property values in Constantia since the 1960s. But if officials have been trying to soft-pedal the restitution option and promote a payout, van der Ross believes that the Property-Owners' Association has a more fundamental problem with the land claims: they "are not keen on having people with a darker hue living there".

Both Pietersen and van der Ross indicate that the claimants are getting very "frustrated" at the slow pace of the process. Many of the people involved are old; some have died since 1990. Frustration has led some people to opt for the payment. But van der Ross fears that others may take another path: "We're probably going to reach a stage when people become so disillusioned they will say, 'look, we just want the land' and we go there and take the land."

But while the Constantia Claimants' Association may have its day, its members are likely too few and too old to redirect the project of the Constantia Property-Owners' Association and

---

[2] There seems to be no official record of how many people were removed. According to George van der Ross, the provincial government's land claims programmes have estimated the figure at between 5000 and 7000 people. Jonathan Hulley, Democratic Alliance councillor for Constantia, also said there was a "vibrant Muslim community in Constantia in the 1950s and 1960s" which numbered in the thousands.

other groups for whom the struggle against encroachment continues. Let us now look briefly at the key actors who are leading the way in this struggle.

The Organisations of Constantia

The Constantia Property-Owners' Association (CPOA)

In terms of municipal affairs and community development, by far the most important organisation is the Constantia Property-Owners' Assocation (CPOA). Founded in 1950, the association presently has a membership of approximately 1 400, about 400 of whom attend the Annual General Meeting. The organisation has a small office in Alphen Common staffed by one part-time administrator. The CPOA also produces a newsletter from time to time. While the CPOA may have a modest formal presence, for years it has found a number of effective ways to carry out its constitutional mandate "to promote and safeguard the interests of the registered property-owners in the Constantia Valley ... to preserve the beauty and rural character of Constantia" (CPOA n.d.). The heart of this mandate is the struggle against encroachment as articulated by Chairperson Anthony Goldstein:

> *If we desire to see Constantia Valley remain more or less as it is now for a long time to come, then we need to understand what pressures exist to change its character; understanding that will help us to manage the problem (CPOA 2001, 5).*

In pursuing its mandate, the CPOA has had a major influence on local government and service delivery issues. According to Goldstein, during the period of the Constantia Valley Local Authority, the CPOA "pretty much ran council". He noted that virtually any development initiative which local government considered in Constantia generally had the approval of the CPOA. This relationship apparently continued, albeit to a slightly lesser extent, even when Constantia was incorporated into the Southern Peninsula Municipality in 1997.[3]

In March 2001, another branch of the CPOA was formed – the Constantia Hills Residents' Assocation (CHRA). This association was set up mainly in response to the closure of Constantia School for Girls and the ensuing plans from the council to subdivide the property and lease part of it to the American International Schools Development Corporation. The CHRA and others in the community viewed this as "a threat similar to the cycle from the 1950s to 1980s when development and subdivision brought dramatic change, population growth, and pressure to the rural nature of the valley" (CHRA 2001). While closely affiliated to the CPOA, the CHRA hoped to add an extra organisational presence on behalf of Constantia property-owners in various local government processes.

As noted by Goldstein, these civic organisations have had a very close relationship with local government. Councillor Joan Heming is also a spokesperson for the CPOA. Both Heming and Constantia's other councillor, Jonathan Hulley, attended the founding meeting of the CHRA. Under the new dispensation, where some councillors are elected to represent wards, the Municipal Structures Act makes provision for the formation of Ward Committees. These are intended to be structures of accountability for local government. In March 2001, the Ward 62 Committee held its first meeting, attended by some 25 people from Constantia, including significant representation from the CPOA. Philip Wheeler, a CPOA member, was elected chairperson.

This has been a brief survey of the structures and methods in which Constantia has organised to protect the interests of their property-owners. The actions of the CPOA and allied organisations have been played out around a number of particular struggles and processes. These will be discussed in some detail below.

However, before examining those issues, an important point needs to be made about representation in Constantia. In terms of race, class, political organisation and representation, Constantia is a virtual monolith. Yet there are other "Constantians". For example, it is one of the few areas in Cape Town where live-in domestic workers are the rule, not the exception. Apart from the

---

[3] Greater Cape Town was divided into 25 municipalities before 1994. However, a restructuring in 1996-97 reduced the number to seven, one of which was the Southern Peninsula Municipality. As from December 2000, these seven were reduced to one: the Cape Metropolitan Area. For details of demarcation issues see Schmidt (2000) and Cameron (1999).

domestic workforce there are hundreds of employees who work in Constantia Village, on the wine farms, and in other commercial ventures. The vast majority of these workers are black or coloured, and from the lower strata of the working class. Yet, these people have no visible organisation or participation in Constantia. In the course of this research, field-worker Monwabisi James carried out a number of interviews with workers. They raised a number of problems with services and other aspects of life for workers in the area. For example, while the absence of street lights may lend a certain rustic quality for propertied residents, for domestic workers who have to travel on foot, darkness facilitates robberies, physical assaults and even rape. While tightly controlling the operating hours of taxis may keep noise and traffic to a minimum, it often means long walks or long periods of separation from families for workers who complete their duties after hours. In the early 1990s, according to academic Jonathan Grossman, a branch of the ANC was formed in Constantia (Grossman was a member). This became an organisational home for domestic workers. The branch played an active role in one of the rare redistributive projects to emerge from Constantia, the Westlake Development[4]. But shortly after the construction of Westlake in 1999, the ANC branch ceased to function on a regular basis (interview, 2001).

Key Moments in the Struggle Against Encroachment

For the propertied residents of Constantia, the struggle against encroachment has taken many forms. There have been three key issues where the realities of South Africa have threatened to encroach on the Arcadian community of Constantia. These encroachments have come in different forms and have been responded to in a number of ways. In each instance, the propertied residents of Constantia have been able to mobilise their resources and develop a workable solution. The three key issues we will explore here are:
* the building and governance of Constantia Village;
* increases in property rate levies; and
* creating a development strategy for Constantia.

The Building and Governance of Constantia Village: Fighting Off "Commercial Creep"

For most communities, attracting investors is viewed as a key measure of success. No doubt many an elected local government official has campaigned on a platform of bringing industry and development to a constituency. For example, most historically disadvantaged areas lack commercial centres and industrial employment opportunities. As a result, residents have to travel long distances to carry out the most simple task – buying a pair of shoes, purchasing a bus ticket, or finding a spare part for a radio. Also, at a fiscal level, rates and taxes from industrial and commercial activity may lend a considerable boost to local revenue. In Constantia, the situation is reversed. Fiscal imperatives of cost recovery are not a priority. The residents of Constantia are willing and able to pay for their services – and for their protection against encroachment. As a result, propertied Constantia wants heavy constraints on what it often refers to as "commercial creep". Signage, subdivision and traffic are enemies to be contained in order to preserve the community.

A key example of the workings of this process has been the development of the Constantia Village Shopping Centre. Unlike many other areas where national chain stores are given *carte blanche* within the broad parameters of municipal by-laws, in Constantia virtually every square meter of the shopping centre is the product of a negotiation process with the CPOA. When Constantia Village was built in 1984, the contours of the shopping centre were carefully set.

---

[4] Westlake is a middle-income residential community located just outside the official boundary of Constantia. It includes a small number of low-income houses, some of which were allocated to people who had built shacks in the area. This was a concession to these informal settlement dwellers but also an attempt to curtail the spread of informal settlement. Westlake is seen as a dangerous precedent by the mainstream of the CPOA. But there is similar concern with much higher-income housing developments, like Reddam, which is also close to the Constantia heartland. While Reddam is a high-income area, its character is very different from Constantia. It is a commercialised area with high security features, including high fences and boom gates to enter. This is in stark contrast to the ambience of mainstream Constantia.

The CPOA's main tool for controlling the development of the centre was a servitude. This is a legal right normally invoked by people with adjoining properties. A servitude ensures that no development undertaken by your neighbour negatively impacts on your usage of your property. For example, a servitude would block a neighbour's attempt to build a wall with obscene paintings on it which faced into your yard. However, the CPOA has obtained a servitude for the entire shopping centre on the grounds that whatever is done in the shopping centre affects the lives of the residents of Constantia.

Hence, the owners and tenants of Constantia Village have to adhere to strict rules laid down by the CPOA. For example, no shop in the Village is allowed to have signage which faces onto the Main Road. Moreover, there is a strict rule about the size of signs and a ban on any flashing or electrically lit signs. To the CPOA, such signage would impact negatively on the nature of Constantia.

Apart from signage, there are constraints on the size and types of shops that can occupy space in the village. According to the dictates of the CPOA servitude, the Village cannot allow any "pubs, cinemas, dancing venues, gambling, betting, escort agencies or sex shops". One fast-food outlet has been allowed, but if it closes, no further fast-food business will be permitted. No shop is allowed to open before 8:00 a.m. or stay open beyond 8:00 p.m. with the exception of restaurants which can stay open until 11:30 p.m. In addition, there is a general ban on national chain stores and hypermarkets. The explanation given by Village Manager Athol Swanson and confirmed by councillor Joan Heming is that Constantia Village should serve the needs of Constantia residents only and should not attract people from other parts of the city. Even the parking space to be made available is subject to regulations – no more than six bays per 100 square meters of floor space in the shopping centre.

A last ban is a predictable one – no selling outside of the designated shop areas. The main targets of this are hawkers and informal sellers. The servitude even specifies how many people may be seated in an indoor/outdoor café/restaurant to no more than one-quarter of the total capacity of the restaurant. All this means that in Constantia Village, unlike in most other shopping areas, you will find no-one trying to give you a leaflet about CV joints, nobody selling baskets, and not a single person offering to look after your car while you shop. Linked to this is an unstated ban on shops which cater primarily to black working-class consumers. Constantia Village contains no Shoprite, no JET stores, not even more middle-class oriented businesses like furniture store Joshua Doore. The Village seeks tenants who operate, as Swanson says, "tastefully" – selling tasteful goods and services to a discrete clientele.

The hidden agenda is that being less tasteful might bring more noise, more traffic and, of course, more people from different class and race backgrounds to Constantia. These are key principles underlying the war against encroachment.

Increases in Property Rate Levies: The LOGRA Court Case

In the absence of a sweeping social revolution in South Africa, it was almost inevitable that the citizens of the black areas of Cape Town would eventually have some confrontation with the residents of Constantia. For the CPOA, this legal test of strength came in the form of a court case over property rates.

The issue of property rates has been a source of great contention in Cape Town. For the residents of Constantia, avoiding taxes which involve cross-subsidy is a key component of the struggle against encroachment. Although councillor Heming states categorically that the residents of Constantia are in favour of cross-subsidy, further comments and actions indicate strongly to the contrary. The argument over rates in Constantia hinges on a number of issues. Firstly, there is the question of the system of valuation. The last general valuation in Cape Town took place in 1974. At that time areas like Hout Bay and Constantia were peri-urban – in the words of Southern Peninsula official Mike Richardson, "like living in the countryside". The rate complexities were compounded by the fact that during the apartheid era, the Cape Metro was divided into 25 local authorities. Each of these had its own approach to taxation. From 1974 to the present, some local authorities carried out valuations, while others did not. Hence gross inequities in valuation and rate payments persisted. As a result, the owner of a property in Constantia which was worth R200 000 in 1997 would pay far less in rates than the owner of a property of equal value in many other areas, including many historically disadvantaged areas. This issue came to the fore in a legal action brought against the city of Cape Town by the Lotus River, Ottery and Grassy Park Residents' Association (LOGRA).

Formed in 1979, LOGRA is an amalgamation of a number of ratepayer and residents' bodies in the area. The organisation has a long history of mobilising residents around issues of municipal service delivery. It summarised its pre-1994 role as follows:

> During the apartheid years, when the genuine political parties who opposed the regime were not allowed to operate, LOGRA filled a very important role as the voice of the people ... Through its campaigns for the improvement of the municipal infrastructure, it created an awareness and political consciousness in the community (LOGRA, 2001).

After 1994, LOGRA continued its activities on behalf of residents, arguing that:

> The new South African constitutional dispensation made it possible for the oppressors to continue to govern our region and our new municipality. Negotiations were started with the new local authority for a fair rates system.

The LOGRA action came in response to an attempt by the Southern Peninsula Municipality to make interim adjustments to rates, while a new general valuation took place. While a general valuation exercise had begun in 1997, completion would have been after the required time for finalising the 1998–99 budget. For 1998-99 the SPM proposed a 19 per cent across-the-board rates increase. These increases were intended to compensate for some of the short-falls in the budgets of the Southern Peninsula which emerged as a result of the amalgamation of a number of local authorities into the SPM. LOGRA largely represented historically disadvantaged property-owners. Their argument was that a 19 per cent across-the-board increase exacerbated the historical disadvantage that resulted from the different dates of valuations. In its case, it pointed out that areas like Constantia and Grassy Park had last been evaluated in 1974, whereas rates for areas such as Ottery were based on 1990 prices.

The municipality's case was legally framed on municipal legislation. The relevant law was the Local Government Transition Act of 1993, which banned any planned deficits in municipal budgets. This forced municipalities to come up with a source of income to cover all expenditure. According to the SPM, to balance the budget with its first expenditure estimate would have required a 28 per cent increase in rates revenue. With a second round of budgeting it slashed costs to reduce the required rates increase to 19 per cent. The argument was that to abandon the rates increase or reduce projected income substantially would violate the conditions of the Act. Lawyers for LOGRA argued that an across-the-board rates increase violated the guarantees of equality contained in Section 9 of the South African Constitution. They pointed out that given the disproportionate increase in property values since the last valuation, a Constantia property-owner would pay less than half the rate of a Grassy Park property-owner if calculations were based on the existing cents in the Rand formula.[5]

The case was dismissed. The court held that although the proposed 19 per cent increase did exacerbate inequalities, the given circumstances of the municipality left it with no other practical option. The court took note of the need for a general valuation to rectify the situation but acknowledged that the valuation could not be completed in time for budgeting for 1998-99.

While the court decision did settle the case, it did not settle the issue. To begin with, the general valuation exercise which began in 1997 was halted because of political-party wrangling between the ANC, the National Party and the Democratic Party. The exercise only resumed after the establishment of new local governments in December of 2000.[6]

Nonetheless, LOGRA office-bearer Richard Arends, who became the legal *persona* who actually brought the case, argued that it was a "victory" since the court supported its view in principle but threw it out on a "technicality". Arends argued that the action also succeeded in putting more pressure on the municipality to move the rates system to a more equitable

---

[5] Cents in the Rand states how many cents in rates per year a property-owner will pay per Rand value of their property.

[6] The valuation was finally completed in early 2002. According to city officials, Constantia was the area where "data capturers trying to accurately value homes met with the most resistance" (Sylvester, 2002).

footing. But while the case may have been a moderate political triumph, it was a financial disaster. The case was dismissed with costs and while LOGRA did manage to get a donation of R50 000, the total bill came to R146 000. The association had no resources to make up the shortfall. As a result, Richard Arends' personal property became the target of the sheriff's collections department.

Despite the legal process, the issue of rates continued to be a target of action for those responsible in the local authority. The SPM tried to make further ad hoc adjustments for 1999-2000. According to Mike Richardson, the attempt in 1999-2000 was to implement an eight per cent across-the-board rates increase combined with an interim rating system to adjust for inequities. He stated that this led to a general increase in rates in Constantia of about 13.5 per cent, although on some individual properties increments reached a maximum of 40 per cent. Rates also changed in other areas like Hout Bay (15 per cent) which had previously been undervalued. In historically disadvantaged areas like Grassy Park, the rise was only three per cent.

But these moves by the municipality hardly calmed the waters. The Constantia property-owners, as an organisational force, and as individual citizens, proceeded with a far-reaching campaign to halt any further rates increases. To support their arguments they raised a number of issues.

Anthony Goldstein said the rates increases amounted to about 60 per cent over four years. His conclusion was that Constantia "got hammered pretty heavily". The CPOA viewed the situation through the spectacles of its version of a cost-benefit analysis. According to Goldstein in 1999-2000 the SPM had only spent R50 000 on capital expenditure in Constantia while receiving some R30 million in rates. He said Constantia's contribution was "way over the top in terms of payment". He even went so far as to call the rates increases a form of "reparations", stating: "we've done reparations, what's next?" Councillor Joan Heming echoed Goldstein's views: "the cost of servicing an area like Constantia is very low compared to the contribution an area like this makes in terms of municipal revenue ... our needs are few."

Within the CPOA there is strong support for cost recovery as opposed to a system which is largely based on cross-subsidisation. Joan Heming argues that the service component of rates should be "on a user-pays basis ... the municipality will have to devise a system of introducing the fairness of 'you pay for what you use'... if I go into Pick 'n Pay Ackerman doesn't ask me to pay more for freshly squeezed orange juice than someone who doesn't have that kind of income". She argues that rates increases are particularly harsh on residents of Constantia because many are older people on fixed incomes. In her view, rates increases could make Constantia unliveable for them. She emphasises that she does not want "forced removal by rates". She believes that if you had a referendum in Constantia, 90 per cent of the residents would not object to making a contribution to disadvantaged areas. But, she warned, there "should be a line between redistribution and robbery".

Like Heming, Liz Brunette of the Constantia Hills Residents' Association expressed concern over increasing rates. She noted that while she had never heard anyone complain about cross-subsidy, they did complain that "they don't see it happening". In her opinion, the key issue for cross-subsidy expenditure was addressing the "population explosion". She said that if you visited certain places in Cape Town, you (would) find "just a teaming mass of under fives". Apart from the population issue, she expressed concern that bills were not transparent. If there was cross-subsidy, she noted, it should be reflected in the bill. Her worry was that "if you look at a bill, you can't really see what you're paying for". She said the lack of transparency was a problem with the rates increases and lamented that "we're a soft target ... authorities know that people living in these areas will pay".

Brunette's perceptions around cost recovery were similar to those of Heming. She praised the implementaion of prepaid electricity, condemning the "expectation of receiving and not paying for anything except food ... you can't go on like that ... with prepaid ... people will start to pay their way. The city will benefit."

Within Constantia, Heming, Brunette and Goldstein represent a voice of moderation on the issue of rates and cost recovery. Far more radical in approach is past office-bearer of the CPOA, Richard Harris. Well known to municipal authorities for his incessant campaigning on behalf of the citizens of Constantia, Harris's latest venture is a legal action against the municipality on the question of payment for sewerage. The smallholding in Constantia which

Harris owns is not connected to the municipal sewerage system. While rates charges in Constantia include a rebate for sewerage charges to those who are not connected, Harris insists the rebate is not sufficient. He is pressing to recover about R4 300 which he argues he has paid for services not received.

The issue of rates, cross-subsidy and cost recovery in Constantia has been the subject of considerable reflection by municipal authorities. On the question of rates, the authorities have aimed to move toward a system of equal cents in the Rand ratios across the board. This would mean that a property of the same value would attract the same rates tariffs regardless of where it was located. Clearly the general valuation is a necessary step in achieving that goal. However, in the interim, the SPM also imposed some differential rate charges on areas within its authority. So, for example, in 1999–2000 there was an across-the-board eight per cent increment accompanied by an adjustment through an interim rating system with some equity component. The adjustment led to a 13.5 per cent increment for Constantia, meaning 21.5 per cent overall. By comparison, the historically disadvantaged area of Grassy Park only received a three per cent increment. Even with these adjustments, Mike Richardson noted that Grassy Park was still paying a slightly higher cents in the Rand rate than Constantia (16.2 cents/Rand as opposed to 15.7 cents/Rand). He pointed out that despite complaints from Constantia residents, the cents/Rand ratio did not actually increase until 1999–2000.

But Richardson adamantly refuted any claims from Constantia residents that they were being "hammered". To begin with, he countered the argument that Constantia had historically consumed relatively few resources, because they were "well organised" and frugal. In his view, Constantia residents' problem was that "they wouldn't accept that they were being cross-subsidised." Richardson estimated that Constantia residents paid about half the rate value of adjacent areas. In addition, he noted, "they paid nothing towards maintenance of the mountain and the major infrastructure that got them into Cape Town every day". Most of these were paid for by the Cape Town City Council. Richardson cited such specific services and infrastructure as the roads that lead out of Constantia to the places where residents worked, and the fire and police services which responded to calls in Constantia although they were not fully funded by the Constantia Valley Local Authority. He also noted the ways in which Constantia residents were able to use the cross-subsidy to block the encroachment of Cape Town's urban life: "Their sewerage ends up in Retreat and that's where the smell ends up." Far from being historical victims or "soft targets" in the present conjuncture, Richardson viewed Constantia as "the little village island that lived a nice existence for quite a few years".

For Richardson, redistribution is an imperative. He argues that there is "no disputing over the question of cross-subsidy". In response to the specifics of issues like non-connection to the sewerage system, he argued that this would be reflected in the value of the property: "we offer a package of services ... you can't say I don't want the mountain, I don't walk on the mountain ... What the council intends is to direct the resources in the most equitable way possible."

LOGRA's sympathies are similar to Richardson's but the organisation calls for more far-reaching and immediate change. For Arends, the first step is implementing an equitable rates system with immediate effect: "these people must pay what's due to the council in one go". For Arends, equity means no rates on property in historically disadvantaged areas. "We've paid enough," he argues, "we'll pay for services". But beyond a total revamping of the rates system, Arends also advocates major adjustments in municipal expenditure. His approach toward Constantia and the privileged areas was to "take them off the maintanance roll" for several years. His argument is that the starting points between areas like Grassy Park and Constantia are fundamentally unequal. He points to the simple example of road maintenance. In Grassy Park, he argues that the base of the roads is inadequate. Hence, if maintenance crews simply resurface, the problems are not solved. In support of his argument, he cited the incident at Klipfontein and DeWet Road the previous winter where a pothole emerged that was so large that a passing bus got stuck in it and could not move. In Arends's view, this is not only an issue for Grassy Park residents but has broader economic implications as well. Arends argues that it is a contradiction that government officials and organisations like the CPOA:

The Struggle Against Encroachment

... shout from the tops of buildings when SAMWU and NEHAWU go on strike ... but what is it costing the country because of the intransigence of local authorities, what does it cost business when their transport breaks down due to inadequate roads? (interview, 2001).

Such arguments go a long way toward refuting the portrayal of Constantia property-owners as beleaguered victims of a government obsessed with retribution. Richardson's historical analysis of metropolitan expenditure details the ways in which the expenditure of the Cape Town City Council provided considerable resources, mostly without cost, to residents of Constantia. While Constantia may draw little from the capital budget today, it was able to concentrate the resources of the CVLA to maintain the standards to which residents had grown accustomed. It should come as no surprise that a wealthy local authority with no expenses on police, fire, library, street lighting, beach and mountain maintenance would be able to focus expenditure. This focus was enabled by the apartheid legislation which protected residents against encroachment, first through forced removals, then through the maintenance of a spatial plan and municipal by-laws which kept Constantia "out of the loop" of informal settlements, industrial pollution, sprawling taxi ranks, and even misbehaving rugby fans, all of which would have brought a range of additional costs.

However, while Richardson's approach to Constantia was steeped in the discourse of equity, there have been considerable shifts away from the equity which he poses as central to the plan of the Cape Metro. When the notion of Metro-type structures first came onto the agenda in South Africa in the early 1990s, they were linked to the notion of "one city, one tax base". To the majority of urban anti-apartheid campaigners, "one city, one tax base" meant that the Sandtons and Constantias of urban South Africa would have to pay up. No longer would they be able to accumulate wealth in isolation from the increasing poverty and degradation amongst the black majority. "One city, one tax base" was a call for social responsibility, equity and redistribution. While Richardson and some other idealists in the new Cape Metro may still be living by these principles, the overall aim of the Metro has changed. Fortunately for the property-owners of Constantia, this shift has provided them with a number of opportunities to advance their struggle against encroachment. One of the most important weapons in this struggle has been the use of consultants to create a development model that moves Constantia in line with mainstream government thinking. We can now turn to this new Constantia, this "brand" Constantia which the property owners, the politicians and the development experts have created in order to bring the past back into the future.

Creating a New Development Plan: Building Brand Constantia

Despite the failure of the ANC to capture the Western Cape in the 1994 elections, the spirit of the RDP infused the development thinking in the province in the early years of democracy. In line with the process which produced the RDP, a provincial stakeholder structure, WESGRO (Western Cape Investment and Trade Promotion Agency) was set up to formulate a provincial development strategy. WESGRO later became the Provincial Development Council (PDC). Drawing up the provincial development plan brought together the stakeholders from the struggle – civic groups, labour and NGOs. Through an extended process of stakeholder meetings, task teams, etc., an agreed policy document, *Shaping the Cape* (PDC 1998), was produced. While not as redistributive as the RDP, *Shaping the Cape* set out a clear process for a progressive economic and social policy in the province. The vision put forward by *Shaping the Cape* was:

"Sustainable development and growth through equity in the Western Cape."

This was supported by a mission to improve human development through:
- the creation of employment opportunities;
- acceptable living standards;
- facilitating economic growth;
- sustainable environmental development; and
- participation by all stakeholders.

The overall aim was "to eliminate the disparities between the advantaged and the disadvantaged in the Western Cape" (PDC 1998).

Yet by the time the document was produced, South Africa had moved on from the days of debating "growth through redistribution" models. With the shift from the RDP to GEAR in June, 1996, business-owners, aspiring business-owners and property owners in areas like Constantia could begin to breathe a protracted sigh of relief. Almost overnight their label moved from "exploiters" to "entrepreneurs". They became the saviours of South Africa in a competitive global economy rather than the heirs of those who had expropriated the land from its original and legitimate owners.

At provincial level, the jettisoning of *Shaping the Cape* was consolidated by the Provincial Economic Affairs Department with the launch of the consultant-driven economic policy Green Paper: Preparing the Western Cape for the Knowledge Economy of the 21st Century in early 2000. The Green Paper was a paradigm leap, moving the main thrust of provincial strategy from equity to creating a province capable of holding its own in the global competition for tourists, investors and information technology resources. With scarcely a mention of the underdeveloped rural areas of the province, the Green Paper focused almost exclusively on building a high-technology "precinct" in the Cape Town Central Business District as the gateway to global trade opportunities with a trickle down to the rest of the province. Gone was the vision of redistributive justice driven by the grassroots struggles of the 1980s; the neoliberal consultants' vision had moved to centre stage.

Although the Green Paper prompted considerable debate and resistance from NGOs and trade unions, the document's resonance with national policy left its ultimate fate secure.

At the level of Cape Town municipal politics, a similar shift unfolded. Instead of growth through redistribution, the keys to economic prosperity became the building of a competitive city which could attract investors and tourists. This shift in orientation was embodied in the process to create a unified Cape Metropolitan Area as part of the final stage of restructuring local government. This restructuring process began in 1995 with the first local government elections. At that point, the notion of mega-cities was driven by the popular early 1990s slogan: "one city, one tax base". As noted above, this slogan was the embodiment of what was seen by civics and the broad democratic movement as the key to urban equity: cross-subsidisation of the black majority by the wealthy white minority. Spatially this meant that rich suburbs like Constantia would necessarily have to be linked under one governance structure to the impoverished townships of the greater metropolitan areas. The motivation was simple: the resources and income of the wealthy could be used to uplift the townships and destroy the apartheid urban social and geographical configurations. But as the processes to create unified metropolitan areas unfolded, the notion of cross-subsidisation lost its centrality. As with national and provincial economic policies, urban strategy looked to the market for salvation. In Cape Town, the culmination of this process was the formation of the Unicity Commission in November 1999.[7] The Commission was a small transformation team which had the task of laying the groundwork for a new dispensation in Cape Town after the second democratic local government elections in December 2000. The Commission, driven by a cohort of external consultants, moved rapidly and decisively toward the neoliberal vision. Calling on the services of global consultants PricewaterhouseCoopers and Arthur Andersen to craft the details of the new Cape Town, the Unicity Commission, like the authors of the provincial Green Paper, moved the goal posts, albeit with a far more subtle choice of terminology and rhetoric. However, the major direction for Cape Town, according to the Unicity Commission, was obvious: fall in line with global trends of building partnerships with the private sector, prioritise attracting tourists and foreign investors, and ensure that residents pay for their services. Despite a smokescreen of pro-equity rhetoric, the documents for the new Cape Metro were enablers of the private sector. Moreover, it was not only at the level of policy documents that the new approach was being implemented. Within the service delivery system, extensive outsourcing, productivity pushes and cost-recovery measures were changing the

---

[7] For a detailed overview of the shift toward the neoliberal paradigm in Cape Town, see McDonald and Smith (2002). For a review of the outsourcing and other pro-market policies in specific sectors, see Pape (2001a and 2001b) and Qotole, Xali and Barchiesi (2001).

shape of life in the Metro, even before the new Unicity was officially launched.[8]

Hence in the "new" Cape Town, as in the "new" South Africa, attracting the mythical foreign investors and tourists became the necessary first step toward development. The basic needs of the majority and the urge to redistribute any ill-gotten past gains would have to move onto the back burner. There was only one road to salvation: the market. To succeed in the market you had to lead with your best, your most experienced foot soldiers, and not those with aspirations, potential, or, even worse, moral claims.

As the shift from redistributive to market justice took shape in Cape Town, the property-owners of Constantia and their allies seized the opportunity. While dozens of consultants, economic experts and spin doctors refashioned post-apartheid Cape Town into a "global city", Constantia's propertied mobilised to claim their piece of the cake.

The key to their strategy was to reinvent Constantia, to put the old wine of quaint village into the new bottles of world-class tourist destination. Not surprisingly they managed to develop a tourist strategy which coincided with the aims of the CPOA: leave Constantia untouched. The building of Brand Constantia became the promotion of what for years in South Africa had been anathema: maintaining the status quo. The CPOA's Anthony Goldstein articulated the position quite clearly: "We believe it is right that it should remain the way it is." The "rarity" of Constantia was proclaimed its value. This noble project of the CPOA was recast to fit into the needs of the province. As Goldstein put it, "the Cape's only long-term resource is as a tourist destination". The place of this "gateway to the South Peninsula" was that of a crowning jewel, a leading asset. And, in Goldstein's terms, the municipality needed to understand that "the best way to develop the asset is to not touch it".

Joan Heming even went so far as to give Constantia's preservation a place on the national agenda. Her argument was that the vision of Constantia was "not separate from that of Cape Town or South Africa ... Constantia is something that the country actually needs." But Heming was quite clear on what type of Constantia was needed and for whom: "if you want to attract people to bring their businesses here, this is the kind of place they want to live in ... Rather than being for the poor, I would see it as being for the kind of people that will help drive the economy forward" (interview, 2001).

For Liz Brunette and the CHRA, a similar conclusion was reached. "Tourism will be the saviour," she emphasised. Another resident echoed these views, arguing that to destroy the "uniqueness of the area" would be to "kill the goose that lays the golden egg". He said further that opening up Constantia for low-income housing would be "as good as putting poor people in the Castle" (interview, 2001).[9]

The strategy of maintaining the status quo in Constantia has gone well beyond the level of offhand comments by CPOA leaders or councillors. Preserving Constantia has been a key aspect of a number of policy papers and studies which have been authorised by the municipality and driven either directly or indirectly by the CPOA. Here we will examine a few of these documents.

Perhaps the most important consultant report in driving Brand Constantia is the *Special Area Study of Historical Constantia* prepared by Professor David DeWar, Barrie Gasson and Piet Louw Architects.[10] This study was commissioned by the residents of the old Ward 10 which included Constantia pre-December 2000. According to DeWar, the aim was to identify the "intrinsic quality" of Constantia. The study attempted to take a 50-year view on Constantia, seeing the area as a "fantastically important Metro resource". While DeWar acknowledged that the general urban trend was for compaction, the formula put forward for Constantia was "diametrically opposed to the general model of the city". For DeWar, a concern in compiling

[8] For a discussion of this process see ILRIG (2000). Details of the waste sector's restructuring are contained in Qotole, Xali and Barchiesi (2001) and Pape (2001).

[9] The Castle was the first major edifice constructed by white settlers when they arrived in the Cape. It functions largely as a museum today.

[10] Other key documents which have contributed to linking Constantia's economic contribution to maintaining the status quo have included the Porter Estate Development Framework (MLH Architects 2001), as well as the Scenice Drive Network Report (Revel Fox and Partners 1998) and the Peninsula Urban Edge Study (VKE Engineers 2000). Like Louw's Study, the Porter Estate Development Framework was driven by forces within the CPOA. The Scenic Drive and Urban Edge studies have provided a tourist- and conservation-oriented framework for areas like Constantia. They have been used as ideological support for the strategy being advanced in Louw's study. For a discussion of some of the ideas and trends that influenced this research, see Watson (2001).

the study was that there was a "political lobby" that "consciously would like to see its quality destroyed". He noted also that "you have to sell the argument" that preserving Constantia "is in the public interest." (Interview, 2001).

There are three assumptions which inform this study. Firstly, that the "unique quality" of Constantia has deteriorated in recent years and remains under threat from a variety of sources including commercial creep, "eyesores and unsightly developments", sub-division and subsequent uncontrolled land use, and the side effects of urban transport systems, especially taxis. Secondly, that the "special features of Constantia are critical to Cape Town which is properly seeking to attract increasing numbers of visitors and new residents ... in this, the city faces fierce competition from many other parts of the world; it requires special features to compete". And thirdly, that any plans for Constantia must be seen in the context of a long-term view. The study claimed to be informed by the position that "if the area is properly managed, it will be priceless: its long-term contribution to the economy of the country as well as to greater Cape Town will be enormous. This must not be destroyed through short-term profiteering or expedient decision-making" (Louw *et al.* 2000, 4).

The study makes a number of recommendations in terms of preserving Constantia and allegedly promoting its status as a tourist destination. The authors of the document promote a comprehensive campaign against the commercialisation of Constantia by calling for no signage on businesses greater than 0.2 square metres; no guest houses; no businesses which impact negatively on neighbours in terms of smell, noise, accessibility; no building of second dwellings on a plot of more than 120 square metres. The study also calls for the maintenance of large plots, recommending nothing in Constantia smaller than 2 000 square metres.

In keeping with the importance of history to the area, the consultants conclude that Constantia should be declared a national heritage site of level-one category. Level one is the highest status of such sites, requiring national management. They are unequivocal in their assessment: "There is little doubt that in terms of historic heritage and in terms of future economic importance, the entire area of historic Constantia should constitute a level-one categorisation".

Taken as a whole, the document amounts to a well-constructed, market-based argument for defending race and class privilege in Constantia. Yet even taken on its own terms, the document amounts to little more than a thinly disguised attempt to advance the dogmatic preservation goals of the CPOA.

To begin with, while Constantia is to be a key "destination", the strategy still shifts responsibility for accommodation and infrastructure to other sites in Cape Town. For example, the banning of additional guest houses and of more than two tourist accommodation establishments side by side shows little evidence of an economic rationality. If Constantia's planners were genuinely concerned with attracting tourist revenue, they could find ways to integrate facilities to blend with the general architectural style and spatial development strategy of the area.

Secondly, Constantia contains some of the most important cramets in the Cape Town area. Indeed, on major Muslim holidays like Eid, hundreds of people come to these cramets. Yet, there is no attempt to incorporate this element of tourist attraction into the Constantia plan.

Lastly, unlike virtually every other document in South Africa which speaks about economic development, these plans contain no mention of trickle-down forms of redistribution. The Constantia vision contains no promises of job creation, no opportunities for small, medium and micro entrepreneurs, no crèches for domestic workers' children and certainly no resource allocation for low-income housing. In short, this is a plan whose central tenet is "Constantia for the Constantians". If there is to be any trickle down, it will have to move through a pipeline which delivers it far away from the boundaries of Constantia.

Conclusion

The shift of South Africa from a developmental approach focused on redistributive justice to creating opportunities for the market has ramifications at many levels. While many researchers have focused on the macro-economic-level impact of the move from the RDP to GEAR, there has been little study done of how this paradigm shift is used by wealthy communities to maintain their privilege and insulate themselves from the class-based conflicts emerging in the new South

Africa. An alternative vision would have viewed the accumulated wealth and municipal infrastructure in Constantia as a resource for advancing social and economic justice. Even a mildly redistributive approach could have used cross-subsidies derived from rates, progressive service tariffs,[11] or a moderate wealth tax to finance infrastructure and consumption on the Cape Flats. Instead, the poor have been made to compensate for their historical oppression by being subjected to a stringent policy of cost recovery.

While even other well-to-do suburbs in Cape Town such as Hout Bay or Newlands have to contend with issues of taxis, informal settlements and crime, Constantia has organised effectively to struggle against such encroachment. Through a combination of mobilising its resources, organising its residents, and effective participation in the government policy process, the residents of Constantia, led by the Property-Owners' Association and local councillors, have been able to mount a campaign to maintain the status quo in their suburb.

Tragically, their strategy may well succeed. The only concession likely to be forced upon Constantia is an increase in rates. But current predictions by those in charge of the valuation, such as Mike Richardson, are that such increases may only amount to the order of 60 per cent. This is unlikely to have major impact on a community where the average sale price of a house exceeds a million Rands.

Ultimately, the shift from an obsession with redress to an obsession with the market has provided a window of opportunity for maintaining privilege. Acts of redress such as land restitution to those forcibly removed or allocating plots for low-income housing will not feature on the immediate Constantia horizon.

It did not have to turn out like this. In 1994, the Constantia property-owners had an opportunity to negotiate redistribution, to manage a process where they would lose some of the their wealth and privilege. They could have maintained considerable physical comfort and discovered a new humanity by participating in building a new democratic order. This option never fully developed. The government did not push it; the residents of Constantia did not push it. Instead, a different type of social contract has been forged: old wealth and new wealth have found common ground and the Constantia of the new millennium remains much like that in the waning years of the previous millennium. But separate development, whether it be under apartheid or in the era of globalisation, is ultimately unsustainable. This is a lesson, it would seem, many Constantians have yet to learn.

Bibliography

ANC [African National Congress]. (1994). *Reconstruction and Development Programme.* Pretoria: ANC.

Bond, P. (2000). *Elite Transition: From Apartheid to Neoliberalism in South Africa.* Durban: University of Natal Press.

— (2001). *Global Apartheid: South African Meets the World Bank, IMF and International Finance.* Cape Town: Juta Press.

Cameron, R. (1999). *Democratisation of South African Local Government: A Tale of Three Cities.* Cape Town: J L van Schaik.

Carew, D. (2001). "The wine that seduced kings." *Saturday Argus,* 25 August, 17.

---

[11] Alan Meehan, a manager in the Southern Peninsula Water Authority, which services Constantia and a number of informal settlements, suggested that prepaid meters would be far more appropriate in areas like Constantia than in the informal settlements and low-income townships where they are concentrated. In Meehan's view, residents of Constantia would be able to afford both the installation costs and be able to maintain the payment. This would have cash-flow benefits for the municipality. By contrast, he pointed out, residents of informal settlements cannot afford the installation costs and often end up disconnected because they cannot afford to "load" the prepaid card. These sorts of "self-disconnections" can lead to illegal connections which cause enormous revenue losses due to both non-payment and increased leakage.

City of Cape Town. (2001). CMA Profile-Housing Services, accessed at http://www. capetown.gov.za/ home/housingservices.asp.

City of Cape Town, Economic Development and Tourism Project Team. (2001). "Cape Town's Economy: Current Trends and Future Prospects". Cape Town: City of Cape Town.

ILRIG (2000). *Survey of Municipal Workers in the CMA.* Research Report for the Unicity Commission.

LOGRA (2001). "An overview of LOGRA Civic." Unpublished paper.

Marais, H. (2001). *Limits to Change: The Political Economy of Transition.* Cape Town: Juta.

McDonald, D. and Smith, L. (2002). "Privatizing Cape Town." Municipal Services Project Occasional Papers Series, Cape Town.

Pape, J. (2001a). "Electricity in Cape Town." Research Paper for Naledi – Local Government Restructuring, Johannesburg.

— (2001b). "A Wasted Opportunity: Workers in Local Government Restructuring in Cape Town." NRF Research Paper, Pretoria.

Qotole, M., Xali, M. and Barchiesi, F. (2001). "The Commercialisation of Waste Management in South Africa." Municipal Services Project Occasional Paper Series, Number 3, Cape Town.

Sylvester, E. (2002)."Glitches in property valuation roll begin to surface." *Cape Argus,* 8 March.

Schmidt, D. (2000). "Summary of Local Government Transition Process in CMA" 1994–97. Unpublished paper.

Xali, M. (2001). PPPs: "A questionable strategy for service delivery" in ILRIG (ed.). *Is There An Alternative: South African Workers Confronting Globalisation,* Cape Town: ILRIG, 131–144.

Watson, V. (2001). "Urban research, planning and action – their relationship in the context of metropolitan Cape Town." Input to the workshop on the spatial form of socio-political change: progress and prospects of post-apartheid Cape Town, University of Western Cape and University of Hamburg, 13 September.

Policy/Consultancy Documents

Cape Metropolitan Council, (2000). *Defining, Mapping and Managing Moss in the CMA.*

— (2000). Statutory MSDF, April.

Constitution of the Constantia. Property-Owners' Assocation, (n.d.).

Constitution of the Constantia Hills Residents' Association, 2001.

Dept of Economic Affairs. (Western Cape Province). (2000). *Preparing the Western Cape for the Knowledge Economy of the 21st Century.* Economic Policy Green Paper, Cape Town.

Fox, R. and Partners. (1998). *Scenic Drive Report.* Prepared for the Cape Metropolitan Council.

Louw, P., DeWar, D. and Gasson, B. (2001). *A special area study of historic Constantia.*

Lotus River, Ottery, Grassy Park Residents' Association and Another v South Peninsula Municipality. High Court, Cape of Good Hope Provincial Division (1999) Case summary, BCLR 440, (c), Case Number 12469/98.

MLH Architects and Planners. (2001). *Porter Estate Development Framework.*

Provincial Development Council [PDC]. (1998). *Shaping the Cape: towards a consensus-based provincial growth and development strategy: a development review.* Cape Town.

Seery, B. (2002). "How the rich like to live it up", Cape Argus, 16 March.

Servitude Agreement between Constantia Property-Owners' Association and Norwich Life South Africa Limited and the Trustees of the Alphen Park Trust, 1999.

South Peninsula Municipality. *Budget 2000/2001.* Department of Finance Return.

Unicity Commission. (2000). *Building a Unified City for the 21st Century: A summary of proposed service delivery and institutional change for the term of office of the new City of Cape Town*. Cape Town.

VKE Engineers. (2000). *Peninsula Urban Edge Study*. Urban Edge Report for the Cape Metropolitan Council Administration.

Interviews

Richard Arends, Chairperson, LOGRA, 8 November, 2001.

Liz Brunette, Chairperson, Constantia Hills Residents' Association, 28 May, 2001.

Professor David DeWar, Georgraphy Department, University of Cape Town, 22 May 2001.

Anthony Goldstein, Chairperson, Constantia Property-Owners' Association, 2 May, 2001.

Jonathan Grossman, Sociology Department, University of Cape Town, 24 May, 2001.

Richard Harris, former office bearer, Constantia Property-Owners' Association, 15 May, 2001.

Joan Heming, Cape Town City Councillor, 21 May 2001.

Jonathan Hulley, Cape Town City Councillor, 5 November, 2001.

Alan Meehan, Southern Peninsula Water Authority, 31 May, 2001.

Christiaan Pietersen, office bearer, Constantia Claimants' Association, 14 June 2001.

Mike Richardson, Southern Peninsula Authority, 31 May 2001.

Athol Swanson, Manager, Constantia Village Shopping Centre, 23 May 2001.

George van der Ross, Chairperson, Constantia Claimants' Association, 19 November, 2001.

Andre van Dijk, Director, Electrical and Mechanical Engineering Services, City of Cape Town, 28 June, 2001.

Philip Wheeler, Member, Constantia Property-Owners. Association, 18 May 2001.

Monwabisi James conducted interviews with workers in Constantia from July to September, 2001. He had one focus group interview with domestic workers, one focus group interview with farm workers and three individual interviews with farm workers. The names and dates of these interviews are not presented due to the agreement of anonymity with those interviewed.

People and Service Delivery

A Fictional Tale of Cost Recovery

In December last year, almost an entire community in a small town in the Northern Cape was scorched to death by a raging fire. The fire was a result of a heat wave that had hit the province over the prevous three weeks. In an attempt to establish how an entire community had burnt to death the reporter uncovered the following: in light of the local authority's stringent enforcement of cost recovery, the fire brigade was unable to attend to the fire before establishing which municipal boundary the area was in, and whether or not the council in the area would accept financial responsibility for the water bill and service rendered. By the time it met these requirements the community had burnt to the ground.

Eye-witnesses then added a most peculiar angle to the tale. They said that while the fire was raging no-one in the community seemed to be using taps or hoses to put out the flames.

Some of the survivors of the freak event were later interviewed and shed light on this peculiar state of affairs:

I was too scared to use my water to save my house. I am so poor I already have nothing. If I used my water, I would have had nothing plus a huge water bill that I cannot afford to pay. Now I just have nothing.

Another survivor stated:

I would really like to have saved my house, I took years to furnish it and turn it into a home, but I had no units on my card and with no water you cannot put out a fire, no matter how hard you try.

But the worst was the experience of an elderly pensioner who managed to escape the jaws of death:

My home was my only possession, I am so poor I cannot even afford to buy water. Since this prepaid system I have never had more than the 50 litres of water a day. You see that is what you get free. In this heat you can't survive. Today I decided to finally take a bath because it was so hot. My neighbour said she will give me some water to drink for the rest of the day. You see once the 50 litres are used up you only get water at 12 o'clock tonight again. I tried to save my house with whatever water was left but when the 50 litres are finished the meter cuts you off. Have you ever tried talking to a meter? I did now with this fire, but it does not hear, it does not care, it just cuts you off even when there's a fire. You just have to stand and watch your whole life burn in front of you. You know they say water is life, without it you die. Well I am here but my soul is dead; it died when my home burnt to the ground. All that is left is ashes.

7

Viva Prepaids, Viva!

Assessing New Technology for Cost Recovery in the Rural Northern Cape

by Hameda Deedat

Introduction

In 1999, the District Council[1] of Benede Oranje District in the Northern Cape signed a contract with South Atlantic Prepaid Water Meters. The purpose of the contract was to replace all conventional water meters in poor towns like Groot-drink, Raaswater, Lennertsville, Cilliers, Alheit, Topline and Lutzburg with prepaid meters. According to the District Council, the motivating factor for the prepaid meters was the high level of non-payment or arrears for service payments that ran into millions of rands (Mapanka interview, 2001).

A process of discussion and community meetings was held around the idea of the prepaid meter. On hearing of the council's intentions, the South African Municipal Workers' Union (SAMWU) called an urgent meeting in a bid to persuade the council against the prepaid system, but to no avail. In July 2000, the first prepaid meter was installed in Alheit.

At the time of my research, implementation was extensive, covering virtually all households. The number of meters installed in the varioius communities was as follows (Seloane correspondence, 2001):

Topline: 168 prepaid meters
Grootdrink: 320 prepaid meters
Raaswater: 380 prepaid meters
Lennertsville: 233 prepaid meters
Lutzburg: 220 prepaid meters
Cilliers: 250 prepaid meters
Alheit: 130 prepaid meters

This chapter will assess the council's programme of prepaid meters. Particular attention will be paid to Lennertsville where we were able to conduct extensive interviews.

---

[1] Throughout the report references are made to minutes or documents of the District Council. Accurate referencing for some of the sources is not possible as they were provided as excerpts from DC documents. The dates for these document were either assumed from the content or synchronised in accordance with the sequence of events as described by both the DC and the community.

Research methodology

Since I did not have much knowledge of the area, I decided to visit at least five of the townships identified above, and to choose one out of the five as a case study. I requested and received the assistance of SAMWU's Northern Province Educator, Maria April, and the union's provincial water coordinator, Steve Seloane.

Alheit

Our research began in Alheit, which is a relatively small township with approximately 300 residents. Interviews were conducted with an elderly pensioner, his daughter, a group of women, and the SAMWU worker who interviewees reported was responsible for cutting off their water. Additional information was gathered through streetscapes. As a result of infrastructural problems with the prepaid meters, the conventional service was resumed. On that basis I decided to move on to the next town and assess the situation there.

Cilliers

The next town was Cilliers, which is much bigger and close to Kakamas. At the time of our visit to the area, one of the engineers from the Kei-Gariep municipality was called out to Cilliers to address a technical problem associated with the meters. We also found that most of the prepaid meters were no longer in operation and were being removed as a result of infrastructural problems. Interviews were conducted with two SAMWU shop stewards, one of whom was the "*Water pompie*", and with a few residents in the area. Many people did not feel comfortable to talk and referred us to the community leader. He was unfortunately at work and could not be interviewed.

Lennertsville

We then proceeded to the next town, Lennertsville. We found that the prepaid meters in Lennertsville were still in operation. Since the meters had been operational for several months, we decided to do more extensive interviews here. We spent the next two days in Lennertsville. We completed two group interviews and eight individual interviews. A brief interview was held with the ANC councillor who was not too keen on our research. Although we had experienced resistance from some of the ANC councillors and the mayor towards the research, we managed to gain their approval and continue. Despite these small obstacles, research in Lennertsville was highly successful and constitutes the core of this report.

Raaswater

Once the interviews in Lennertsville were complete, we proceeded to Raaswater. We completed a streetscape of the area and conducted an interview with two residents.

Topline and Grootdrink

Although these towns would fall under a new local authority as a result of the changes in demarcation, we did interview ANC councillors in the relevant townships.

Apart from the community interviews, we also spoke with officials from the various local authorities: Mr. JP Mapanka, Mr. Feris, and the Town Treasurer Martin Papier from the Lower Orange River District Council; Mr. Andrew Swartz, known as "Pastoor" from Kei-Gariep; the Upington Municipality, as well as various ANC councillors.

Historical overview of services

During the apartheid years, areas like Alheit, Cilliers, Topline, Raaswater and Lennertsville, received virtually no services. The white local authority only serviced the white areas. Communities had to find sources of water for drinking and other day-to-day necessities. Since most of these towns arose from of the need of local farmers for labour, the underground canal used for irrigation became the source. Using the canal meant that people in the community had to roll drums of water to their homes (Alheit community interview, 2001).

By the 1960s, these communities decided to implement their own kind of water delivery in the area. The Alheit community, for example, sourced water from an underground canal, and started a donkey-cart water-delivery service. A member of the community who owned a donkey and a cart was given two shillings for each 200-litre container that he filled and delivered.

In 1989 the divisional councils responsible for the surrounding area in the Lower Orange River District amalgamated to form the Lower Orange River Regional Council. One of the spin-offs from this was an extension of a water and sanitation service to the seven townships.

Each household received access to water through a yard tap. However, since the infrastructure was connected to the canal, the water remained impure. Each household was also fitted with an outside toilet with water-borne sewerage. This first level of service in these seven areas was completed in 1995.

By 1997, however, in response to requests from communities in the seven towns, the regional council decided to implement a water-purification system in the area. The community in Alheit, for example, appealed to the council for a purified-water service after the canal was drained and corpses were discovered in it. There were also complaints of the occasional outbreak of diarrhoea-related illnesses resulting from the use of contaminated water. Apart from improving the water quality in these areas, the council began to provide electricity and refuse removal as well.

But these services were not delivered for free. Residents were required to pay a flat rate of R72 a month. For these communities, where permanent unemployment is common, and seasonal or casual farm labour the only work, R72 was a high tariff. The result was that many households were unable to pay for the services, and arrears began to accumulate.

Given this socio-economic context, we interviewed officials in the District Council, the Kei-Gariep municipality, as well as a number of ANC councillors, in order to gain an understanding of why local authorities chose to install prepaid meters in a bid to recover costs.

Cost Recovery: The Official Explanation

A document furnished by the District Council contained a description of the infrastructural problems within the existing water service. The document ascribes the need for prepaid meters to wastage and irresponsible management of water by residents. Water is identified as the biggest problem facing the District Council (DC minutes 1998).

This problem was most severe during the summer months in the high-lying areas of the towns, when temperatures frequently reach 40 degrees. Increase in consumption caused an uneven pressure flow of water which in turn caused unequal distribution. In some households, water gushed from the taps, while others received only a trickle or none at all. According to the DC, the purification system is of RDP standard, and so the fault therefore is not in the system, but in the community.

Therefore, in the DC's view, a mechanism to control and or limit water was required. An ordinary water meter would allow the council to employ a policy that correlated the fee to water usage. However, it would supposedly not stop or reduce consumption.

The use of prepaid meters was therefore recommended as an effective tool to a) limit/control the level of water usage while maintaining a high level of hygiene and b) deal with the problem of non-payments (DC, 1998).

The executive committee of the DC on 18 June, 1998 commissioned three of its officials to visit the areas of Hartswater and Vryberg. The aim of the visit was to assess the use of prepaid water meters which had been installed in these areas. On 31 July, 1998, the three officials presented the findings of their visit, which are detailed below.

Description of service in Hartswater and Vryberg

Six-hundred meters were installed in six residential areas in March, 1998. There was a drastic reduction in the overall use of water in these areas. The average use of water per household was between nine and fifteen litres a day, which is less than the 25-litre provision made by the local authority. Community members were spending R20 to R25 a month on water at the rate of R2 per kilolitre. The system was made financially sustainable through the use of the progressive block tariffs (where low consumption is in effect subsidised by higher consumption which earns a higher charge). As a result of the system being connected to a computer, effective water-loss management was possible for both the communal and yard taps. The central computer also produced a record of all water sales made by each individual user that was printed out quite easily. This avoided any fraudulent use of the card or false claims regarding water purchases.

Community Response to the System

There was initial resistance by the community towards the prepaid meters and even "vandalism" of 13 of the meters. However, this changed, and it soon appeared that there was a positive attitude towards both the prepaid meters and the service.

The communities were also positive about the employment opportunities that resulted from this system. A cashier was appointed from the community to manage the administration side of the system. A few people with technical skills were employed to address any such problems if and when they arose. Finally, another person was employed to operate and manage the computer, replace the battery every three weeks, and provide advice and assistance when necessary.

The only concern raised at the end of the visit was that one meter was tampered with in such a way that it continued to allow water to flow through in site of attempts to fix it (DC minutes August 1998).

In light of the outstanding payments in the seven aforementioned towns and the positive account presented to council, a decision was taken in favour of the installation of a prepaid water service. Steps were then initiated and interested parties were encouraged to tender for the contract. The companies that tendered were Bambamanzi and South Atlantic Prepaid Water Meters. South Atlantic won the tender and a process was set up to inform the relevant communities of this decision.

In response to SAMWU, Mr. Mapanka (correspondence, 2000), CEO of the DC, justified the decision to implement a prepaid water metering system by arguing that the council was not only bound by law to deliver services to communities, but also to ensure payment for service. This payment, in conjunction with the subsidy received from government, was the only way to ensure the successful delivery of service. In spite of the ANC government writing off the debt in 1995, the DC was R7 million in debt resulting from non-payments from 1995 to 2000. The expected income from services rendered to communities should have yielded R227 000 a month, but the actual income received was only in the region of R90 000 to R100 000 (Mapanka 2000).

We also interviewed Mr. Mapanka. He alluded to the above and added that this problem was further compounded by the substantial increase of water use by the communities in these towns during summer. Besides increasing the costs incurred by the DC, the rise in demand for water resulted in a crisis in the actual water delivery. According to the DC the separation between water use and water cost resulted in communities mismanaging water as a resource. Prepaid meters yet again rose to the occasion as the most apt tool to attend to this problem as well. In spite of SAMWU's attempts to engage the council on its decision to implement a prepaid metered service to the community, the response from the CEO indicated that council had decided on the issue. On 1 July, 2000, the installation of the prepaid meters in the seven towns began.

Kei-Gariep Municipality (KG)[2]

As a result of the new demarcation process that occurred all around South Africa in November 2000, four of the seven towns found themselves located under a new local authority. The responsibility of the delivery and maintenance of this prepaid meter system now rested with the newly formed Kei-Gariep Municipality.

Despite the recent change in authority, the municipality's view on cost recovery was investigated. Although the Municipal Director, Mr. Andrew Louis Swartz ("Pastoor") spoke favourably of cost recovery, he was aware of the possible problems that such a service could pose for poor communities. He also indicated that he would not have opted for such a system, but they had inherited it, and that neither he nor his council were in a position to remove all the meters. He added that a large amount of money had been put into the system and it would not make financial sense for KG as a municipality to revert to an old system.

For me to discredit a community who are struggling that will be a problem. If it is true that we have inherited a problem then we need to sort it out. So what I am saying is if we inherited a system that is discrediting other people somewhere we need to sort it out – doing so will not only benefit the communities that we serve but us as a municipality as well.

He also mentioned that KG was briefed by the DC about infrastructural problems experienced since installation of the prepaids:

We do recognise that there are infrastructural problems with the prepaid meters. We hope to use some of the areas where the meters are currently as a pilot. From an admin point of view we are aware of what the problems are and we will rectify it immediately.

During the course of the discussion, both Pastoor and Mr. Meaer Clarke, the technical engineer for KG, expressed views that favoured subsidisation of the use of water by the poor from the large farms. Pastoor added that KG was planning to implement free basic water and electricity to the poor,[3] and that the increase in tariffs to farmers would create the funds required for subsidisation.

I was part of a task team that investigated the amount of water and electricity that the municipalities should be subsidising and I believe that we can offer even more water to the people and even more electricity because I believe we are in a position to subsidise poor communities with 12kl of water and with sufficient electricity.

His position was supported by the technical engineer who added that:

Through my experience I have learnt that most people in the poor communities use between 1 and 12kl a month. The problems that we are having with regards to arrears is not with the poor but with those who can afford to pay (Clarke interview, 2001).

At the end of the interview, an attempt was made to assess whether or not Pastoor would remove the prepaid meters should they prove to be detrimental to the well-being of poor communities. He stated that as an individual his hands were tied since communities in the area go through their ANC councillors and that in this instance the councillors were all in favour of the prepaid meters. As director of the municipality, he did not feel he could challenge the voice of the councillors who were the chosen representatives of the communities:

You need to speak to the politicians, the councillors and the mayor; they are the real power behind the decisions. I just carry them out.

---

[2] Prior to the demarcation process that occurred on 1 November, 2000, the seven towns of Lennertsville, Cilliers, Alheit, Raaswater, Topline, Lutzburg and Marchant all fell under the control of the Lower Orange River District Council (DC). As a result of the demarcation process, four of the seven towns were placed under the jurisdiction of the newly amalgamated Kei-Gariep municipality. The four towns were Lennertsville, Alheit, Cilliers and Lutzburg. Raaswater was placed under the newly formed UPNAM municipality and Topline and Grootdrink were placed under the newly formed Kakamas Municipalities.

[3] Part of the ANC local government election campaign promises was a monthly free lifeline of 6 000 litres of water and 50kWh of electricity per household. The policy was to be implemented as from 1 July 2001.

The ANC Councillors

Since its councillors were elected in most of these townships we also wanted to interview ANC leaders.

Unfortunately, only one ANC councillor, Gina Cloete, was prepared to grant an interview.[4] At the time, she was quite active in, and familiar with, the developments around the prepaid water service in the area. This is how she understood the problem:

> The prepaid meters were implemented in the areas in 2000 and we as councillors do not have a complete understanding of how the system currently operates. But we feel that it is a good thing as it teaches the community to be responsible and to appreciate the fact that water has now been made available to it. If the entire area has the meters it will be a good thing. Our only problem is the electricity, but this is an inherited problem from the previous council. We feel that it is important to provide services for those who were previously disadvantaged under apartheid and we will not ask for that for the farmers. Since July this area is now under a new authority. There are problems in these areas with the existing infrastructure. We are currently investigating and meeting with councillors in the area and trying to assess what the needs are of the communities and how they can best be addressed. We are also looking into the possibilities of using or accessing other sources of income for the provision of these services.

Community Response

The next section of this paper is a sampling of the Lennertsville community's response to the implementation of prepaid water meters. While this may only be the voice of one small community, we think its members' experience and reflections are important for all those involved in debates and struggles around prepaid meters.

Background on Lennertsville

Lennertsville is a small, predominantly coloured township, with 232 plots and an informal settlement situated on its outskirts. Like the other six towns in our research, it was earmarked for the installation of a prepaid water service. This service was to replace the flat-rate system introduced in 1995. According to the documents furnished by the District Council who was responsible for the service at the time, the percentage of payments for the period Oct 1999 to February 2000 were:

	Oct	Nov	Dec	Jan	Feb
Number of households paying	105	92	65	65	65
% of households paying	45%	40%	28%	28%	28%
Total households = 232; Average payment: 34%					

As a result of the high level of arrears, the installation of the prepaid system began in early February 2001 in Lennertsville. By 21 February, 233 prepaid meters were installed.

According to the residents interviewed, prior to 1994, Lennertsville had non-purified water delivered via yard tap. In 2000, this service was improved by the installation of a simple purification system which was meant to service the 233 households in the area. The

---

[4] Those who refused were: Mr. Roy Orlyn (Lennertsville), Mr. Barry Andrews (Alheit), and Mr. H. Basson (Marchant, Lutsburg and Cilliethe). Interviews with Lennertsville residents are from the focus group conducted on 11 July 2001. Quotes are anonymous.

improvement in the service had an accompanying fee increase from R18 to R23. This was a monthly flat rate, payable by each household.

According to one resident:

> Before 1994 we had communal taps. From 1990 to 1992 we had yard taps. The cost was first R12, then R18, then R21, and then R23 just for water. In 1998 we were charged R71 for all the services: this was a monthly flat rate. Our water was impure up until last year. People in the community are poor and therefore could not afford to pay these rates. Most people are in arrears. We cannot keep up with arrears of R8 000 or more. My husband earns R150 so I cannot afford to pay. I went to explain my situation to them and so they left me. They have not cut off my services.

> We never paid for water. Some people say we did but we never. When we eventually were made to pay we paid R18 and that was for our yard tap. The council gave each house a tap in its yard for water. In 2000 they gave us clean water. The water was purified in that tank there and we had a water "weegskaal" or "water pompie" to check the water and put in the chemicals. In Lennertsville the water weegskaal is Fanie Mowers.

According to the interviews, the community was relatively pleased with the improvement in the service in spite of the increase. In the words of one of the residents: "it's much better than walking to the canal and carting buckets of water". Although most of the interviewees shared this sentiment, some residents raised some of the problems related to the service. For example, the reservoirs were not large enough. They only had a 26kl capacity.

Residents stated that for 233 households and approximately 300 families this was fine in winter. In summer, however, the temperature soars to 40 degrees and the water is not enough. When empty, each reservoir or dam takes almost an entire day to refill.

> We had this problem last year December [2000]. We complained to Mr. Roy Orlyn but he did nothing. Eventually he landed up running around and trucks had to come and bring us water. The tank did not have enough water for us. It is too hot in summer and we need more water. (Anonymous resident, interview, 2001).

Water pressure was another problem. Houses close to the tank receive water first and with high pressure, whilst those further away have very little pressure.

According to interviewees, contamination of the water was a consequence of some pranksters in the community. It was soon put to a stop by the council.

> When the council put in the tank they did not cover it and one day not too long after the tank was brought here, we started to get sick and had tummy problems. The water had a funny smell and was stinking. Eventually someone complained to the council and they came to put a cover on the dam. Some kids in the community thought they were funny and threw something in the water, but we no longer have this problem. (Anonymous resident, interview, 2001).

According to residents, this system worked well, and the community was quite content. But in November 1999, representatives of the District Council, ANC councillors, and Mark Reineke from South Atlantic Prepaid Water Meters addressed the community. Community members were informed of the DC's decision to replace the flat-rate yard tap with prepaid meters. According to the minutes of the meeting, Mr. Lategan addressed the community on behalf of the DC. He expressed the motivation for the prepaid meters:

> The prepaid meter will be able to assist the community to pay for their arrears, for example, if you buy water for R30, R5 will go towards your arrears. You will be able to conserve water and you will only pay for the water that you use. There will no longer be any account sent to people and the tariff for the refuse removals will be included in the overall cost and will be deducted through the prepaid system. The hours of work for office administrators will change. For those who are poor and earn below R800, there are indigent forms that need to be filled out. It is important that the owner of the house completes the form (L.O.D.C Minutes November 1999).

The interviewees from the community presented a somewhat different account. One resident described the community meeting as follows:

When we got to the meeting our ANC councillor was there, someone from the DC and this guy from Cape Town, a white guy; I think his name was Mark. Ja, he spoke to us and told us that the meters are good because it will stop this problem that we have in the community. People used to steal each other's water. (Interview, 2001).

The community felt that the problem of "water theft" was of the council's own making. Before speaking directly about theft, residents emphasised the issue of affordability:

The council tried to get us to pay for the services and when we cannot pay they cut off our water – this has been happening for the past four years.

When the council started to cut off people's water in the community, that's when the problem started. As you can see we are a poor community; most people are unemployed. It is very difficult to find work and those who do have work pay very little. Also they work on the farms so the work is seasonal. If the farmer does not have work for you then you are like the rest of us – unemployed.

Only a few people here have permanent work. So you see, to pay for water or the R72 a month which is for water, electricity, refuse and our rates, is too much. Most of us cannot afford to pay and we have not been paying for years now. All of us in the community are in arrears, not a hundred rands but thousands, I owe R8 000, that lady over there owes R12 000, some people owe a bit less. But we are all poor so we cannot afford to pay.

This view was shared by yet another resident who added:

As she was explaining, because we are so poor we cannot pay and we have arrears. The council began to cut off our water to force us to pay. Some people went to the council and tried to make an arrangement and got their water reconnected but you need to pay R250 first. If you don't pay they cut you.

One resident then narrated an incident that had occurred in the community:

There is a woman in the community who was far behind with her payments. The water pompie went to close her tap but she refused to allow him into her yard. He then went to the police who then forced her to give in. As soon as her tap was closed she had another tap put in for another year until they found out. She does not have an income and her husband does not work – sometimes she has to smuggle here and there just as long as she can keep her children alive and she will do whatever is necessary to provide water for them. The money that she has goes towards the food and clothes and keeping a roof over their heads – so she refuses to pay a reconnection fee. They do not have an answer for her when she explains her problem. There is no answer – her situation is desperate.

Residents then explained how cutoffs by the DC had led to the problem of "water theft" in the community:

Ja, things were bad, like they are explaining some people could afford to pay for water and others could not. And that's where the problem came. Before the cutoff people used to share and used to be friendly towards each other, but since the cutoff started there have been many fights and neighbours who were friends for years don't talk and curse and used to swear each other because of water. Those who are paying or who have water no longer gave water to those who did not have because they have to pay for that person's water as well. We can barely afford to pay for our own. You see the problem.

Many interviewees also highlighted conflicts that began to emerge within communities as a result of the water cutoffs:

We used to help each other before but we now have to pay for the water and they cannot help me pay so I cannot give them. Other times it results in an argument in the community so the council told us not to give each other water. It is still causing problems in the community amongst neighbours – people fighting with each other. So what happens is when you go to town or you go to sleep people come and steal water.

> *Our taps are outside, and you cannot guard your tap 24 hours a day. Then at the end of the month the council shows you a water bill that is sky high and you don't understand. You are too scared to use the water and yet you owe so much.*

This conflict, along with other problems, led to a certain enthusiasm amongst community members for the installation of prepaid meters.

> *This became a big problem for the council and for us in the community too and when we used to complain, the council used to encourage us not to give the other people water. I think they realise how much of a problem it was becoming; that is why they brought this Mark guy to explain how the prepaid meters will put an end to the theft of water.*

> *We were very happy to hear this, because there was so much fighting between the neighbours already. He told us that the meter would be inside the house and the section for the card outside. He said the card would act like a key. When you put the card into the unit water will flow from the tap, and when you pull out the card the tap will shut off. No-one can get water from your tap and no-one can use their card in your unit. He explained that because the meter was attached to a computer it would be able to deduct about 10 per cent of what we pay for water towards our arrears, so we would be paying for water and arrears at the same time. We were also told that the water would be much cheaper than the R23 that we are paying and that we will be able to save.*

> *You know we were so happy to hear this that everyone in the hall shouted "Viva pre-paids, Viva!".*

> *The community accepted the prepaid meters since we could control our water.*

According to both the minutes of this meeting and the consent forms filled out, all 233 households registered and signed in favour of the installation of the prepaid water metered system in Lennertsville. The community seemed to have embraced not only the prepaid system but that they were responsible for their own access to water. Many expressed the need to work carefully with the water rather than interrogate the fact that the amount they could afford would not sustain their needs.

After a period of actually using the system, only a few people maintained a positive perspective. Their views highlighted the fact that the system generally ran smoothly, after a few obstacles at the outset:

> *Initially many of us had problems with our cards. When you bought R10 of water the deduction on the R10 was so much that you hardly had any water. I was not the only one; there were so many people who had this problem so we had to go to the municipality to get another card. They gave me a new one so now when I buy R10 it does not deduct so much and in fact I can get a lot of use out of the R10 water if I work nicely with my water.*

> *I don't have a garden, just a small creeper, so I wet it here and then I fill my drum with water and then I have my bath which I fill to do my washing and another bath for bathing – and so on. So I work carefully with the water. I don't think I will manage in summer though. The children get very hot and they want to bath and play in the water to cool down. It gets very hot here in summer and I don't think I will be able to manage with R10 water. I might have to use more. I use R10 every second week but I will never be able to do that in summer. We are four in my family but in summer R10 will not be enough, plus there are three people that are renting a room from me who need to also use that water.*

> *The only problems were infrastructural problems – it lasted a few weeks – three weeks but then everything was sorted out. I was trained to do the maintenance of the meters. My husband and I were both trained and we were paid.*

> *We never had water meters. Before the prepaids we paid a flat rate. The prepaid is a good system because before the meters they used to come and close your water if you*

had arrears and then you were cutoff. Now you have a prepaid meter and it deducts arrears as well so they won't come and cut you off.

Such positive views, however, were a distinct minority. Most of the residents interviewed expressed frustration and confusion. Their inability to pay for water coupled with the constant infrastructural problems made access to water almost impossible.

Here is how one resident described her experience:

I bought R10 of water but I never got R10 water, I just got R4 and my slip did not show me R10 of water. For four people, two adults and two children, I bought water on Monday, and the meter shows me four. I don't know what it is, four litres, kilolitres, now it is showing four. I don't know how it got to that; I never used so much.

Another resident said:

I used to pay R23 for water but I cannot afford to pay this every week – There are 10 people in this house and when I buy water for R10 this week I go and buy water again – I have to fill my 25l drum and I have to be careful. When the drum is empty I just fill it again, and if I don't have money I have to stay without. Sometimes I use the emergency water⁵ – R250 a month is all that I get so I am struggling to keep up. My husband will be a pensioner soon and will have to stop working. When he stops working it will be difficult. All the expenses are too much for us. I only use the emergency water once. I try and save water for emergencies.

One resident explained how her misunderstanding of the emergency water system, coupled with infrastructural problems, cut her off from water for three days:

Everyone is using the emergency water, but not all of us have access to emergency water. I sat without water for three days and then I went to the office and told them to come and take out this meter. They did and now I have emergency water. If the box is on 000 then there are some who are fortunate and others who are not so fortunate to get the water.

Another highlighted how problems with the cards had the same result:

If you use 3kl for the day then the box switches off automatically – it only goes on again at midnight the next day. That is for all of us; you cannot use more than 300 litres a day whether you have money on the card or not. This was in the beginning, then all our cards were taken and returned and since then this no longer happens.

Residents also complained about the payment office and the administrative difficulties related to this system:

We have a problem with the office as well – it closes at five in the evening and if you are late you cannot get water. It is closed from 5pm on Friday and most of us have to go without water for the entire weekend and there are many of us who have been forced to do this.

The interviews also indicated quite strongly that daily access to drinking water had fast become a struggle for this community:

There are many incidents of people in the community who don't have money to buy water. There are many who beg for water even though people shout at you and insult you; you just take the water and keep quiet. Other people when they are drunk they go and beg for water and then they get told you cannot buy water but you can afford to get drunk. Ja, we are begging for the water because of the prepaids but we are the ones who said "Viva" for the prepaids. We said viva because we thought it was a good system but we were not informed properly.

If I don't have water then I must go and borrow money or beg for water. But eventually if we don't have money for water I will take my bucket and walk down to the river and

---

⁵ The notion of emergency water was introduced as a tide-over measure in case of emergencies. The amount allocated for emergency water was three litres. According to the treasurer at the DC an emergency was defined as a water cutoff which resulted from people either forgetting to buy credit, not monitoring their water use effectively, or the cash office being closed. Emergency water was also only made available once a month.

fetch water like we did before the taps. I will have to pull out the plants and forget about my garden and as for the toilet, well, I will have to find a way around that one.

Many of the interviewees also expressed a sense of despondence with, and disappointment in, their ANC councillor Mr. Orlyn, whom many felt did not guide them enough or provide them with enough information to take a decision around the prepaids.

He is being blamed by the community for the problems because he does not talk. He just keeps quiet. He does not explain to us what is happening or what we need to know. He just keeps quiet. He does not call meetings or gatherings to explain issues. We in Lennertsville are a community but our councillor is not accountable to us. He owes us an explanation. All we know is that two women came to us and made us fill out forms and asked us about our income and how many people are living in the house. This was done by the Kei-Gariep Municipality.

There were forms that we had to fill out – now recently but we did not get an explanation as to how or why we are filling in the forms – the councillor was involved but when we ask him what is happening he does not provide us with an answer.

We use the water mainly for our yards and gardens and toilets and general household use – washing machines, animals, children. Everyone in the community filled out an indigent form but we are currently not receiving free water.

This section concludes with voices in the community that capture the resentment, frustration and apathy felt by this community as its right to access water was prevented by a prepaid system.

There were many problems with the prepaid. There was an incident of a woman in the community who almost stabbed someone because he came to install the prepaid meter. There were not too many of this kind of incident – most people accepted the fact that there was a decision in the meeting and there was not much that could be do about the prepaids now. So we just accepted it; there was no real choice.

There are a lot of people who have been fighting against the prepaid meters – they had to bring the police – that woman and her husband at that house, they almost stabbed the person who put in the meter.

The problem is that the day of the meeting everyone either agreed or kept quiet regarding the prepaids but when they came to put in the meters that is when the problem started. The community does not want the prepaid meters – we don't want the prepaid. We want the taps.

We are struggling for 10 years to get water and our struggle is not over and now we cannot go to the boer in the office and say he has cut us off because with the prepaids we have cut ourselves off.

Assessment of Cost Recovery

Analysis of the prepaid meters

The use of prepaid meters in poor communities around South Africa is fast becoming commonplace. I have researched prepaid meters in Hermanus (Western Cape) and in KwaZulu-Natal[6] but I found the Northern Cape situation in July 2001 to be the most disconcerting.

As a result of their apartheid history, the Lennertsville community, did not seem to perceive their struggle to access clean water as unusual. But what makes this situation so alarming is the way in which the DC sold the concept of the prepaid meters to this community. Instead of conducting an investigation to uncover the root of the problem of non-payment, the DC labelled the community "defaulters" and subjected them to a prepaid water service.

---

[6] For details of the research for Hermanus see Deedat, Pape and Qotole, (2001); for KwaZulu-Natal see Chapter 4 in this volume.

What made matters worse was how the DC then proceeded to manipulate the social upheaval caused by cutoffs in these communities as a basis for the installation of the prepaid system. As explained in an earlier section, the first measure of cost recovery applied by the DC was water cutoffs. To the DC's dismay, this action did not have the desired response, i.e. an increase in payment levels, but rather resulted in so-called "water theft" and a breakdown in social relations within communities. This schism was further exacerbated by the DC encouraging members of the community who had access to water to refuse to give any to those who were cutoff.

The culmination of this division played itself out during the community meetings wherein the prepaid meter service was proposed. Instead of sketching the realities that would confront the poor using a prepaid service, the DC proclaimed that a prepaid meter would put an end to water theft. It also was alleged to provide a solution for those who found their arrears figures intimidating. Ten per cent of their monthly water bill was to be deducted and paid towards their arrears. The presentation of this to a community with a poor literacy level was both deceiving and unethical.

The average monthly water bill of a household is in the region of R30. Ten per cent of this is R3. The arrears are in the region of R4 000 to R12 000, with interest accumulating. A deduction of R3 per month would only cover a fraction of the interest on the arrears. Such a system would clearly lead to an increase, not a decrease, in residents' debt.

The communities were also told that only their card regulated the use of water and no-one could use their water source or tap. What was not emphasised was that they needed credit on that card to access the water, and that without credit they would cut themselves off from the service.

In addition, residents were apparently made false promises about the costs of water under the prepaid system. Many interviewees said they were told that they would pay much less than the previous R23-a-month flat rate and would get more water than they did before. As we have noted some residents were so impressed by the prepaid system at first that they even shouted "Viva prepaids, viva". But after four months of usage, the scenario had changed. Many residents expresssed the view that both the DC and their councillors had misled them.[7]

While many of the interviewees had strong criticisms of their water service, there was no talk of organising around the issue. Community-based organisation in these areas was/is non-existent.

The irony of it all is that the DC can wipe its hands clean as it attends to new responsibilities under the new demarcation. In the meanwhile the Kei-Gariep municipality and the communities of the four towns must continue to endure the consequences of the prepaid system.

In closing, I would like to state how disillusioning it is to see local authorities perpetuating the inequalities of the apartheid regime against communities who over the past 45 years, were already subjected to third-class services on racial grounds.

The goal has become balanced budgets rather than improving the lives of the citizens they serve. In their quest to recover costs, councillors and officials go against the grain of the equality and redress enshrined in the Constitution of South Africa. These are rights which are given to every South African regardless of class, race or gender. But in communities like those researched here, these rights are being eroded with every tick of the prepaid meter.

---

[7] In late 2001 the KG council implemented the free basic water policy in these communities. This was a campaign promise by the ANC and other political parties during the December 2000 local government elections.[7] The lifeline was supposed to make 6kl of water available free to each household every month. At the time of this research the free water had not been implemented.

Bibliography

Deedat, H., Pape, J. and Qotole, M. (2001). "Block Tariffs or Blocked Access?" The Greater Hermanus Water Conservation Programme, Municipal Services Project Occasional Paper Series 5, Cape Town.

Documents of the Lower Orange River District Council in chronological order:

No Dates:

Beskrywing van Probleme: Water voorsiening

August 1998: *Gemeenskapdienste:- terugvoering: Afbetaalde Water meters: besoek aan Hartswater.*

October 1998: *Aanstelling vir ondersoek aan meer ekonomiese dienslewering.*

October 1999: 3.5: Installering van voorafbetaaldemeters.

October 1999: Minutes of the District Council on the 15/10, p. 2.

November 1999: Minutes of the District Council on the 18/11, p. 3.

November 1999: *Raadslede betrokke by bestuurstelsel van prepaid meters.*

1999/2000: Tender NR. 8: *Voorafbetaaldewatermetersstelsels en meters. Projek spesifikasie*, pp. 13–21.

1999/2000: Tender NR. 8: *Verskaffing en of instaleering van.*

December 1999: *Menings van erfeienaars oor die voorafbetaaldewatermeters.*

December 1999: *Vergadering: Voorafbetaaldewatermeters.*

February 2000 -*Betaalpresentasie: Oktober 1999 - Februarie 2000.*

March 2000: Minutes: *Notule van vergadering gehou in verband oor prepaid/Tenderkommittee wat gehou was op 23/3, pp.–2.*

July 2000: *Kennisgewing van vergadering: Installeering van voorafbetaaldewatermeters. Brief aan SAMWU Northern Cape President, Mr. Mdhululi.*

April 2000: Minutes: *Notule: Spesialeraads vergadering 3/4, p.2.*

April 2000: *Voorafbetaaldewatermeters, 14 April, verslag oor brief met SAMWU.*

May 2000: *Installering van voorafbetaaldewatermeters in die Benede Oranje Distriksraad Dorpies, brief aan SAMWU vir die aandag van Steve Siloane.*

SAMWU Correspondence documents:

February 2000, letter to Mr. Mdhululi, from SAMWU head-office, media officer Anna Weekes.

Mapanka April 2000: Letter to the CEO of the Benede Oranje Distriksraad, Mr. Mapanka, from SAMWU Northern Cape, Steve Siloane.

Seloane February 2001, Letter to SAMWU head-office, attention of Lance Veotte, from SAMWU Northern Cape, Steve Seloane.

Interviews

Alheit Community, 7 July, 2001
Pastoor Swartz, 10 July, 2001
Gina Cloete, 10 July, 2001
Mr. Mapanka, 11 July, 2001
Mr. Meaer Clarke, 7 July, 2001

Lennertsville Group Interviews

6 July
Groups 1 (4 people)
Group 2 (6 people)

9 July
Group 3 (8 people)
Group 4 (5 people)
Group 5 (4 people)

11 July
Group 6 (4 people)
Group 7 (6 people)

12 July
Group 8 (5 people)
Group 9 (8 people)
Group 10 (4 people)

People and Service Delivery

The RDP integrates growth, development, reconstruction and redistribution into a unified programme. The key to this link is an infrastructural programme that will provide access to modern and effective services like electricity, water, telecommunications, transport, health, education and training for our people. This programme will both meet basic needs and open up previously suppressed areas. In turn this will lead to an increased output in all sectors of the economy, and by modernising our infrastructure and human resource development, we will also enhance export capacity. Success in linking reconstruction and development is essential if we are to achieve peace and security for all.

Reconstruction and Development Programme (1994, 6)

8

The Bell Tolls for Thee
Cost Recovery, Cutoffs, and the Affordability of Municipal Services in South Africa
by David A. McDonald

The case studies presented thus far in this book provide detailed, qualitative information on people's experiences with cost recovery and municipal services. The studies are based on ethnographic research methods with open-ended questionnaires and contextual analysis of people's life histories.

Rich as they are in detail, these case studies are necessarily limited in their ability to speak to the wider national experience on a given subject matter. This chapter, therefore, looks at the results of a national survey on South African attitudes towards, and experiences with, cost recovery. This random, stratified sample of 2 530 people, conducted in July 2001, is representative of the entire South African population over the age of 18 years and offers the first-ever glimpse into the national experience with cost recovery and service cutoffs.[1] Designed and implemented in collaboration with the Human Sciences Research Council (HSRC) as part of its annual public-opinion survey, the questionnaire covered a wide range of service delivery issues as they relate to cost-recovery: attitudes towards service costs, free services and block tariffs; access to services; experiences with service arrears, service cutoffs, evictions and other legal actions for non-payment; ability to pay for services; and coping strategies if services are cut.

---

[1] The Department of Constitutional Development (now the Department of Provincial and Local Government) ran a series of questionnaires with local authorities from late-1995 to mid-1998 on issues of cost recovery rates, service cutoffs and debt levels, but these surveys relied entirely on official local-government statistics. Moreover, these statistics were highly unreliable because of the fragmented nature of local government at the time, and the fact that by June 1998 only 76 per cent of municipalities had bothered to file their reports (DCD 1998). The only other national survey of this nature was conducted by the Helen Suzman Foundation (Johnson 1999), but this was focused primarily on urban/town areas and was biased in terms of sampling towards the Gauteng area (where it was deemed non-payment for services was highest). Most importantly, the survey by the Helen Suzman Foundation did not benefit from any of the detailed case-study research material used to cross-evaluate our survey results.

The results of this national survey[2] allow us to compare the case studies with the larger country-wide situation. There is a basic congruence in the findings of the two. Both suggest that cost recovery on municipal services imposes enormous hardships on low-income families, contributes to massive numbers of service cutoffs and evictions, and jeopardises the potential for millions of low-income families to lead healthy and productive lives.

It is estimated that close to 10 million South Africans have had their water cut off for non-payment of service bills, with the same number having experienced an electricity cutoff. Approximately two million people have been evicted from their homes for the same reason. And although it is low-income African households that bear the brunt of these service cutoffs, lower-middle-income families are also being affected, with the highest proportion of cutoffs (within a given income bracket) taking place in households that earn between R2 001 and R3 000 per month. It should be noted that this survey was conducted just as free water and electricity policies were being introduced in South Africa (July 2001). Extensive public education campaigns combined with considerable media attention contributed to widespread public knowledge of these free service policies, but few respondents would have experienced the impact of them at the time of their interview. It is possible, therefore, that attitudes towards service affordability and cost recovery have changed since that time and that fewer households are having their water and electricity cut off for non-payment (because of the free units of service).[3]

Access to Services

At the time of the first democratic elections in South Africa in 1994, it was estimated that 12 million South Africans did not have access to clean drinking water, and 21 million people did not have adequate sanitation (ANC 1994, 28). Ten per cent of the population did not have access to a toilet of any kind, a further one-third of South Africans had to rely on pit latrines, and 14 per cent of South Africans had no form of refuse removal (RSA 1995, 10). Over 20 million people did not have access to electricity (RSA 1998, 21).

Since then, there have been major expansions of service infrastructure, particularly in the areas of water and electricity. As of February 2002, the South African government claims to have provided seven million additional people with "access to clean, running water" and to have connected 3.5 million additional people to the electricity grid (Mbeki, *Cape Argus* 9 February, 2002).

Nevertheless, more than six million South Africans are still without access to piped water (RSA 2001), and four million people (or 37 per cent of all households) still do not have access

---

[2] The following methodology notes accompany the HSRC'S National Opinion Survey in July 2001, from which the questions used in this chapter were taken: "The Human Sciences Research Council (HSRC) has for several years been conducting regular national surveys on public opinion. Topics that have been investigated included satisfaction with service delivery, perceived national priorities, political preferences and the economy. The survey instrument comprised a questionnaire containing questions on a variety of themes. It was divided into different topics and the duration of interviews of respondents was between 60 and 90 minutes. A sample of 2 704 respondents was selected throughout South Africa in clusters of eight households situated in 338 Primary Sampling Units (PSUs)/enumerator areas (EAs) as determined from the 1996 census. In order to ensure adequate representation in the sample from each province and from each of the four dominant population groups, the sample was explicitly stratified by province and urban/rural location. This added up to 18 strata (see below). Disproportional samples were drawn from less populated provinces such as the Northern Cape, Free State, Mpumalanga and North West.

Number of PSUs/EAs per province and strata.

	EC	FS	GT	KZN	MPL	NC	NP	NW	WC
URBAN	14	21	56	24	12	21	4	11	29
RURAL	25	9	2	32	18	9	28	19	4
TOTAL	39	30	58	56	30	30	32	30	33

The realised sample [2 530] was only slightly less than the intended 2 704. In terms of province and population group, the spread was sufficiently wide to facilitate statistical generalisations about opinions prevailing within each province and amongst persons of each of the four main population groups. Each case was then weighted so that the resultant weighted data set would approximate the distribution of the population of South Africa in terms of population group, province, gender and educational qualification."

[3] There are fundamental problems in the way in which free services have been conceptualised and implemented in the country (see Chapter 1 for a detailed discussion). Moreover, many households are not receiving free blocks of water and electricity because of their payment arrears, and there are widespread reports of continuing cutoffs of water and electricity despite the free services policy.

to electricity (RSA 2002b). These figures are consistent with our own survey findings (Table 8.1). Central government has committed itself to providing access to "basic supplies" of water and electricity to all of these remaining households by 2008 and 2012 respectively,[4] but the bulk of the remaining water and electricity connections will be in difficult-to-access rural areas where capital and operating costs per unit are significantly higher than urban areas because of lower population densities and longer distances from water and electricity sources. These service extensions will therefore take longer to complete, will be significantly more costly to install, and could result in substantially higher per-unit costs for consumers should direct cost-recovery principles be applied.

Table 8.1: Access to water and electricity	
Q: How do you get your drinking water? (%)	
Piped – internal with meter	34
Piped – internal with prepaid meter	4
Piped – yard tap with meter	13
Piped – yard tap with prepaid meter	2
Piped – yard tap with no meter	9
Piped – free communal tap	12
Piped – paid-for communal tap	2
Borehole/well	10
Rainwater tank	2
Flowing river/stream	6
Dam	4
Stagnant pond	2
Other (specify)	2
Q: Do you have access to electricity in your household? (%)	
In-house meter	31
In-house prepaid meter	35
Connected to other source which I pay for (e.g. connected to neighbour's line and paying neighbour)	1
Connected to other source which I do not pay for (e.g. connected to neighbour's line and not paying)	1
Illegal connection (e.g. connected to ESKOM line)	2
Generator/battery	–
Other	1
No access to electricity	28
Uncertain/Don't know	1
N = 2520, 2515	
Note: Figures rounded off to the nearest per cent and therefore may not add to 100 per cent. A dash (–) represents a figure greater than zero and less than 0.5 per cent.	

[4] Basic Water Provision for All by 2008: Kasrils, Sapa press release, 12 February, 2002; Electrification Plan "Will Need Huge Subsidies", *Business Day* 7 March, 2002.

It is in the area of sanitation and refuse collection that the service delivery record is most wanting. Our survey demonstrates that only half of the country's population has access to flush toilets, many of which are outside of the house and/or shared with many other families,[5] while close to a third of South Africans continue to use ordinary pit latrines and chemical toilets which are often unsanitary, and always unpleasant (Table 8.2). A full 10 per cent of respondents do not have access to any form of toilet, while five per cent are forced to use the bucket toilet – a degrading and unhealthy system.

With regards to waste management, 42 per cent of respondents in the survey do not have access to any form of refuse collection (with most of these being in rural areas), while close to 10 per cent still rely on communal skips.

Table 8.2: Access to sanitation and refuse collection	
Q: What type of toilet does this household use? (%)	
Flush	50
Improved or VIP pit latrine	2
Ordinary pit latrine	31
Bucket toilet	5
Chemical toilet	1
No toilet access	10
Other (specify)	2
Q: Does your household have refuse collection? (%)	
Curbside collection	43
Communal skip (within 100 metres of household)	8
Communal skip (more than 100 metres from household)	1
Other (specify)	1
No refuse collection service	42
Uncertain/Don't know	5
N = 2517, 2472	

Affordability of Services

Service costs vary dramatically across the country, and even within municipalities. But for those who have service infrastructure and who receive regular bills, the median total cost per month for water, electricity, sewerage, and refuse removal ranges from R224 to R400 (Table 8.3).

Table 8.3: Monthly Costs of Services								
Q: Approximately how much does your household pay per month for each of the following services that you have access to? (%)								
Service	Does not pay	R0–R20	R21–R50	R51–R100	R101–R150	R151–R200	R200+	Uncertain/Don't know
Water	24	11	12	14	11	7	11	10
Electricity	5	11	15	16	14	12	21	6
Water-borne sewerage	14	8	23	13	5	3	3	32
Refuse removal	13	13	24	12	4	2	2	30
N = 2406, 2403, 2330, 2330								

These figures are noteworthy for at least two reasons. First, they indicate an enormous cost burden for low-income households. With 57 per cent of the sample earning less than R1 000 per month in household income, even the lower figure of R224 per month for services is close to a quarter of household income and suggests considerable pressure on the household budget. For many poor households with extended families, the actual service charges are significantly

---

[5] See Ramphele (1993) for a detailed discussion on this issue.

higher than the national median, forcing difficult choices between the use of municipal services and essentials like food and clothing. For example, 16 per cent of respondents with household incomes of R751 to R1 000 per month are spending more than R200 a month on electricity alone.

The second notable feature of these costs is how relatively cheap these services are for upper-income families – a group composed overwhelmingly of white urbanites who have long benefited from heavily subsidised municipal services (Ahmad 1995). For this relatively small but economically powerful group, the payment of municipal services is simply not a major budgetary concern (despite complaints about prices being too high). Nor are these upper-income groups being asked to pay prices that are out of line with international practice. In fact, according to ESKOM (*Mail & Guardian* 15–21 March, 2002), South Africans enjoy "virtually the lowest-cost energy available anywhere in the world", with average electricity prices having decreased by 15 per cent in real terms between 1994 and 2001 (ESKOM 2001). South Africans also pay considerably less for water than many countries – less than a third of the average price per litre in the UK, for example.[6]

Also worth noting are the high numbers of households that do not know what they pay for sewerage and refuse removal. The costs of these services are included in the general rates bill (as opposed to direct tariffs), and are therefore not easily separated from municipal taxes. Charging tariffs for these services could raise these costs considerably as cross-subsidisation potentials from the general rates base are reduced. In the City of Cape Town, for example, it has been estimated that the price of water and sanitation services could increase by 30 to 50 per cent if these two services are combined into a single, ringfenced, tariff-based "business unit" separated from other service sectors in the city (McDonald and Smith 2002, 48).

Respondents were asked whether they thought the price they paid for services received was "too high", "too low" or "about right". Responses were largely split between "too high" and "about right", with very few saying that prices were "too low". Water and electricity topped the list of services in the "too high" category, with 47 and 43 per cent of respondents indicating these opinions respectively (Table 8.4).

Table 8.4: Perception of service prices				
Q: In your opinion, is the price you pay each month for the following services too high, too low, or about right for what you receive? (%)				
	Too high	Too low	About right	Uncertain/ Don't know
Water	47	6	36	11
Electricity	43	6	45	6
Water-borne sewerage	30	4	42	24
Refuse removal	28	5	45	22
N = 1579, 1758, 1133, 1216				

A breakdown of these responses by income, race and location (rural/urban) provides some interesting insights (Table 8.5). Only water is shown in the table for space reasons but it is representative of responses for electricity and other services as well.

Not surprisingly, it was respondents from low-income households who were most likely to say that the price for municipal water is too high, but significant numbers of respondents from middle- and upper-income households felt the same way, including a third of those respondents with household incomes of more than R20 000 per month.

Ironically, it was the most marginalised group (African, rural and low-income) who were the most likely to say that prices for water were *too low*. Why this would be so is unclear. These are the respondents who are least able to afford services while at the same time being the most likely to have to pay higher per-unit costs for the services they do receive, because of poor economies of scale, distances from service sources, and the legacies of apartheid-era pricing biases.

---

[6] According to the International Water Resources Association (IWRA 2001), the average water price in South Africa is US$0,34 per kilolitre compared to US$0.37 in Canada, US$0,52 in the United States, and US$1,11 in the United Kingdom.

Q: In your opinion, is the price you pay each month for water too high, too low, or about right for what you receive? (%)

Household income	Too high	Too low	About right	Uncertain/ Don't know
No income	53	14	27	7
R1–R500	52	6	30	12
R501–R750	40	8	38	14
R751–R1 000	56	5	25	14
R1 001–R1 500	53	4	35	8
R1 501–R2 000	59	3	32	6
R2 001–R3 000	51	2	4	6
R3 001–R5 000	36	2	52	10
R5 001–R7 500	41	4	47	8
R7 501–R10 000	48	0	46	5
R10 001–R15 000	45	6	47	2
R15 001–R20 000	36	0	41	23
R20 001–R30 000	33	0	67	0
R30 000 +	32	0	55	13
Race				
African	46	9	32	13
Coloured	52	1	42	5
Asian	69	0	29	1
White	42	0	51	8
Rural/urban				
Rural	41	10	36	13
Urban	49	6	32	12
Metropolitan	51	2	39	8
N = 1579				

Respondents were also asked how easy or difficult it was for them to pay for services received (Table 8.6). A slight majority (53 per cent) were able to pay for their services fairly easily", but 17 per cent said they could only pay for services if they "cut back on other essential goods like food and clothing", and close to one-fifth (18 per cent) of all respondents said that they "cannot afford to pay for these services no matter how hard [they] try" (the remaining 12 per cent were "unsure").

In other words, for every one million adults who receive bills for basic municipal services, 170 000 can pay for these services only if they cut back on other essential goods like food and clothing, and an additional 180 000 are unable to pay the full cost of their services "no matter how hard [they] try".

It is conceivable that some respondents said they could not pay for services "no matter hard they try" because they were concerned that the data might be used against them, but all precautions were taken to assure respondents of confidentiality by professional fieldworkers. More importantly, the case study research for this book and elsewhere (e.g. Desai 2001, Fiil-Flynn 2001) overwhelmingly supports the argument that affordability is the biggest concern when it comes to the payment of service bills. With 57 per cent of the sample earning less than R1 000 per month in household income, it is not difficult to imagine the scale of the problem. Johnson (1999) takes a very different view on this, as we shall see below, but his conclusions are based on a much narrower set of empirical data and what would appear to be a pre-determined commitment to the "culture of non-payment" thesis.

Table 8.6: Ability to pay for services	
Q: How easy or difficult is it for you to pay for the services that you have in terms of the total budget of your household? (%)	
I can afford to pay for these services very easily without really worrying about the cost	16
I can afford to pay for these services but it requires some budgeting	37
I can pay for these services only if I cut back on other essential goods like food and clothing	17
I cannot afford to pay for these services no matter how hard I try	18
Not sure	12
N = 1809	

Not surprisingly, it is those with the lowest household income that say they find it the hardest to pay, with 25 per cent of respondents living in households earning less than R1 000 per month saying that they are unable to pay for services "no matter how hard [they] try" (as opposed to just three per cent of those with household incomes of R3 001 to R5 000 and none with household incomes of more than R15 000). Racially, it is African and coloured households that bear the biggest budgetary burden, with 22 per cent of African respondents and 20 per cent of coloured respondents who live in households that receive services indicating that they cannot afford to pay their bills "no matter how hard [they] try" (as opposed to seven per cent of Asian respondents and just one per cent of white respondents). These racial dynamics are highly correlated to household income, of course, but do underscore the continuing racialised character of poverty in the country.

However one looks at it, these figures are startling and reveal a major affordability crisis. If, for example, 18 per cent of the seven million people who are reported to have been given access to water since 1994 are unable to pay their water bills "no matter how hard [they] try", then 1.26 million of these new recipients are unable to afford this water and an additional 1.2 million have to choose between paying for water and buying other essentials like food. Similar percentages apply to the 3.5 million South Africans who have been given access to electricity.

These figures also challenge the so-called "culture of non-payment" thesis that is so popular in South Africa. At the heart of the state's Masakhane ("let's build together") campaign is the notion that poor households continue to use the anti-apartheid boycott rhetoric of the 1980s as an excuse not to pay for services. This is a line adopted by many politicians and civil servants who have been quick to blame the poor for cheating on payments. The only other report to have been undertaken on this topic adopts a similar line. Johnson (1999), having conducted a quasi-national survey for the Helen Suzman Foundation, describes the service payment issue as a "community-wide culture of non-payment ... which enables widely disparate groups to find different reasons for the same behaviour" (81). This stems from a "weak civic culture" (91) and the "lawless nature" (18) of many townships and informal settlements. He describes the situation in Germiston, for example, as requiring a "completely new social and cultural climate".[7]

The popular media is also rife with references to the "culture of non-payment". It is invariably aimed at poor, black households despite the fact that white-owned businesses are

---

[7] He later goes on to say, however, that the "non-payment crisis is all too comprehensible" when seen in the context of worsening household incomes and unemployment (Johnson 1999, 49-50). Moreover, his own data contradict his "culture of non-payment" thesis. When respondents were asked why they think people do not pay for services, unemployment (59 per cent) and inability to pay (59 per cent) top the list of reasons, with "service boycotts" (seven per cent) and "No-one else is paying; why should I?" (eight per cent) barely registering (Johnson 1999, 72). In the end, though, Johnson simply does not believe the people who told him that they cannot afford to pay for services: "The nearer we pressed towards the really hard questions about non-payment, the greater this evasive smokescreen grew so that by the end it was quite clear that a very large number of our respondents were not telling the truth" (95).

amongst the worst defaulters.[8] The perception has entrenched itself in the public imagination, and forms the basis of many an indignant letter to the editor from suburban residents who feel they are carrying an unfair burden (morally and financially) for the payment of services accounts.[9]

To be sure, there are some township residents who do not pay for their services because they feel they can get away with it and because others are not paying. With non-payment rates in rural and township areas averaging between 22 and 33 per cent in the mid-1990s (DCD 1998), and as high as 75 per cent today,[10] it is not surprising that some residents would take advantage of the situation. But from the data collected in this survey, and from evidence gathered in the more qualitative, ethnographic work in this book, it is clear that "ability to pay" is at the root of the payment crisis, not a "culture of non-payment".

Research in Soweto has shown that the overwhelming majority of respondents keep careful records of their electricity bills, and file the bills away safely for many years (Khunou, this volume; Fiil-Flynn 2001). Some households have expressed confusion over the intro-duction of volumetric charges for electricity (flat-rate systems were in place for decades), and have trouble understanding the structure of their bills (difficult at the best of times, but exacerbated by illiteracy). Most residents spoken to for the Soweto research knew exactly what they had to pay for electricity, and expressed a deep concern about how they would manage to pay these bills. These are not the sentiments of people steeped in a "culture of non-payment".

Service Arrears

Many low-income households find themselves heavily in arrears for basic services like water and electricity. Close to one-quarter of all respondents (22 per cent) said they were in arrears for water (with an average debt of R2 274), while 13 per cent said they were in arrears for electricity (with an average debt of R2 189). Some respondents were in arrears for as much as R10 000 while other case study data show arrears of R30 000 and more (Fiil-Flynn 2001). Over a third of the arrears encountered in the survey had accrued over a two-to-five-year period, and a further ten per cent were more than five years old (see Table 8.7).

In terms of ability to pay, more than half (51 per cent) of those with arrears said that they "cannot afford to pay these arrears no matter how hard [they] try", while an additional 13 per cent said they could only pay if they cut back on other essentials like food and clothes. Once again, it is respondents from low-income households who are most affected by arrears, with a third of all respondents from households earning less than R1 000 per month being in arrears for water, and about 12 per cent being in arrears for electricity.[11] In both cases the arrears average is two and a half times the respondents' monthly household income, indicating the seriousness of these debts relative to household earnings, and the virtual impossibility of being able to pay these debts off.

There are two other trends worth noting here. Firstly, respondents from households in urban and metropolitan areas are more likely to be in arrears than respondents in rural areas,

---

[8] For example, approximately one-third of the R2.1 billion owed to the Cape Town City Council for services is from businesses, many of whom owe more than R100 000 ("Council Takes Aggressive Action to Claim Arrears", *Cape Argus* 26 February, 2002).

[9] For example, the following letters were sent to the *Cape Argus* on 26 February, 2002, in response to an article critiquing the unfair distribution of municipal resources in the upper-income suburb of Durbanville as compared to that of the low-income township of Khayeltisha – both in Cape Town: "What articles like this always fail to point out is that all the people living in Kenridge Road [in Durbanville] pay all their rates and taxes, whereas very few of the people in Khayelitsha pay anything at all. In fact, those of us who live in the Tygerberg are subsidising Khayelitsha to a very great extent and our suburbs do not have as high a quality of upkeep as we are used to"; "The *Cape Argus* makes no comparison of the rates paid by residents in Durbanville and those in Khayelitsha ... only about ten per cent of what we pay in rates is actually spent on services in our area – the balance of 90 per cent going to more needy areas. What is going on here?"; "What a stupid article about different suburbs. You thankfully highlight the arrears in both areas."

[10] "Khayelitsha is City's Top Debt Headache", *Cape Argus* 20 February, 2002.

[11] Electricity arrears may be lower because most new electricity connections are installed with prepaid meters which do not allow for a customer to go into debt.

Table 8.7: Statistics on service arrears			
Q: Do you have any arrears for payment of water or electricity? (%)			
	Yes	No	Uncertain/ Don't know
Water	22	69	8
Electricity	13	80	7
N = 1702			
Q: If so, what is the approximate value of these arrears? (Rands)			
Water		Mean = R2 274	
Electricity		Mean = R2 189	
N = 557,329			
Q: If so, how far back do these arrears go? (%)			
< 6 months		28	
6 months–2 years		30	
2–5 years		34	
5–10 years		8	
> 10 years		2	
N = 554			
I can afford to pay these arrears very easily		12	
I can afford to pay these arrears but it would require some budgeting		17	
I can afford to pay these arrears but only if I cut back on other essential goods like food and clothing		13	
I cannot afford to pay these arrears no matter how hard I try		51	
Uncertain/Don't know		7	
N = 538			

owing in part to the fact that metered connections are less common in rural areas. The second is that arrears do not just occur in extremely poor households. A quarter of respondents from households with incomes of R2 001 to R3 000 per month were in arrears for electricity (average of R2 293), and 30 per cent for water (average of R2 796). The percentage of respondents in arrears drops off significantly after this income bracket, but there is still a noteworthy percentage of respondents with monthly household incomes of R3 001 to R5 000 and R5 001 to R7 500 who are in arrears on their water bills (12 and seven per cent respectively). Whether this represents a creeping crisis of affordability into the middle classes – a deepening of the "bell curve" discussed below – is difficult to say from this survey, but it does indicate the enormity of the problem.

Service Cutoffs

In an attempt to force service users to pay their bills and/or arrears for water and electricity, municipalities and other service providers (e.g. ESKOM, the parastatal electricity provider) instituted policies of service cutoffs, i.e. having water, electricity and other basic municipal services discontinued to a household. Seldom used prior to 1994,[12] service cutoffs have become a major mechanism of payment enforcement and have been implemented throughout

---

[12] The more common form of service cutoffs during the apartheid era came in the form of housing evictions which were done largely for political reasons as opposed to non-payment of municipal services (although non-payment of rent in council houses constituted grounds for evictions in many cases (Desai 2001). In the 1980s, the highly volatile nature of anti-apartheid protests in urban townships made it both dangerous and politically unwise, in an era of neo-apartheid reforms, to attempt service cutoffs. Nevertheless, de facto cutoffs took place because of the high rates of infrastructure breakdown and the lack of proper maintenance.

the country. In Soweto, up to 20 000 homes a month had their electricity cut off by ESKOM in early 2001 (Fiil-Flynn 2001), while in Cape Town, close to 100 000 households had their water cut off for non-payment between 1996 and 2001 by the various municipalities that now make up the Cape Town Unicity (McDonald and Smith 2002).[13] Ashwin Desai's (2001) graphic description of service cutoffs and evictions in Chatsworth, Durban, is another case in point.

Nor are these merely isolated incidents. Our survey data suggest that the level of service cutoffs for non-payment has reached serious levels in South Africa. Thirteen per cent of respondents indicated that they had had water cut, and an additional 13 per cent said they had had their electricity cut (with 39 per cent of these respondents having experienced both) (Table 8.8).

Assuming an adult population over the age of 18 years in South Africa of approximately 25 million people (i.e. the sample from which this survey was drawn), this means that 3.25 million people have had their water cut off for non-payment of bills and 3.25 million have had their electricity cut off. But since water and electricity cutoffs affect the whole household (not just the individual interviewed) the actual number of people who have *experienced* a service cutoff must also take into account household members under the age of 18. At the very least we can multiply these figures by 1.7 persons (which would take us to the total population of South Africa of 42 million people). But given that low-income households have considerably higher concentrations of children it is not unrealistic to extrapolate these figures out further.

If we use a figure of three additional persons the number of people affected by water cutoffs is just under 10 million, with the same number being affected by electricity cutoffs (and about 7.5 million people having experienced both). Using the same calculations, approximately two million people have been evicted from their homes for failure to pay their water and/or electricity bills and a further 1.5 million people have had property seized.

These startling figures are supported by statistics from the Department of Provincial and Local Government (RSA 2002a, 30–31). Based on data collected from 88 per cent of municipalities in the country, there were 256 325 electricity disconnections and 133 456 water disconnections in the last three months of 2001. If each household had an average of five people, this translates to more than 1.2 million people having been affected by electricity cutoffs and close to 700 000 people having been affected by water cutoffs during this short period of time – all of which have taken place *after* the free services programme began on 1 July, 2001. But even these figures are not complete given that many municipalities did not provide reports. Nor do the electricity figures include cutoffs by the parastatal energy provider, ESKOM, which had been cutting off as many as 20 000 households a month in Soweto in early 2001 (Fiil-Flynn 2001).

It is also worth noting here that Telkom – the state-owned telecommunications provider – has disconnected 40 per cent of the 2.1 million phone lines it has delivered over the past four years. Most of these disconnections have been with low-income households and have been driven, according to Robyn Chalmers of *Business Day*, by "Telkom's need to become more efficient in the run-up to competition, due to be introduced soon, and to prepare for its listing later this year or next [i.e. privatisation]".[14]

---

[13] Data collection by the Department of Constitutional Development from 1996 to 1998 also showed quite dramatic cutoff rates with national figures ranging from 50 000 to 90 000 electricity cutoffs every three months. It is quite likely that the actual figures were much higher since only 47 per cent of municipalities filed reports (DCD 1998).

[14] *Business Day* 15 May, 2002.

The Bell Tolls for Thee

Table 8.8: Experience with service cutoffs for non-payment			
Q: Has your household ever experienced any of the following? (%)			
	Yes	No	Uncertain/ Don't know
Having your water cut off for non-payment	13	81	6
Having your electricity cut off for non-payment	13	81	7
Eviction from your home for failure to pay for water or electricity	3	89	8
Seizure of property for failure to pay for services	2	90	9
Threats of legal action by the municipality for failure to pay for water or electricity	7	84	9
Actual legal action taken against your household for failure to pay for water or electricity	3	88	9
N = 2327, 2300, 2285, 2290, 2292, 2280			

These cutoffs of essential services are tough medicine, and perhaps the most damning indictment of how aggressive cost-recovery policies have undermined the physical delivery of infrastructure in South Africa. Moreover, these are only figures for those who have had their services cut off by an external agent. There are untold numbers of households who impose their own form of "cutoffs" by consuming less water and electricity than they really need in order to avoid payment defaults and arrears. Prepaid meters have the same basic effect, with low-income households purchasing only as much water or electricity as they can afford, regardless of the amounts they need in order to live healthy and productive lives. This issue has received considerable attention in the UK, and has led to the banning of certain prepaid meter devices, as well as the passing of legislation which prohibits the disconnection of the water supply to homes and a variety of other institutions for reasons of non-payment (UK 1999).[15]

In terms of demographics, it is the poorest of the poor who make up the largest *absolute number* of respondents who have experienced cutoffs, but it is respondents from households with monthly incomes of R2 001 to R3 000 who have experienced the largest *proportion* of cutoffs within their income category (Figure 8.1). Close to a third (32 per cent) of this group have experienced electricity cutoffs, and 23 per cent have experienced water cutoffs.

This "bell curve" effect – the bulge in the lower-middle-income category of Figure 8.1 – may be due to the fact that these households have enough money to purchase or rent a house with metered service delivery, but do not have enough income to pay for all the services they use/need on a monthly basis. Widespread water cutoffs in lower-middle-income neigbour-hoods like Tafelsig in Cape Town epitomise this phenomenon, diminishing many of the hard-fought gains that these households thought they had made in the "new" South Africa. Unless one has managed to climb solidly into the post-apartheid middle-class, the demographic "bell" of cost recovery tolls for anyone unfortunate enough not to be earning a sufficient income to pay their bills.

---

[15] Section 1.4 of the UK Act states: "The Act removes water companies' powers to disconnect water supply for non-payment, or to limit the supply with the intention of enforcing payment, from a list of different premises. These premises are: private dwelling houses, caravans, houseboats, houses in multiple occupation and sheltered accommodation (where these are someone's main home); children's homes; residential care homes; prisons and detention centres; schools, premises used for children's daycare, institutions of further and higher education; hospitals, nursing homes, GPs' and dentists' surgeries (including surgeries set up as primary care pilot schemes); and premises occupied by the emergency services." The Act goes on to state (in Sections 1.6 and 1.7) that "No person should have to face the prospect of cutting down on essential water use for washing, cooking and cleaning because they cannot afford their bill ... The Government is therefore using regulations to take forward measures which it considers are essential to protect vulnerable people from hardship". I am indebted to Alex Loftus for this reference.

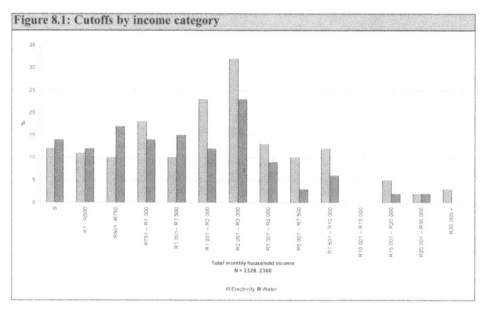

Respondents were also asked how they coped with service cutoffs (Table 8.9). Their answers provide a wide range of survival strategies, from accessing the service of a neighbour to using alternative energy sources such as paraffin, to simply "going without the service until it is reconnected by the municipality". The percentage of respondents who said that they "go without" suggests that many of these cutoffs are for short durations, but other coping strategies suggest much longer-term cutoff periods. Case-study research has shown that electricity and water cutoffs of up to nine months in duration are not uncommon (e.g. Fiil-Flynn 2001; Xali, this volume).

Table 8.9: Coping strategies for service cutoffs

Q: When you experience water cutoffs, how does your household cope with these disconnections? (%)

We go without the service until it is reconnected by the municipality	25
We get water from our neighbours	50
We get water from a community tap	8
We get water from a nearby river	11
We get water from a nearby dam	2
We get water from a nearby stagnant pond	1
We get water from government trucks that provide potable water for free	2
We get water from private traders that sell potable water	2
We reconnect our water illegally (or have someone else do it for us)	1

Q: When you experience electricity cut offs, how does your household cope with these disconnections? (%)

We go without the service until it is reconnected by the municipality	38
We get electricity from our neighbours	3
We use alternative sources of energy like paraffin and coal	45
We reconnect our electricity illegally (or have someone else do it for us)	4
Other (specify)	6

NOTE: Figures based on percentages of those who had experienced a water or electricity cutoff. Responses were unprompted and more than one answer could be given. As a result, figures do not add to 100 per cent.

Another concern here is the use of alternative sources of water and energy as a coping mechanism. Water cutoffs, for example, can lead to the use of contaminated water supplies such as rivers and stagnant ponds, with dire health consequences. For example, the introduction of cost-recovery measures on water services in KwaZulu-Natal in mid-2000 forced many people to use unsafe water sources, contributing to the cholera outbreak in that province that resulted in over 100 000 cases of infection and 250 deaths (Deedat and Cottle, this volume). The use of paraffin and coal in place of electricity is also problematic, with shack fires, respiratory disease, and the dangers to children (especially poisoning through the drinking of paraffin in the mistaken belief that it is water) amongst the leading causes of illness and death in low-income households (see Eberhard and Van Horen 1995).

Finally, it is worth noting that the figures shown in Table 8.9 for "reconnecting illegally" are probably understated because of fear of reprisal. One study in Cape Town found an illegal reconnection rate of 60 per cent after water cutoffs were implemented by the Tygerberg Municipality (McDonald and Smith 2002). Illegal reconnection of electricity is also widespread in Soweto under the community-led Operation Khanyisa (light up) (Fiil-Flynn 2001).

Free Services

One response to the issue of affordability and cutoffs has come in the form of "free services". Initially developed by the national office of the African National Congress (ANC) in the lead-up to local government elections in December 2000, and subsequently adopted by the Democratic Alliance (DA) as part of its election campaign in the same year, the free services policy is based on the concept of providing a "lifeline" supply of water and electricity to every household in the country free of charge.

There are concerns with the manner in which these policies have been designed and implemented (see Chapter 1), but free lifeline services remain a potentially powerful method of addressing affordability concerns. Consequently, respondents were asked their opinion of this policy, and who they thought should be entitled to free water and electricity, as well as if they felt there were any other services that should be offered on a "lifeline" basis.

The results were mixed. There is strong support for free water and electricity for households with incomes of less than R500 per month (78 per cent in favour), but this support drops off rapidly as recipient income increases. Households with marginally higher incomes of up to R1 000 per month received 52 per cent support while only 27 per cent of respondents were in favour of providing free services for households with incomes of up to R2 000 per month (Table 8.10).

What these figures demonstrate is highly qualified support for "free services", with only the poorest of the poor deemed eligible for this assistance. The fact that *all* households in South Africa, regardless of income, are to be provided with a free block of water and electricity under current policy plans clearly runs counter to the sample of public opinion we obtained in our survey.

Table 8.10: Attitudes towards free basic services

Q: In the recent local government elections, various political parties made promises to provide free water and electricity. Which of the following groups do you think should be entitled to enough free water and electricity to meet their basic needs? (%)

	Yes	No
Those who earn less than R500 per month	78	22
Those who earn less than R1 000 per month	52	48
Those who earn less than R2 000 per month	27	73
Those who earn less than R3 000 per month	19	81
All households	38	62
No households	11	89
N = 1968		

There are differences in attitudes to free services along race and income lines. Respondents from low-income households gave the strongest levels of support for free services to households with less than R500 per month in household income (88 per cent support), while those with higher incomes were less likely to support the policy (with 41 per cent support) (Table 8.11). In other words, the bulk of support for free services comes from households that are themselves in the greatest need of the lifeline assistance while middle- and upper-income households are much less likely to be supportive of free service policies. Racially, black respondents were most likely to support free services to poor households (with Asians showing 89 per cent support), while white respondents were least likely to support free services (57 per cent support).

Table 8.11: Attitudes to free services by income and race

Percentage in each category who believe that households which earn less than R500 per month should be entitled to enough free water and electricity to meet their basic needs (%)

	% of support
Total monthly household income	
No income	75
R1 – R500	82
R501 – R750	88
R751 – R1 000	86
R1 001– R1 500	87
R1 501 – R2 000	77
R2 001 – R3 000	88
R3 001 – R5 000	66
R5 001 – R7 500	76
R7 501 – R10 000	60
R10 001– R15 000	57
R15 001 – R20 000	41
Race	
African	81
Coloured	78
Asian	89
White	57

When asked who they thought should pay to cover the costs of these free services, most respondents were in favour of having government pay (76 per cent), but this support fell off dramatically when asked if they thought this should be financed by extra taxes on wealthy households and businesses (40 per cent and 49 per cent support respectively). The option of relying on "donations" from the wealthy and from business also received mixed support (Table 8.12).

But here again there were differences along race/class lines. In general, white and upper-income respondents were far less likely to support increased taxes and donations from business as methods of financing free services to poor households than were black and lower-income respondents. For example, 48 per cent of respondents from households earning between R501 and R750 per month were in support of introducing extra taxes on wealthy households to pay for free services while only 10 per cent of those in households earning between R10 000 and R15 000 were in favour of this approach. And while 43 per cent of African respondents were in favour of increased taxes on wealthy households only 19 per cent of white respondents were in favour.

Table 8.12: Attitudes towards covering the costs of free services			
Q: Where do you think the money to pay for these free services should come from? (%)			
	Yes	No	Don't know
The government	76	16	8
Extra taxes on wealthy households	40	47	13
Extra taxes on businesses	49	38	14
Donations from the wealthy	40	43	18
Donations from businesses	46	36	19
N = 2472			

In sum, white, upper-income South Africans are the least likely to support free basic services for poor households and are also the least likely to support financing these free services by increased taxes or donations. In fact, opposition to free services increases as income rises, with 59 per cent of those with household incomes of between R15 000 and R20 000 per month being outright opposed to free services and 69 per cent being opposed to increased taxes to pay for these services (for a detailed discussion of this kind of opposition to cross-subsidisation from upper-income communities, see Chapter 6, this volume). But it is not just white South Africans who are opposed to this kind of redistribution of household income. Upper-income blacks are also more likely to oppose these measures, highlighting the increasingly class-based character of South African politics.

With respect to other services that might be offered for free, the highest levels of support were for primary healthcare (79 per cent) but there was a majority support for most other services as well (Table 8.13), suggesting considerable public sympathy for an expansion of free services to other sectors. Nevertheless, the same race and class dynamics apply in terms of who does and does not support such policies.

Table 8.13: Support for other possible "free services"			
Q: How about the following services? Do you think any of these should also be provided for free to certain groups? (%)			
	Yes	No	Uncertain/ Don't know
Regular refuse collection	57	31	12
Basic road maintenance	63	27	10
Storm-water drainage	53	32	15
Fire protection	61	28	11
Primary healthcare	79	16	5
Access to libraries	67	23	10
Access to recreational facilities like sports fields	63	27	10
Public transportation	38	52	10
N = 2530			

Block Tariffs

Respondents were also asked about their support for "block tariffs" – a system whereby the per-unit cost of a service increases with consumption. The City of Cape Town, for example, does not charge for the first block of water (0 to 6kl), while the second block (7 to 20kl) is charged at R2,60 per kilolitre, the third block (21 to 40kl) at R4,10 per kilolitre, the fourth block (41 to 60kl) at R5,50 per kilolitre and the final block (61kl+) at R7 per kilolitre (City of Cape Town 2001).

The rationale behind block tariffs is twofold. First, they act as a cross-subsidisation mechanism by charging more for higher levels of consumption (generally by middle- and upper-income households with swimming pools, many electrical appliances, etc.). These revenues are then used to pay for the initial cheap or free blocks of consumption (i.e. the "lifeline" supply for poor households). Second, if done properly, block tariffs can also curb over-consumption of environmentally sensitive resources such as water and electricity by acting as a price disincentive at higher levels of consumption (see Deedat, Pape and Qotole 2001).

Block tariffs have been used sporadically in South Africa for decades but have only recently been integrated into more holistic demand-management systems for resources like water and electricity. Moreover, fragmented local governments have long had highly disparate tariff rates, with rationalised tariffs only being introduced since the last round of municipal elections in December, 2000.

It was therefore necessary to give respondents a brief description of block tariffs before asking them their attitudes towards this policy (Table 8.14). Although we cannot be sure that all respondents understood the full implications of this pricing system, the question did highlight the cross-subsidisation potential of block tariffs.

The results show that a slight majority of respondents support block tariffs (53 per cent). In this case, the support is consistent across race, income and urban/rural location. In other words, progressive block tariffs as a cross-subsidisation mechanism would appear to enjoy fairly widespread support and may be a useful way to help subsidise free services and reduce the negative impacts of cost recovery on poor households.

Fifty-three per cent does not constitute overwhelming support for block tariffs, however. There could also be a backlash against this method of cross-subsidisation as block tariffs are introduced and enforced across the country. White, middle-class South Africans have always enjoyed heavily subsidised services, and rising tariff rates may come as a shock to some. Given the resistance by this demographic group to other forms of taxation to subsidise free services for the poor, resistance to block tariffs may also increase as they are implemented.

Nevertheless, progressive block tariffs offer policy-makers another potentially powerful cross-subsidisation mechanism, while at the same time addressing long-standing environmental concerns with wasteful patterns of water and electricity consumption, waste disposal, etc. This will likely require public education campaigns to inform and educate service users as to the potential benefits of block tariffs.

Conclusion

The statistics presented here are sobering. They offer a picture of post-apartheid service delivery that is at best plagued by affordability problems and overly aggressive bureaucrats bent on recovering costs, and at worst, a deep failure on the part of government (both local and national) to ensure an affordable supply of essential services to all. That government has not been closely monitoring and evaluating the scale and character of service cutoffs and affordability is itself deeply concerning.

Table 8.14: Attitudes towards block tariffs as a cross-subsidisation mechanism

Q: One of the ways that has been proposed to help pay for free services is a "block tariff". This is a system where the price of a service like water or electricity increases the more you use of it. For example, if you use water to fill a swimming pool you will have to pay much more per litre than someone who just uses water for washing dishes or cooking. Do you think this is a good way to help pay for the cost of free services? (%)	
Yes	53
No	29
Uncertain/Don't know	19
N = 2487	

Perhaps the most important conclusion to draw from this survey is that there is an urgent need to debunk the myth of a "culture of non-payment". If, as I have argued here, *ability* to pay is more important than *willingness* to pay, then no amount of moralising or threatening is going to alleviate the payments crisis in the country. You cannot squeeze blood from a stone.

Furthermore, essential services need to be made more affordable for poor households if the promise of service access for all is to be met. The introduction of "free services" is a step in the right direction, as are (steeply) progressive block tariffs. However, there are problems with the design and implementation of free services, and there is stiff resistance from middle- and upper-income ratepayers to redistributional mechanisms. This makes it very difficult to produce the kinds of cross-subsidisation revenue flows required at a local level to improve and expand service delivery in low-income areas. In this case, it will be up to national government to provide the funds needed to make up for the dramatic cuts that have taken place in intergovernmental transfers over the past ten years, and to re-evaluate its own fiscal priorities (e.g. the R40 billion deal for military hardware and the February 2002 budget announcement of a R15 billion tax cut for middle- and upper-income households).

And finally, there is a need for major debt relief for service arrears. This is a sensitive matter, and must not be seen to penalise those who have struggled to pay for their services in the past. But the heartless, and perhaps unconstitutional, practices of household evictions and water and electricity cutoffs are simply unsustainable – socially, morally, and economically. Without some kind of reform it is likely that the backlash to cost recovery will continue in South Africa.

Acknowledgements

Thanks are due to Meshack Khosa for his assistance with the design of the service delivery questions in the survey and for his support for this project from within the HSRC. Thanks also to Anneke Jordan of the HSRC for her assistance with the data set and to Bob Mattes with advice on extrapolating the data figures to the household level.

Bibliography

Ahmad, J. (1995). "Funding the Metropolitan Areas of South Africa". *Finance and Development*, September.

ANC [African National Congress]. (1994). *The Reconstruction and Development Programme*. Johannesburg: Umyanyano Publications.

Business Day, 7 March, 2002.

Business Day, 15 May, 2002.

Cape Argus, 9 February, 2002.

Cape Argus, 20 February, 2002.

Cape Argus, 26 February, 2002.

City of Cape Town. (2001). *Proposed Tariff Reports for the 2001/02 Financial Year: Addendum W-D*, May.

DCD [Department of Constitutional Development]. (1998). *Project Viability Report*, March, accessed at http://www.local.gov.za/DCD/dcdlibrary/pro/pvindex6_98.html.

Deedat, H., Pape, J. and Qotole, M. (2001). "Block Tariffs or Blocked Access? The Greater Hermanus Water Conservation Programme". Municipal Services Project Occasional Papers Series, 5. Cape Town.

Desai, A. (2001). *The Poor of Chatsworth: Race, Class and Social Movements in Post-Apartheid South Africa*. Durban: Madiba Publishers.

Eberhard, A. and Van Horen, C. (1995). *Poverty and Power: Energy and the South African State*. Johannesburg: Pluto Press.

Eskom. (1996). *An Analysis of the Implications of Supply Capacity Limitations in Low Income Residential Areas*. Mimeo, 1996.

– (2001) Annual Report 2000. *African and Globally Competitive*. Johannesburg: Kagiso BM Printing.

Fiil-Flynn, M. (2001). "The Electricity Crisis in Soweto". Municipal Services Project Occasional Papers Series, 4. Cape Town.

IWRA [International Water Resources Association]. (2001). "Update", July.

Johnson, R.W. (1999). "Not so Close to Their Hearts: An Investigation into the Non-payment of Rates, Rents and Service Charges in South Africa's Towns and Cities". Helen Suzman Foundation Special Reports, Johannesburg.

Mail & Guardian, 15–21 March, 2002.

McDonald, D. A. and Smith, L. (2002). "Privatising Cape Town: Service Delivery and Policy Reforms Since 1996". Municipal Services Project Occasional Papers Series, 7. Cape Town.

Ramphele, M. (1993). *A Bed Called Home: Life in the Migrant Labour Hostels of Cape Town*. Cape Town: David Philip Publishers.

RSA [Republic of South Africa]. (1995). *Municipal Infrastructure Investment Framework*. Ministry in the Office of the President and the Department of National Housing, 12 June. Cape Town: Government Printers.

— (1998). Department of Minerals and Energy, Draft White Paper on the Energy Policy of the Republic of South Africa. Pretoria: Government Printers.

— (2001). Minister of Water and Affairs and Forestry Budget Speech to Parliament, 15 May. Pretoria: Government Printers.

— (2002a). Department of Provincial and Local Government, Quarterly Monitoring of Municipal Finances and Related Activities, Summary of Questionnaires for Quarter Ended 31 December 2001. Pretoria: Government Printers.

— (2002b). Briefing by the Parliamentary Portfolio Committee on Minerals and Energy, 6 March. Cape Town: Government Printers.

Sapa Press Release (2002). "Basic Water Provision for All by 2008": Ronnie Kasrils, 12 February.

UK [United Kingdom]. (1999). *Water Industry Act of 1999*. London.

People and Service Delivery

In this campaign, COSATU demands:

- Government must stop privatising basic services and national infrastructure at once. Basic services are water, sewage, rubbish disposal, electricity, welfare, and basic housing, health, transport, education, telecommunications and cultural services such as stadiums, parks and libraries; these services must remain in the hands of the people.

- Any restructuring of the state must improve services for our communities and especially for the poor. It must keep and create quality jobs.

- Restructuring must be negotiated with communities and labour, and be approved by parliament or local government councils.

So far, government has not seriously negotiated these demands with us. We hope that we will be able to make more progress in the coming weeks. If not, we will continue to take action to oppose privatisation.

COSATU (2001)

We are searching for viable alternatives for a politics that can just give people hope. We need efficiency and the optimal use of resources but rational planning must not forget the people. We have to be very careful about the centralised state because it failed in the Soviet Union. We need more participatory and decentralised decision-making.

Trevor Ngwane, leader of the Soweto Electricity Crisis Committee (SECC) (Focus, 2002)

9

Looking for Alternatives to Cost Recovery

by John Pape

In the previous chapters we have compiled an extensive critique of cost recovery. While we have worked hard to bring together this collection, in a sense such a critique is easy. The extent of cutoffs and hardships visited on impoverished South Africans by cost recovery provide ample material for our research. But our work must not end there. We also need to pose alternatives.

The struggle to create alternatives to cost recovery has already begun. Grassroots actions like Operation Khanyisa (light up) of the Soweto Electricity Crisis Committee, and the extensive mobilisations against privatisation on the part of organised labour, are steps towards an alternative. But while these actions are important, there is much work to be done.

Here we will consider three aspects of an alternative path:

- Short- and medium-term measures which would improve people's lives and advance an alternative agenda;
- An investigation into the type of organisation(s) required to develop and consolidate an alternative; and
- The nature of the alternative paradigm itself.

Steps Along the Way: Short- and Medium-Term Measures

There are a number of measures which have already become the focal point of mobilisation in communities. Many of these have become the source of campaigns or programmes of action.

The first such measure is an end to punitive measures against residents who are in arrears. This means an immediate end to all residential cutoffs of water (including the use of devices which reduce water to a trickle), electricity, and the stopping of any evictions or attaching of property. These actions by government are a fundamental violation of human rights and go against the South African Constitution which guarantees access to these services. Without this as a first step, there can be no move towards an alternative.

But linked to ending cutoffs are two other key issues: scrapping arrears, and providing lifeline services. As our national survey has shown (see Chapter 8), arrears are a reality for nearly a quarter of South African households. More than half of those in arrears stated that they could not afford to pay them "no matter how hard [they] try". Hence, there can be no sustainable development unless affordability dominates the thinking of municipal authorities. There can be no transformation in South Africa when millions of households remain ensnared in a debt trap from which they cannot possibly escape.

If arrears are scrapped, citizens must also have an assurance that the debt mountain will not rise up again. To avoid such a debt trap, effective lifelines must be implemented.

Since 1 July, 2001, every municipality in South Africa is supposed to provide minimum free household lifelines of 6 000 litres of water and 50kWh of electricity per month. These provisions are a direct response to pressure from below for more affordable service delivery. The lifelines are a great victory for the poor of South Africa. However, in the context of cost recovery, the victory is not secured. According to the Department of Local Government, in the last quarter of 2001 alone, 296 325 households had their electricity cut and 133 456 had their water cut (DPLG 2002, 30). Lifelines cannot be contingent upon payment of previous bills.

But apart from the linkage of cost recovery to lifelines, the present proposals have other shortcomings as well. To begin with, the level of services provided is questionable. In particular the 50kWh of electricity severely constrains what can be considered "basic needs". With this amount of electricity, for example, regular operation of a fridge, a heater and an electric stove would be difficult. According to Bond (2000, 88) the average prepaid meter consumption for five to six people is 80kWh per month. Since prepaid meters are mainly in low-income households, 50kWh is likely to provide only the bare essentials – lighting and one or two appliances.[1]

The current lifeline policy has raised other queries as well. The RDP (ANC 1994, 29) called for a medium-term on-site water supply of 50 to 60 litres per person per day. The government's current provision is based on 25 litres per person per day (with eight people per household). At present there seems to be no plan to upgrade to medium-term RDP levels. To do this would entail an extensive improvement on existing infrastructure which in many places could not bear additional water flows.

But water and electricity are not the only "basic" or "essential" services. There is an ongoing debate as to whether other services such as refuse removal or sanitation should not also be included in the lifeline system.[2]

Any expansion or upgrading of services will not come free of charge. This brings us to our next measure: cross-subsidies from large-scale users. At present, businesses and the wealthy contribute little to such redistribution. Instead, they are subsidised by taxpayers in a number of ways. Many large-scale users have huge arrears which are ignored by municipal accounts departments. The collusion is such that even attempts by organised labour to get a list of these delinquent firms have been met with silence. While impoverished residents with prepaid meters have to go without electricity because they may lack five or ten Rands, bulk users get virtual tariff holidays, often accumulating arrears into six or even seven figures for years.[3] This is hardly in line with equity.

But cross-subsidisation need not only come from payment flows. As a number of researchers (McDonald and Smith 2002; Qotole et al. 2001) have pointed out, the distribution of service infrastructure and resources in South African municipalities remains profoundly unequal. From refuse collection vehicles to skilled electricians, the historically white areas remain extremely privileged. Hence another important form of cross-subsidy would involve a reallocation of these resources.

---

[1] This situation is further complicated by the power of the connection that is installed. The government's Municipal Infrastructure Investment Framework (MIIF) recommends 5-amp connections for basic service levels. This would mean that even if a household could afford a stove and a fridge, its system would not have the capacity to run them.

[2] There is a broader ideological question concerning the issue of lifelines as well. This relates to the notion of defining and quantifying needs, especially "basic" needs. The central concern is whether needs are determined by a scientific analysis of the minimum required for human survival or are socially determined by the particular context in which they arise. For a detailed discussion of this in the South African context, see Ruiters (2000). Similar issues are also raised in Bond (2000).

[3] For example, the Sunday Times (7 April, 2002) estimated that businesses and government departments owed some R400 million in unpaid rates. City officials said that the city had taken no action "for fear of hurting the local economy". The same article told how an 89-year-old partly blind and deaf woman had been evicted from her home the previous month. In the process "a chair was plucked from under her by council officials".

The last key short-term measure is halting privatisation and honouring commitments to prioritising public-sector delivery. On many occasions, government has declared a preference for the public sector. In the National Framework Agreement signed by SAMWU and SALGA (South African Local Governments' Association) in December 1999, the public sector was agreed upon as the "preferred option". Clause 78 of the Municipal Systems Act (RSA 2000), which built on the Framework Agreement, states that before a local authority can bring the private sector into service delivery, it must follow a number of steps, which include assessing:

a) the municipality's capacity and potential future capacity to furnish the skills, expertise and resources necessary for the provision of the service through the "internal mechanism" (the existing municipal system);

b) likely impact on development, job creation and employment patterns in the municipality; and

c) the views of organised labour.

A restructuring of public-sector delivery, or what the Systems Act calls the "internal mechanism", could build the capacity of a development-oriented local authority to deliver more effective services while reducing costs and redistributing existing resources. These sorts of options could take a number of forms, from public-public partnerships to more direct cooperation with community-based structures. If such a process made use of the vast experience and knowledge of municipal workers in service delivery, a new form of service could begin to emerge. Apart from improving service delivery, such an approach could enhance solidarity between municipal workers and communities.

Instead of following the path outlined in the Framework Agreement and Systems Act, most local authorities have opted for privatisation in all its forms – selling off municipal assets, financial ringfencing of departments, and outsourcing of a host of functions. In most cases, this has been done without even considering how to increase existing capacity. These moves toward involving the private sector in service delivery have been facilitated by the government's Municipal Infrastructure Investment Unit (MIIU), which has spent tens of millions of Rands promoting public-private partnerships in service delivery. No wonder that in many instances, rather than work with labour, municipalities have chosen to scapegoat workers for the failures of service delivery strategies, and proclaimed, in contradiction to their own policies, that only the private sector has the capacity and expertise to deliver.

These, then, are the short-term measures which have already been the object of consider-able action by community structures and trade unions. In the short-term, all of these could significantly change the quality of life for millions of South African households. For the most part, they are not technically complex issues requiring unavailable expertise or world-class technology. But their non complexity, does not mean they will not be contested. In the era of globalisation, securing even the basic needs of poor people always involves a struggle. And usually those promoting cost-recovery models have the resources on their side. While the above measures can have immediate impact, there are also a number of more medium-term steps needed to curtail the hegemony of cost recovery.

Perhaps the most important measure is job creation. The primary reason that millions of South African households are in arrears is that they have little or no income. The February 2002 Mesebetsi Labour Force Survey put the national unemployment rate at between 32 and 45 per cent (FAFO 2002).[4] If the national average is in this range, there must be many communities with much higher rates. How can a community with an unemployment rate of 50 to 60 per cent be expected to cover the cost of services? Only once there is income flowing into households can there be talk of payment for services. As Ms. Thekiso of Diepkloof noted, for many citizens, employment is linked to ensuring rights:

If I had a job I would believe that there was democracy and rights. This would make my life easier; I would be able to pay and therefore would not get cut off. However since I do not have a job I do not have rights, therefore ESKOM can just come in and cut me off.

---

[4] An MSP micro-survey of Soweto found that 22 per cent of "heads of households" were unemployed, with another 40 per cent being pensioners. Not surprisingly, 61 per cent of these households had experienced electricity cutoffs in the previous 12 months (Fiil-Flynn 2001).

We cannot separate the viability of service delivery from an economy which is losing more than 100 000 formal-sector jobs per year. Job creation cannot be left to trickle down from corporate profits. The state, through expanded public-works programmes and other initiatives, must play a proactive role.

Increased funding from national government to local authorities

The assumption of the present model is that municipalities have the capacity to raise additional money apart from national government funding. This is largely founded on the neoliberal visions of cities as business entities which compete for investment, tourists, and other sources of funding. Yet, the reality in many municipalities is vastly different. In most rural districts, there is very little possibility to become "competitive". With minimal infrastructure and severely limited potential for attracting either tourism or investment, these municipalities will remain at the margins of any competitive process. If there are tourist or investment "dollars" to be captured, they will most likely flow to the best-resourced areas such as Johannesburg and Cape Town. Furthermore, in these rural districts, other sources of revenue such as rates and taxes are also extremely limited. To make matters worse, most residents are unable to afford payment for services, let alone tariffs for much-needed additional infrastructure. But this is not only the case in Category C municipalities. The overwhelming majority of South Africa's urban population faces dire circumstances as well. With rising unemployment rates, there is little hope of an immediate turn-around. Hence, the only solution to the problem in the short and medium term is more funding flowing to local authorities from the national fiscus. Without this, cutoffs and evictions are more likely to increase than to abate.

Policy Measures Toward Alternatives

The measures mentioned above have all been the target of extensive campaigns by community structures and trade unions. But other measures, such as progressive block tariffs and the use of prepaid technology, could also contribute to both reform and the building of an alternative.

Progressive block tariffs: These are already used by many municipalities in their water billing systems. But while progressive block tariffs have redistributive potential, they are not a substitute for central government financing. For example, in municipalities which encompass large rural areas, there is little scope for mobilising funds through block tariffs. Most of these districts have relatively few industrial or large-scale domestic users. An area like Hermanus, which was one of the pilots for an integrated water conservation programme including block tariffs, is ideal for such a policy. But Hermanus is a tourist centre which trebles its population in season.[5] This is not a typical municipality in South Africa. A second important point is that in most instances progressive block tariffs have only been applied to water. In many areas electricity pricing remains extremely regressive. In Johannesburg, users in Soweto pay higher unit costs than do users in Sandton (Fiil-Flynn 2001). In other areas, the more electricity a consumer uses, the less he/she pays per unit. Such a billing system is yet another expression of the dominance of neoliberal orthodoxy in service delivery. Since low-income users consume only three per cent of total electricity output (Bond 2000, 112), there is no genuine financial logic in escalating their tariffs. Ultimately, lowering unit costs for increased consumption sets a clear agenda: providing incentives to corporate users far outweighs the need to meet apartheid backlogs. In addition, such a policy fails to take into account the massive socio-environmental impact of bulk service delivery. For those driven by neoliberal costing, there are seemingly no social or environmental limits to supply. The alternative vision would be that if users must pay, let them pay in a way that reflects equity. In particular, tariffs need to reflect socio-environmental costs for corporate users. In a society with a long history of resource-based industries, such costs cannot be left in the orthodox economists' category of "externalities". They are an integral part of economic development

---

[5] This is not to say that progressive block tariffs were an unqualified success in Hermanus. Over the course of three years they succeeded in reducing water consumption by about a third while increasing revenue. Yet the policy focused on the former white suburbs. At the same time, strict cost recovery was being applied in the townships, leading to massive cutoffs and some selling off of houses to pay arrears. For a detailed discussion of the Hermanus experience with block tariffs, see Deedat, Pape and Qotole (2001).

and service delivery systems.[6] Billing should reflect the social opportunity costs of increasing provision to corporate users, not simply economies of scale and costs as measured in the narrow accounting sense.

Usage of prepaid technology: To date, prepaid systems have largely been used to pressurise the poor. A far more effective use of prepaid technology could be applied to large-scale corporate users. Through on-line systems, bulk users could prepay for consumption. This would generate massive cash-flow benefits and interest income for local authorities and ESKOM. This revenue could become a key source of cross-subsidy. As noted earlier, bulk users are some of the most delinquent bill payers. Yet in absolute numbers, they are relatively few. Setting up a prepaid system for these users would be far more administratively manageable than fighting the war of installing prepaids in households which clearly cannot afford either the cost of the meter or the full cost of the service.

Lastly, there is the issue of public participation in issues of service delivery. Various policy documents and pieces of legislation call for public participation. The Systems Act (RSA 2000), for example, outlines a public participation process for the formulation of Integrated Development Plans (IDPs). This process includes inputs from communities and labour. The organisational rights agreement signed between the unions and the South African Local Governments' Association (SALGA) mandates the formation of Local Labour Forums (LLFs). These LLFs can be sites for considering issues related to service delivery, especially the outsourcing of functions. Yet, in nearly all municipalities, such participatory structures have been stripped of their powers. In the IDP, the typical consultation process has been for the municipality to set up a series of poorly publicised public meetings in communities. These meetings then constitute the legal requirements of the Systems Act in terms of consultation.[7] In the meantime, key decisions about the IDP are taken by council exco or even by consultants who have been contracted to develop the actual plan. While Local Labour Forums have been created in many municipalities, they seldom consider matters of substance for service delivery. At present, structures for participation in South Africa often serve more to marginalise than to empower. But there are alternatives.

In other communities around the world, the political will of local-government leaders has produced processes where citizens have a voice in the decisions that affect their communities. Perhaps the best-known example is the participatory budgeting process in Porto Alegre, Brazil. Here, more than 20 000 citizens, mandated by their communities, consider the relative needs of different areas of the city, and decide on the municipal budget (Public Sector International/ILRIG 2000). Like Brazil, South Africa has a long history of participatory democracy. Trade unions, civics and many other formations operated on a system of mandates and accountability throughout the 1980s and early 1990s. Some organisations still follow such a practice. But the government has chosen not to build on this model. Instead, top-down processes like the IDP consultations are given the name of participation.

Political Questions: New Organisational Forms

We have outlined some of the key short- and medium-term measures which could contribute towards an alternative to cost recovery. Scrapping arrears or state-led job creation are crucial. However, the process for attaining such victories is also critical. If such gains are to be part of building an alternative, they must be the result of mobilisation at grassroots level. The precise form of an organisation or social movement which can successfully advance an alternative is difficult to delineate. Past formulations such as vanguard parties, national liberation

---

[6] At a parliamentary briefing in March, 2002, officials from the Minerals and Energy Affairs Department estimated that they would need to spend R150 million to treat 68 asbestos mines. "Treating" means cleaning up the toxic waste left behind over the course of the past century and a half. The officials stressed that this did not include any costing for doing the same for "coal, gold or any other mine." Nor did it include payments to workers and citizens whose health had been adversely affected by asbestosis or other mining-related ailments (*Business Report* 22 March, 2002).

[7] This description of the IDP process is based on workshops conducted with local government workers from the South African Municipal Workers' Union (SAMWU) from a variety of municipalities in all nine provinces. This was complementary to the research undertaken by the MSP. The process described here was the norm. In only one municipality did participants report that they were satisfied with their participation in the IDP process. In that case, the mayor of the city was a former shop steward in the union.

movements, green parties or even traditional trade unions do not have a grand track record of success. It is likely that new organisational forms will emerge from new struggles.

Nonetheless, such a political force requires at least four major features which are rarely seen in community or labour organisations today. Firstly, it must bring together the interests of organised labour, the broader working class, and poor rural communities. The knowledge of workers needs to become a resource for transforming both service delivery and the relationships between labour and the community. For example, instead of hiring expensive consultants to design service delivery strategies which bring in the private sector, workers themselves can be used as researchers to define and analyse problems. In many communities, municipal workers who collect refuse or maintain facilities are the most direct interface between local government and the public. Yet, there are few instances when these workers take part in a "needs assessment" of the community. At the same time, workers need education in how to build such relations. In many communities, the face of the municipality is a rude or uncaring clerk who ignores or abuses citizens who are carrying out a routine transaction. At times, even some layers of the workforce have joined business and their employers in condemning those who have arrears as "irresponsible" or perpetuators of a "culture of non-payment".

This schism between labour and the community is further exacerbated by the notion that workers form an "elite" simply because they are employed. This absurdity has become a battle cry for employers who want to drive down wages and working conditions. That a South African worker earns perhaps ten per cent (in hard currency terms) of what his/her US or German counterpart earns, and that the vast majority of South African workers have to support more than a handful of unemployed family members, is somehow missed in the perpetuation of the "workers as elite" myth. At the same time, communities must avoid shooting the messenger. Throwing stones at municipal vehicles, or holding municipal workers hostage because they want to read meters or even disconnect services, is not a viable way to build political alliances.

Secondly, such a political force must find ways to extend women's participation in building an alternative. The majority of the services provided by municipalities overlap with what is traditionally viewed as "women's work" in the household. When there is no money to load the prepaid electricity card, women's workload in cooking or accessing fuel increases. When local governments increase charges for services like childcare or primary health provision, they are in most instances shifting work onto women and young girls. If toddlers cannot go to crèche, it is most likely a woman or a young girl who will have the task of looking after them at home. If there are no accessible healthcare facilities, it is most likely a woman who will have to look after the sick family members at home. When we look at the mobilisations around service delivery issues in communities like Soweto, Tafelsig and Chatsworth, we find many women involved. But in most cases, when we look to the leadership of the organisations in these communities, men are in the majority. Similar gender-based problems also exist in the trade union movement. Even unions which have a majority of women members typically have a male-dominated leadership. Until women's centrality in leading these struggles and their special skills and experience are recognised, a political force capable of contesting the neoliberal local government agenda is unlikely to emerge.

Thirdly, while service delivery and payment systems may seem like the most local of issues, there is an increasingly international dimension to what is taking place in local government. Municipalities draw their models and their policies from "international best practice". When assets are sold off, or services are contracted out, particularly in water and electricity, transnational corporations are often involved. Indeed there is a roll of international players in service delivery. Companies like Vivendi and Suez Lyonnaise des Eaux, and brokers like Price Waterhouse Coopers are included on the list of usual suspects. The global character of these companies requires a global perspective to contest their cost-recovery policies. Hence, at times, local movements fighting for an alternative will have to draw on the lessons from organisations in other parts of the world who have had direct experience with the particular corporation or issue they are confronting. The local is global, just as the global is local.

Finally, there is the overall question of building an alternative ideology. The ideology of neoliberalism is individualism, as exemplified by possession of symbolic "branded" goods and consumption of global culture – from *The Bold and the Beautiful* to CNN to Manchester

United. At municipal level, this ideology is manifested in the notion of "competitive" or "world-class" cities and citizens as consumers. Under these notions, the main aim of a municipality is no longer working together to meet the needs of the people. Instead, meeting the needs of the people becomes a byproduct of a competitive, business-oriented process to attract tourists, to lure foreign investors, to project the appropriate image in the international arena, and to satisfy the most important consumers. As in all competitions, there are winners and losers. In most cases, the winners will be the cities with the most resources, the corporations with the most power and influence, the citizens with historical privilege on their side. Also-rans in these competitions are those with little to offer the global market: underdeveloped rural municipalities, workers from the pre-information technology age, subsistence farmers who have not yet imbibed the export gospel. Any alternative must ultimately take on the need for everyone to become a Pop Idol or win the Lotto. Enhancing service delivery can become a process to build citizens' capacity to work together to ensure that their rights remain a reality. As long as a municipality puts recovering costs above building this type of community, the rich will continue to prosper and the poor will resort not only to illegal connections, but to putting more direct forms of pressure on those who continue to ignore their suffering.

The Ultimate Vision: An Alternative Paradigm

The ultimate vision must take us away from the reliance on market forces and measures like cost recovery. Under the current paradigm, certain reforms may bring temporary relief to those on the receiving end of cut-offs or prepaid technology. But overall, as long as cost recovery remains hegemonic, even attempts at meaningful reform will be riddled with attacks on the poor.

Describing the Alternative Paradigm

In advancing an alternative paradigm, there is a strong temptation to go back to the RDP and other progressive policy documents from the 1980s and early 1990s. The notion of a developmental state which drives the national economy through various non-market interventions is an important component of leaving behind the neoliberal policy framework of Growth, Employment and Redistribution (GEAR) adopted in 1996. Also, the concept of "people-centred development" offers an appropriate starting point for an alternative: meeting people's needs. This is a far cry from the current ideology of "ensuring" or "facilitating" private-sector profitability.

Yet, attempts at "restoring" or going back to the RDP pose two serious problems. Firstly, the struggle for the RDP itself has been lost. A programme for the future may draw on some of the content of the RDP, but the Reconstruction and Development Programme cannot be resuscitated *in toto* as the manifesto of an alternative. New programmes, charters and platforms will have to developed in the course of contestation.

Secondly, and more importantly, the ideas within the RDP form the starting point for moving away from GEAR, but fall far short of a comprehensive alternative. For this, we need to turn to a broader discussion of what informs much of our present understanding of alternatives, including the RDP.

Public Goods: A Limited Alternative

For the most part, the current discussion remains confined to the welfare state notion of public goods. In mainstream economics, public goods are those for which consumption is collective. In the more orthodox version of defining public goods, they are also said to be "indivisible" in the sense that individual consumption cannot be calculated. Classic examples of public goods are public security and street lighting.[8] Both of these are generally seen as necessary,

---

[8] It should be noted that the wave of privatisation and the advance of technology have rendered the indivisibility of some goods questionable. For example, private security companies have a number of ways to bill consumers for services. With the increasing privatisation of security in many areas of South Africa, the logic of the indivisibility thesis is no longer unassailable.

but billing according to use is difficult. Because of the importance of public goods, the general assumption of Keynesian economists was that they should be provided by the state. The notion of public goods is linked to another category, that of merit goods. Merit goods are those which benefit the society as a whole but are not profitable if run as a private enterprise. Classic examples of merit goods are mass education and preventative healthcare.

In comparison with neoliberal practices such as ringfencing and business units, the declaration of some goods as "public" is a clear-cut advance. Viewing services like water and electricity as public goods is one way of situating a service in a broader developmental paradigm. In a market economy, this is directly connected to whether we regard such services as commodities or resources for development. Since this question of commodification has important consequences for developing an alternative framework, let us explore it in some detail.

When water is viewed as a commodity, we assess the water service on the same terms we would a business: does the provision of water earn a profit for the provider? In a public-goods perspective, water becomes a resource for development. With this approach, we cannot assess water services solely through traditional accounting methods. For example, in underdeveloped rural areas, access to affordable water enhances potential for agricultural production. But water does not only have economic benefits. An adequate supply of water for drinking and hygiene is essential for maintaining health. In turn, these health benefits have positive socio-economic spin-offs. At the level of individual or collective productivity, reducing incidents of diarrhoea or cholera will enhance the productivity of a workforce. Moreover, if fewer people are ill because of poor water and sanitation service, health-care resources will be freed up. Instead of having to respond to cholera epidemics, the health-care system can focus on HIV/AIDs or primary healthcare.

Apart from this, an effective water service has important gender-equity benefits. In most households, accessing water is seen as "women's work". When water is far away or in short supply, women have to spend more hours in the day sourcing water. The load of domestic labour, already disproportionate in most households, becomes even more gender-biased.

While the public-goods concept stresses the developmental aspect of services, this does not imply that service provision comes without any costs. There are costs to providing services – both budgetary and social. In the developmental sense, every service delivery strategy has an economic and social opportunity cost (i.e. a foregone alternative). Under the model of cost recovery, the foregone alternatives are typically those developmental impacts which benefit the poor. For example, when cost-recovery models are chosen, pro-poor alternatives are left behind. Instead of having a purified water-supply to contribute to their health, those who cannot afford to pay for services must bear the risk of water-borne diseases. Instead of turning on a household tap, women in poor households must walk to the river or visit a distant communal tap after dark.

Similar problems occur with electricity, where allocation of infrastructure to large-scale users typically means bypassing provision to informal settlements or rural areas. For the poor, electricity brings many benefits. Domestic tasks like cooking and heating become easier. Students can study more effectively. In informal settlements, electricity reduces the likelihood of shack fires often caused by paraffin.

Delivering services as public goods also contributes to social sustainability by building links of solidarity amongst community members. If your water or electricity cuts out, your neighbour can help you. By contrast, many of our case studies have shown how cost-recovery measures stratify already fragile communities. The law of competition prevails. Those who cannot afford to pay become ostracised or become the commercial prey of their neighbours who may resort to selling them water from their own taps.

As we can see, viewing services as public goods presents considerable potential for addressing the needs of the population. While traditional economics defined public and merit goods quite narrowly, the analysis can be extended to include a number of other goods and services which relate to socio-economic rights and equitable sharing of the benefits of an industrialised economy. Ultimately, in an advanced welfare state, clean air, recreational facilities and Internet access could be seen as public goods. In contemporary South Africa, production of anti-retrovirals or adult basic education materials could easily be classified as merit goods.[9]

Stretching the Boundaries: Toward Decommodification

However, despite the positive aspects of the public-goods perspective, a genuine alternative needs to push the boundaries considerably further. The essential problem with the public-goods perspective is that social welfare and development as a whole remain at the margins of a mainstream market economy. While state ownership and provision of water may guarantee lifelines and adequate supply to all residents, the bulk of the economy still remains driven by a profit motive. While state provision may, as the free-marketeers say, "crowd out" the private sector, the fundamental dominance of corporate power remains unchallenged. In an era of globalisation, where the rapid increase in corporate power has fast-tracked the rise in poverty and inequality, grabbing a small piece of the economic cake will not change the fundamentals. More likely, in fact, is the possibility that, as a result of resistance to globalisation, some aspects of the public-goods position will be captured under aid programmes, social safety nets, and the Poverty Reduction Strategic Plans of institutions like the World Bank.

While the extensive provision of "basic needs" to historically disadvantaged communities remains a high priority, such a strategy also leaves much of what was created by apartheid capitalism unchanged and unquestioned. For example, most urban areas in South Africa still bear the spatial configuration of the apartheid city. The apartheid city was a carefully crafted strategy to institutionalise race and class separation.[10] In the debates of the 1980s and early 1990s, dismantling the apartheid city was the central aim of alternative planners. In Johannesburg, for instance, researchers linked to the civic movement carried out an extensive survey of the metropolitan area to identify land in historically white areas which would be suitable for settlement by black working-class households. More than enough land to accommodate such an alternative was uncovered. Yet, such notions have dropped off the planning agenda. The struggle has become one to maintain access to existing services or extending access to the communities structured by apartheid logic. Separate development has not been challenged. As Greg Ruiters (2001, 19) has pointed out, we may be headed for a "kind of economic quarantism", far from the non-racial society based on participatory democracy that was once the vision of the liberation struggle.

A second example of the shortcomings of the public-goods perspective takes us closer to the heart of the matter. The public-goods perspective assumes that the allocation of resources remains primarily in the hands of the owners. Some public goods may be subsidised, but the heart of the productive economy remains essentially unchanged. In the case of South Africa, this quasi social contract largely means the same transnational corporations who dominated the apartheid economy remain in the driver's seat. The world the mine-owners made stays intact. But a genuine alternative must shake the roots of this power. Citizens must not simply take part in a consultation process, or sign a petition to get refuse removal in their community. An alternative scenario puts citizen power at the heart of economic decision-making power. This means that allocation of resources would ultimately be made on the basis of priorities decided by the majority. In the current context of South Africa, the majority are overwhelmingly black and poor. Such an alternative would likely involve new forms of collective or cooperative ownership of resources, new structures and processes of political democracy which extend beyond free and fair elections, and new methods of controlling the influence of the owners or controllers of mega-resources.

At one level, this would incorporate aspects of the public-goods perspective by removing certain services from the logic of the market. But other choices would also have to be subject to democratic political processes, beyond parliamentary review committees. For example,

---

[9] Some people within Oxfam have already begun a campaign for information as a "global public good" (Oxfam, 2000). Ex-World Bank economist Joseph Stiglitz (1999) echoed this view in a speech to the UK Department of Trade and Industry (1999). The debate over public goods took on another dimension with the suggestion by Michel Camdessus, former head of the International Monetary Fund, that international financial and monetary stability be categorised as a global public good (1999).

[10] For a critique of the apartheid city, see Smith (1992).

should motorcar factory technology be used to produce luxury sedans for the export market or mass transport vehicles for citizens of South Africa and the region? Should the mining houses which have shaped the rural and industrial landscape of the country for nearly a century be left free to pursue the agenda of global capital accumulation? The issue of alternatives addresses not only the outcome of such decisions, but who makes them and how. With respect to services, and ultimately all goods as well, they are no longer seen as commodities, but become decommodified. The production and allocation of goods and services is no longer decided on the basis of profitability, but on the basis of societal welfare as determined through participatory democracy.

For the foreseeable future, the social movements in South Africa are not likely to take up such lofty issues. Defensive struggles like fighting cutoffs and evictions, or opposing privatisation and retrenchments, will be full-time occupations. But as leaders of these social movements are well aware, their efforts are part of a much broader contestation of the agenda of globalisation and corporate power.

While the proponents of globalisation have repeatedly asserted that there is no alternative, millions of people have been mobilised under the slogan: "A better world is possible". And for those looking for an alternative, that better world needs to be far more than the present reality with a few public goods attached.

Bibliography

ANC [African National Congress]. (1994). *Reconstruction and Development Programme.* Johannesburg: Umenyanu.

Bond, P. (2000). *Cities of Gold, Townships of Coal: Essays on South Africa's New Urban Crisis.* New Jersey: Trenton, Africa World Press.

Camdessus, M. (1999). International Financial and Monetary Stability: A Global Public Good? Remarks At the IMF/Research Conference: Key Issues in Reform of the International Monetary and Financial System: Washington, D.C., 28 May.

Deedat, H., Pape, J. and Qotole, M. (2001). "Block tariffs or blocked access: The Greater Hermanus Water Conservation Programme". Municipal Services Project, Occasional Paper Number 5.

DPLG [Department of Provincial and Local Government]. (2002). Quarterly Monitoring of Municipal Finances and Related Activities, Summary of Questionnaires for Quarter Ended 31 December 2001, 30).

FAFO. (2002). *Mesebetsi Labour Force Survey Report.* Johannesburg: FAFO.

Fiil-Flynn, M. (2001). "The Electricity Crisis in Soweto," *Municipal Services Project Occasional Papers Series,* 4. Cape Town.

Focus. (2002). Interview with Trevour Ngwane, accessed at www.hof.org.za./focus 25/focus 25 interview.html.

Oxfam. (2000). Information as a global public good: A right to knowledge and communication, Oxfam International Campaign Proposal, accessed at http://danny.oz.au/free-software/advocacy/oicampaign.html.

Pape, J. (2001). "Poised to succeed or set up to fail: A case study of South Africa's first public-public partnership in water delivery". Municipal Services Project, Occasional Paper Number 1.

Qotole, M., Xali, M. and Barchiesi, F. (2001)."The Commercialisation of Waste Management in South Africa" Municipal Services Project Occasional Paper Series 3, Cape Town.

RSA [Republic of South Africa]. (2000). *Municipal Systems Act*. Pretoria: Government Printer.

Ruiters, G. (2001). "After basic needs: social justice and water politics". *Debate: Voices from the South African* left, March, 16–23.

Public Sector International/ILRIG. (2000). *There is an alternative: The public sector*. Cape Town: Logo Print.

Smith, D. (ed.). (1992). *The Apartheid City and Beyond: Urbanisation and Social Change in South Africa*. London: Routledge.

Stiglitz, J. (1999). "Public Policy for a Knowledge Economy". Remarks at the Department for Trade and Industry and Center for Economic Policy Research, London, U.K., January 27.

Wallerstein, I. (1999). "A Left Politics for the 21st Century? or, Theory and Praxis Once Again". Paper presented to the Fernand Braudel Centre.

Index

A

Ability to pay (service bills), 66–67
Access to services, 162–164
Affordability, 7, 11, 95, 164, 167
African National Congress (ANC), 1, 20
    Reconstruction and Development Programme, 1
Alheit, 144
Alternatives to cost recovery, 183–193
Apartheid, 1, 20
    and bantustans, 82
Apartheid city, 191
Arrears, 185

B

Bantustans, 20
Bhofolo, 45
Bill of Rights, 4
Biwater, 6
Block tariffs, 28, 175, 186
    and free services, 28
Brutus, Dennis, viii

C

Capitalism, 191–192
Cape Town, 20, 28
Cholera, 11, 30, 81–97
    and cost recovery, 95
    causes of, 82, 90–92
    financial implications, 93–94
    pre-paid meters, 82, 90–92
Cilliers, 144
Commodification, 12–13, 53
    decommodification, 33–34, 72
Communal taps, 29
Congress of South African Trade Unions (COSATU), 3, 62
Constantia, 123–139
Constantia Claimants Association, 126
Constantia Property Owners' Association, 12, 123, 127
Constitution, 4, 24, 32, 115
Consumer municipal debt, 48
Consumerism, 189
Corporatisation, 6, 26
Cost recovery, 2, 4, 5, 7–8, 10, 11, 13, 17–36
    block tariffs, 18
    and cholera, 95
    and democracy, 117
    commercialisation argument, 25
    community response, 115–116
    definition of, 18, 19
    enforcement, 31
    environmental arguments, 25
    fiscal arguments, 22
    full, 18, 21, 24
    inequality in, 27, 114, 154
    lack of monitoring/evaluation, 32
    health implications, 114
    moral arguments, 24
    near full, 26
    problems with, 26
    "ringfencing", 18
    volumetric measurement, 18
    voluntarism, 27

Cost reflexivity (cost reflexive), 21, 26
Crisis of service delivery, viii
 crisis of legitimacy, 2
Cronin, Jeremy, 2
Cross subsidies, 176, 184
"Culture of non-payment", 7, 49–50, 54, 167, 177
Culture of non-servicing, 7
Cutoffs, 5, 11, 19, 171–172
 of electricity, 19
 water, 19, 105, 170
 illegal reconnections, 69–70
 number of, 162
 permanent, 53
 UK experience, 32

D
Democratic Alliance (DA), 21
Department of Constitutional Development, 5
Department of Minerals and Energy
 Draft White Paper on Energy Policy, 24
Department of Provincial and Local Government, 29–30
 cost recovery questionnaires, 161
 tracking program, 32
Department of Water Affairs and Forestry, 4, 24
Development
 approach, 1
 failure of, 3
Development finance, 3
Diarrhoea, 114
Diepkloof, 11, 61–74
Draft White Paper on Energy Policy, 21
Draft Local Government Property Rates Bill, 23
Durban Chamber of Commerce and Industry, 23

E
ESKOM, 31, 62–63, 64–67, 74
 and democracy, 74
Evictions, 162

F
Fort Beaufort, 10, 43, 46, 52, 55
French investment in South Africa, 43
Free services, 29–30, 173–175
 electricity, 29

G
Globalisation, 2
Gordhan, Ketso, 6
Growth, Employment and Redistribution (GEAR), 2, 23

H
Hartswater, 146
HIV/AIDS, 83–84
Human Sciences Research Council (HSRC), 9, 161
 and National Opinion Survey, 162,

I
iGoli 2002, 6
Indigent, 5
Indigent policies, 5
Infrastructure expansion, 4
Integrated Development Plans, 187

J
Johannesburg, 6
Job creation, 185–186

K

Kei-Gariep Municipality, 147
Khayelitsha, 112, 116
Klipgat, 5
KwaZulu-Natal (KZN), 10–11, 81–97

L

Labour
Lennertsville, 12, 144, 148–153
Lifelines for the poor, 184
Local government and service delivery, 2
Local Government Transition Act, 4
Local Government White Paper, 4
LOGRA, 130

M

Madlebe, 82–90
    and communal tap consumption, 90
    comparison with Empangeni, 94
Maeda, Pricilla, 64
Makhaza, 9–11, 101–119
Mandela, Nelson, 24
Mandela Village, 67
Masakhane ("Let's build together"), 1, 2, 24
"Massive cutoffs", 64
Mayekiso, Moses, 1
Medium Term Expenditure Framework, 5
Meters, 19, 53
    for water, 22
    for electricity
    prepaid, 12, 19–20, 31, 81–97, 145–146
Mlungisi, 50
Moosa, Mohammed Valli, 103
Muller, Mike, 26
Municipal Finance Bill, 5
Municipal Investment Infrastructure Unit, 5
Municipal Services Project (MSP), 8, 27
Municipal Systems Act, 22

N

Naidoo, Jay, 1
National Economic Development and Labour Council (NEDLAC), 4
National Water Act, 21
Nelspruit, 5
Neoliberalism, 4, 10, 25, 188
New National Party and Democratic Party, *see* Democratic Alliance
Non-payment of bills, 22, 106
Northern Cape, 12

O

"One city, one tax base", 3
Operation Khanyisa, 6
Operation Vulaamanzi, 6
Outsourcing, 5–6

P

Participatory action research, 9
Payment withholding, 1
People-driven development, 1
Perception of service prices, 165
Perception of water prices, 166
Phambili Nombane, 108, 112
Planact, 3
Prepaid meters, 53–54
Pricing (of services)
Privatisation of municipal services, 26, 43, 185
Public-private partnerships (PPPs), 5, 185

Q
Queenstown, 10, 43, 48, 49, 51, 52

R
Raaswater, 144
Rates boycott, 1
Reconstruction and Development Programme (RDP), 2, 189
Research methodologies, 8
Ringfencing, 30
Rural Development and Community Development Forums, 4

S
Sanctions, 2
South African Communist Party (SACP), 2
Service arrears, 168–169
Selebi, Jackie, 3
Shona Khona, 85
"Snowball sampling", 8, 11, 85
Soobramoney legal battle, 4
South African Municipal Workers' Union (SAMWU), 5, 8, 116
South African National Civics Organisation (SANCO), 3, 70–71, 74, 106, 108–111
Soweto Electricity Crisis Committee, 6, 183
     and Operation Khanyisa, 61
Street lighting, 51
Stutterheim, 10, 48, 50, 51
Structural Adjustment Programmes, 2
Systems Act, 187

T
Table of Non-Derogable Rights, 4
Tafelsig, 6
Topline, 144
Tripartite Alliance, 46
Tutu, Desmond, 2
Tygerberg Administration, 108

U
uMthlathuze Water Board, 81–82
Unicity Commission, 103
Urban Foundation, 20

V
Vryberg, 146

W
Water and Sanitation Services South Africa (WSSA), 10, 42–44, 55
     and privatisation, 43
Wellman, Peter, 4
Water Supply and Sanitation White Paper, 23
White Paper on Local Government, 103
White Paper on Water and Sanitation, 21
White Paper on National Sanitation Policy, 21
Women, 28, 114
     and services, 10
     and cutoffs
     participation, 188
World Bank, 2, 5, 22, 25
World Health Organisation (WHO), 29

Y
Youth for Work, 11